Gworge Shaw-Lafevre Eversley

English And Irish Land Questions

Collected Essays

Gworge Shaw-Lafevre Eversley

English And Irish Land Questions
Collected Essays

ISBN/EAN: 9783744724104

Printed in Europe, USA, Canada, Australia, Japan

Cover: Foto ©Thomas Meinert / pixelio.de

More available books at **www.hansebooks.com**

ENGLISH AND IRISH

LAND QUESTIONS.

COLLECTED ESSAYS,

BY THE

RT. HON. G. SHAW LEFEVRE, M.P.,

*First Commissioner of Her Majesty's Works and
Public Buildings.*

CASSELL, PETTER, GALPIN & CO.:

LONDON, PARIS & NEW YORK.

1881.

PREFACE.

In view of the many questions affecting the Tenure of
Land, whether in Ireland or in other parts of the United
Kingdom, which are now under discussion, I have ventured
to reprint in a connected form various essays and papers
which during the last few years I have written on different
branches of this subject. With one exception they are
republished without addition or alteration, save that a few
redundant passages have been omitted. To the article on
"Common Lands," which was published in the *Contemporary
Review* of 1879 under the title of "The Rescue of Epping
Forest," I have added an historical account of the origin
of Commons, and a fuller account of the movement of
late years for their preservation than has yet appeared. In
this, as in other subjects dealt with in this volume, I have
endeavoured to explain in popular language the legal
principles involved, and to show how the present state of
our Land Laws has been evolved even more from judicial
decisions than from legislation of past times. Before any
reforms on such subjects are effected, it is necessary that

public opinion should be persuaded thoroughly of the necessity for change; when this is effected, it will be found that even legal principles are not so inflexible as to be incapable of adaptation, and the judges on the bench, equally with Parliament, will find the means of giving effect to public opinion, and of reconciling to a greater degree than is generally supposed to be possible ancient doctrines with modern requirements.

G. S. L.

February 10, 1881.

CONTENTS.

FREEDOM OF LAND.*

—◇—

THE NEW DOMESDAY BOOK.

The modern Domesday Book, as the Parliamentary Return, giving the list and acreage of the Landowners of the United Kingdom, has been happily termed, enabled the Country for the first time since the Domesday of the Conqueror, to form an estimate of the ownership and distribution of its landed property.

Compared indeed with the original, it is very deficient in details. It is so framed as to give very little local information as to the ownership of land in particular parishes or districts, or the number of tenants of the various owners, or as to the nature of the ownerships. It does not distinguish between leaseholders, copyholders, and owners in fee ; it omits all reference to the owners of land let on long lease ; it does not distinguish what is mere house property from landed property ; it does not enable us to estimate how many members still exist of the class formerly so numerous, the yeomen of England, cultivating their own lands, or how many may be considered as forming a class of peasant proprietors ; it is,admittedly inaccurate in many of its details.

These inaccuracies, however, do not, it is believed, disturb the general results ; and faulty though it may be in many respects, it is still most valuable ; it enables us to compare the numbers of landowners of different classes with those in other countries. At first sight, indeed, the aggregate is apt to mislead. A total of 1,153,816 landowners is given for the United Kingdom : of these, however, no less than 852,438 are entered as owners or lessees of less than one acre of land, with an aggregate of 188,000 acres only, valued at £36,300,000 per annum. It is obvious that with rare exceptions these must be owners,

---

* An Essay published December, 1879.

and most of them leaseholders, of mere house properties. From the 301,378 entries of owners of above one acre, further reductions must be made in respect of dupli-cate entries, holders of glebes, corporations, and charities. A careful examination of the Return has shown that, after making these deductions, there are certainly not more than 166,000 owners of land, as distinguished from houses, in England and Wales, 21,000 in Ireland,* and 8,000 in Scotland.

It may be safely stated, then, that the number of land-owners of the United Kingdom is under 200,000. How then is the land divided among these owners?

A careful analysis has shown that of the 72,000,000 acres accounted for, exclusive of manors, woods, forests, property let on long lease, property within the metropolis, and house property generally—

1,000 persons own about 30,000,000 acres, averaging 30,000 each.
4,000   „   „   20,000,000   ,,   5,000 „
10,000   „   „   10,000,000   ,,   1,000 „
50,000   ,,   „   9,000,000   ,,   180 „
130,000   ,,   „   1,750,000   „   13 „

These figures, however, rather understate than overstate the proportion of land held by large owners as compared with small owners. An addition should be made to the acreage of the former, in respect of woods and manors which are not accounted for in the return, and which pro-bably amount to nearly 4,000,000 acres. Making an addi-tion on this account, it may be safely said that 15,000 persons own between them 64,000,000 acres out of a total $76\frac{1}{3}$ millions; of the remainder about 1,500,000 acres are held in mortmain, by the Crown, the Ecclesiastical Com-missioners and other Church Corporations, the Universities, Public Schools, Hospitals, and Charities.

It will be seen, however, from the above figures, that the distribution of land is very different in the three countries. Of Scotland, rather more than half consists of mountain and moor, of little agricultural value, and held in immense blocks. The remaining half is owned by a very small number of persons; peasant proprietors do not exist there.

---

* Including about 5,000 holdings bought by their tenants under the Bright clauses of the Church Disestablishment Act (1869) and the Irish Land Act (1870).

One person only out of every 400 owns land; and one in twenty-eight owns a house.

In Ireland the proportion of landowners would have been about the same as in Scotland, but for recent legislation promoting the purchase of land by tenants, which has added about 5,000 to the number of-small owners, or nearly 30 per cent. of the previous number; with this addition, one person in 257 owns land, and one in 120 owns a house.

In England and Wales it appears that the number of owners of land is proportionally larger. There are parts of the country, such as Cumberland and Westmoreland, where the class of yeomen has not altogether died out. There are considerable numbers of owners of small properties in the neighbourhood of towns, which would be more properly classed as owners of villas. In Lincolnshire and Cambridgeshire there are a certain number of owners of small holdings. With these exceptions there cannot be said to exist a class of yeomen farmers or of peasant proprietors. One person out of 130 is probably an owner of land, and, omitting London, one person in twenty-six the owner of a house.

LANDOWNERS IN OTHER STATES.

If we compare the state of landowning, as thus disclosed, with that existing in others of the civilised countries of the world, whether in Europe or in the New World, we cannot fail to be struck by the extraordinary difference. Nowhere is there anything at all comparable to the state of this country, except in parts of Spain, in Bohemia, and in Southern Italy and Sicily. Throughout the whole of Western, Central, and Northern Europe the greater part of the soil is everywhere owned by a large body of persons, including large numbers of what we should call the yeomen class, or small farming proprietors, and still more of the class of smaller owners, more properly called peasant proprietors.

France is said to be owned in respect of two-thirds of its total cultivated area by small farmers and peasant proprietors, and one-third of it only is owned by larger proprietors, who let their lands on farming leases to tenants. M. de Lavergne, the highest authority on this subject, stated a few years ago, before the separation of Alsace and Lorraine, that the owners and occupiers of land in France might be divided into three classes, as follows :—

FRANCE (OWNERSHIPS).

	Total Acres.
5,000,000 owners averaging 3 hectares (7½ acres)	37,000,000
500,000 medium sized owners averaging 30 hectares (75 acres)	37,000,000
50,000 large proprietors averaging 300 hectares (750 acres)	37,000,000
5,550,000	111,000,000
State domains and communal property	10,600,000
	121,600,000

FRANCE (AGRICULTURAL HOLDINGS).

	Total Acres.
1,815,000 occupiers of less than 5 hectares (7½ acres)	12,540,000
1,256,000 occupiers of between 5 hectares and 40 hectares (100 acres)	43,800,000
154,000 occupiers of over 40 hectares (100 acres)	27,142,000
3,225,000	83,482,000
Woods and forests	19,980,000
Moors and uncultivated land	18,200,000
	121,662,000*

* It is of interest to compare this table with a similar one for the United Kingdom :—

OWNERS.

	Total Acres.
130,000 small owners averaging 13 acres...	1,750,000
50,000 medium-sized owners with an average of 180 acres	9,000,000
15,000 large owners averaging 4,260 acres	64,000,000
195,000	74,750,000
Crown lands and lands in mortmain	1,600,000
	76,350,000

AGRICULTURAL HOLDINGS.

	Total Acres.
750,000 occupiers of less than 10 acres	4,500,000
316,000 occupiers of from 10 acres to 100 acres ...	14,700,000
92,000 occupiers of above 100 acres	28,000,000
1,158,000	47,200,000
Mountains, moors, and woods	29,000,000
	76,400,000

From these figures it appears that France is neither owned nor cultivated to the extent that is generally believed by peasant proprietors; one-third only of its area is owned by this class; one-half of its cultivated land is held on tenancy; and the farms of over 100 acres very much outnumber those in the United Kingdom. Compared with this, five-sixths of the area of the United Kingdom are owned by 15,000 persons, and not one-fiftieth part of it by small owners. The number of small cultivators, however, is considerable; they number three-quarters of a million, and hold one-tenth of the cultivated land; the large farms are under 100,000 in number, but they contain about two-thirds of the cultivated land of the United Kingdom.

Switzerland, Baden, the Rhine provinces of Prussia, Bavaria, and Hesse are almost wholly owned and farmed by their cultivators, varying only between the moderate-sized farmers and peasants. The same may be said of Sweden and Norway. Belgium, in respect of one-half of its area, is cultivated by its owners, and in respect of the other half by a very numerous class of small tenants farming the lands of others. Throughout the remaining parts of Germany, whether Austria or Prussia, the land is owned by large proprietors and small proprietors in about equal proportions: large properties are not unfrequent, but among them are dispersed an immense number of small owners, for the most part cultivating their land themselves. The same may be said of Piedmont, North Italy, and of the northern parts of Portugal and Spain.

In none of these countries does there exist the entire and absolute separation between the three classes of landowners, farmers, and day labourers, which is the distinguishing feature of the English system; in many of them there are numerous large properties cultivated by tenants and labourers; but the tenant-farmers are members of a class of whom many are themselves owners, and a great proportion of the labourers are also owners of land. Throughout all the countries named at least 50 per cent., and in France probably 75 per cent., of the labouring population in the rural districts are owners of small properties, which they either cultivate themselves, or let out to their neighbours or relations to cultivate, while working for wages themselves.

In the United States, also, the separation of the rural community into landowners, farmers, and labourers has not begun to show itself. The land is owned by its cultivators. There are more than three millions of landowners cultivating their own lands. Even in the oldest settled States, in the neighbourhood of large cities, where wealth has accumulated to an extent quite as great as the great manufacturing towns of this country can show, and where land has attained a very high value, the same features exist. Ownership everywhere prevails as opposed to tenancy. The State of New York may be compared in extent with Ireland. It contains 22,190,000 acres of land held in farms. Of these there were, by the last census, in 1870, 216,000 owners, as compared with the 21,000 owners of land in Ireland. These owners have increased since 1860 by 20,000, or 10 per cent. ; and this increase has been mainly in the class of persons owning between three acres and twenty acres. Of these there were 17,800 in 1860, and 31,000 in 1870.

CAUSES OF DIFFERENCE.

What then is the cause of this extraordinary difference ? Why is it that land in England is in the possession of so few, and in every other part of the world of so many ? Is it the result of economic laws only, working freely, without any artificial aid or encouragement by the state, or is it the result of legislation, and of political or social causes ? Has it resulted in the full development of the resources of the land ? Has it tended to the well-being of all classes, and stimulated the industry and promoted the thrift of the lowest, as well as subserved the enjoyment of the highest ?

Where a very marked difference is observed in the conditions of one and more countries, the political inquirer instinctively looks about for other differences, and on finding them concurrent in all cases, connects them together as cause and effect. In the case, therefore, of landownership, it is not strange that we should at once have our attention called to the fact that this country differs not only in its condition but in its laws. In every other country above referred to, the laws either give no sanction to the accumulation of landed property upon eldest sons, or, as in the case of France and some others, compel its distribution equally among all the children on the death of their parent, and generally offer no facilities for the maintenance of property in particular families by means of entails. In this country the law gives prominent sanction to the one practice and facilities for the other.

There are, however, economists, and by no means an unimportant class, who believe that the present distribution of land in England has no reference whatever to these laws, and that it is due solely to economic causes, which they conceive tend in a wealthy country to the inevitable aggregation of land in a few hands, and to a complete separation of the functions of landowners, farmers, and labourers. In the view of such persons, the existing condition is defensible on the ground that it leads to the best development of the resources of the land, and is inevitable, as with the growth of wealth and luxury, land itself must become a luxury of the highest quality, the ownership of which can be indulged in only by the rich.

According to this school the existing tendency will be carried much further, and we may look forward, as wealth increases in this country, to the gradual but certain extinction of those few small ownerships of land which still exist in rural districts, and to the absorption of all small estates in larger properties ; and they preach the doctrine that the further this monopoly of land, as they frankly admit it to be, is carried, the better will it be for the country, as the greater prospect there will be of the duties of landlords being carried out. Land is, and should be, in this view, an article of luxury which only the rich can afford to hold ; and it is only to be expected, and is certainly to be desired, that the smaller proprietors should convert their capital as landowners into tenants' capital, by selling their land and becoming the tenants of five times as much land as they can hold as owners.

It may be replied to this, that in other parts of Europe, where there is great accumulation of wealth, there is no such tendency. Belgium is one of the wealthiest parts of Europe. It compares with the manufacturing districts of England. In proportion to its size and population, there is certainly as much of capital invested in manufactories and railways ; and yet, so far from the tendency being to a reduced number of owners, the reverse is the case, and the movement of property is towards a gradually increasing number of landowners. Small capitalists outbid the larger capitalists for landed property ; and not only is a greater part of Belgium cultivated by its owners, but of the remaining half a large portion is owned in very small portions, and is let out to farming tenants at very high rents. Land is there the luxury of all classes, although there are many very large proprietors.

The same may be said of Normandy—the wealthiest, happiest, and most populous part of France. It is a rich manufacturing district. There would be the same motive there, as is alleged to exist in England, for small proprietors to sell their lands, become tenants of what they previously owned, and to invest their money either in industrial enterprises returning a much higher rate of interest, or in tenants' capital, enabling them to hire more land than they can own. Yet such is not the fact. Small proprietors give higher prices than large proprietors, prices that would appear to be excessive in the agricultural parts of England, and there is no tendency for land to fall into few hands. There is great variety of ownership in this part of France ; large owners and small owners intermix ; large farms and small farms are found side by side ; but the large owners are not prone, like pike in a pond, to swallow up the smaller fry of their kind.

The price of land in rural districts of France is generally forty years' purchase of the annual value, and often more. The peasants are not without appreciation of other investments giving higher returns ; it is well known that the great loans raised of late years to meet the war expenses, and the German indemnity, have been mainly raised from the savings of the peasants ; they are not the less ready, however, to purchase land returning one-half less interest. M. de Lavergne has shown that the common belief as to the indebtedness of the small proprietors in France is not true ; the mortgages on their properties average no more than ten per cent. of the value of the land.

The same may be said of Holland—a country where there is more accumulation of savings than in any other part of Europe ; whose inhabitants are accustomed to lend out money to every borrowing power in Europe, and often in loans of the most risky nature. They appear none the less able to understand the value of safe investments in land at a very low interest. Land is even more valued there by the small capitalist than by the wealthy.

So far, then, from being able to draw any conclusions from other countries in favour of the proposition that, with advancing civilisation and with increasing wealth and luxury, land tends to fall into fewer hands and to become more exclusively the luxury of a particular class, the very reverse is the case ; and everywhere we find other classes competing for land with the wealthy, and giving for it prices which would be considered very high even in this country.

We are not, however, left to the resource only of comparing existing things and tendencies in other countries with what we experience in this country ; we are also able to point to the changes which have been made in those countries, with the very object of bringing about their present condition, and of avoiding that which this country presents.

It is important to recollect that the condition which exists in England was that exhibited not many years ago throughout the greater part of Europe, that the laws such as we now have in England were the laws of the whole of Europe, and that Europe has within the last hundred years almost universally abandoned them ; and, further, that our colonists took these laws with them to the New World, but there speedily got rid of them, finding them opposed to the principles on which their communities were founded, and intolerable in their results upon the free commerce of land.

LAND LAWS OF FRANCE.

In France, before the Revolution of 1789, large properties prevailed throughout a great part of the country. They were held and preserved in families by laws very similar to those which still prevail in England. Primogeniture and entail were almost universally in practice among the upper classes. These laws, however, were the exclusive privilege of the nobility. The law was different for inferior classes. There existed even in those days a large number of small owners. This class had existed from time immemorial, and were either descendants of small freeholders, or of Roman coloni, holding on payment of small and hereditary rents, and who had been brought within the range of the feudal system, or were emancipated serfs who held by certain tenure, but subject to most arbitrary and galling services and dues, under feudal lords. These people had inherited from the Roman law the principle of equal and compulsory division of property on death. The principles of feudal law had never been extended to them. Primogeniture was not their privilege; entail was expressly prohibited to them.

Even before the Revolution great complaints were made of the effect of entails, in causing multiplicity of suits, in creating uncertainty as to title, in depriving creditors of their just rights, in promoting clandestine arrangements of property, in withdrawing from the freedom of commerce so large a portion of the land, and in tending to the accumulation of property in few hands; many attempts were made by the executive government to restrict and curtail this process, and to make it as little noxious as possible.

The celebrated Chancellor D'Aguesseau wrote of entails in the year 1750, in language which might be used of England in the present day. The President of Aix, another distinguished lawyer, had wrritten to him as follows :—

"One may doubt whether it would not be advantageous to the interest of the state wholly to abolish entails (substitutions); they help to preserve family property, but it is only by sacrificing the creditors of the family, who have lent their money in good faith. Nothing is more unjust than this; and as it is a matter of indifference to the State that the property of such families should be preserved, it seems that no general reason exists for permitting the maintenance of entails, which were invented by people possessed of a foolish obstinacy to prolong their names, but who forget that a bankruptcy, occurring in every second generation, dishonours them."

D'Aguesseau, in reply, wrote as follows :—

"The complete abolition of entails would probably, as you say, be the best of all laws; and there might be found more simple means of preserving a sufficiency of property in great families to sustain their position. But I fear that in order to arrive at this, we should have to commence by reforming men's brains, and this would be the enterprise of one whose own head might be in danger of being reformed away. It is, in truth, a great misfortune that the vanity of mankind is the predominating influence of legislation." *

It was by the inspiration of D'Aguesseau that a law was passed in 1747 greatly limiting the power of entails, and compelling publicity of them. In the preamble of this law it is stated that, among other evils of entails, they provided an order of succession different from that of the state ; that what had been intended for the benefit of the family often ended in its ruin ; and that entails interfered with the freedom of commerce in land. The statute, however, effected little ; it left untouched all the existing entails, which still continued to spread their noxious influence throughout France.

One of the earliest efforts of the French Revolution was to deal with the land question. In the celebrated meeting of the National Assembly of the 4th of August, 1789, it was at the instance of Vicomte de Noailles and the Duc d'Aiguillon—the foremost and weathiest members of the nobility—that all feudal rights and privileges were abolished, and among these were the privilege of primogeniture and the power of making entails. Of the spirit which animated the Assembly on these subjects we can best judge from the well-known speech of Mirabeau on the law of succession. " Is it not sufficient," he said, " for society, that it has to bear the caprices and passions of the living ? must it also suffer from those of the dead ? Is it not enough that society should be charged with all the evil consequences resulting from testamentary despotism from time immemorial to the present ? must we also subject it to all that future testators may add to this evil by their last wishes, so often whimsical and unnatural ? Have we not seen a multitude of wills which breathed of pride or vengeance ; in some an unjust, in others a blind preference ? The law cancels those wills which are termed *ab irato*, but does not and cannot quash those which we may call *a decepto, a moroso, ab imbecilli, a delirante, a superbo.* How many are there of these acts of the dead towards the living, where folly seems to dispute with passion, and where the testator makes a disposition of his property which he dared not confide to any one when alive—a disposition in respect of which he must have

* See letters of D'Aguesseau, quoted in Treatise on Substitutions by Cossé.

detached himself from all regard to his memory, and have
thought that the tomb would protect him against ridicule
and reproach ? . . . . There are no longer eldest sons
or privileges in the great family of the nation ; there should
be none in the smaller families of which each state is
composed. How many are there who, born without fortune,
succeed by some means or other in enriching themselves.
Puffed up by this accident, they often conceive a respect
for their name, and they will not let it pass to their
descendants except under escort of a fortune which may
recommend it to consideration ; they choose an heir among
their children ; they decorate him by will with all that can
sustain the new existence which they prepare for him, and
their ambitious pride paints for itself by anticipation, even
beyond the tomb, a line of descendants who will do honour
to their blood.   Let us, then, stifle this germ of useless
distinctions ; let us break these instruments of injustice and
folly ! ”

Under the influence of this passionate oration, the
Assembly not only voted the repeal of the laws of primogeniture and entail, but would not even permit primogeniture ;
it made universal and applied to the nobility that which had
been previously the law of the lower classes—namely, the
compulsory division of the greater part of the paternal
property, of whatever nature, equally among the children,
leaving only a small proportion to the discretion of the
testator.

In 1792 the Assembly carried the same principles
further; it abolished all existing entails ; the expectant
heirs under entails were irrevocably deprived of their
expectations ; and property subject to these settlements was,
in the interest of the public, freed from all limitations and
placed at the absolute disposal of existing holders.

It is worthy of notice that these great changes speedily
commended themselves to the habits, customs, and
opinions of all classes, even of the upper classes and of the
nobility, and the principle of equal division of property on
death very rapidly gained acceptance ; and when, after the
restoration of the Bourbon monarchy, the reactionary
government of 1826 endeavoured to restore, to a very
limited degree, the principle of primogeniture and the power
of entail, so great was the force of public opinion against the

project, so strongly was the family feeling, even of what remained of the old nobility, opposed to a restoration of such privileges, that the Chamber of Peers rejected the proposals; the leading members of the old nobility voted against them, and hundreds of eldest sons petitioned against them, on the ground that they would introduce disagreement and discord into families. It is not too much to say that there is no institution in France so popular and so immutable as that which requires equal division of property among children. The law indeed permits a father to dispose by will of a portion of his property, and to accumulate this upon any favoured child; but the universal custom of France is to disregard this power, and to distribute equally among the children.

The French Revolution did more than merely alter the law. It took further measures to promote the wider distribution and ownership of property. The vast possessions belonging to the Church were appropriated by the state, and sold; 600,000 tenants became purchasers of their holdings, paying for them probably in depreciated "assignats." A portion of the property of the Emigrés, though less than is generally supposed, was dealt with in the same way. A portion of the communal property was also sold. Not less than a million tenants were thus enabled to become owners. Long after the Revolution, speculators, known under the name of *bandes noires*, bought up large properties and sold them to the tenants. The result of all these operations was vastly to increase the number of landowners, and to produce the state of ownership which we now see there. Has the condition of the peasants improved? Who can doubt it who reads the description given of them before the Revolution and compares it with their present condition? Has France gained or lost in a political, social, or economic view, by this great accession to the number of her landowners? There is only one answer possible for those who look back at her history of the last few years. It is universally admitted that she was able to emerge from her difficulties of foreign invasion, of a crushing war indemnity, of the gravest political convulsion, and of struggles with the Commune of Paris, by the conservative force of her great mass of property owners, and the vast accumulations of wealth created by their industry and thrift.

The principles of the Revolution, especially as regards the land laws, were carried by the triumphant arms of the new Republic, and yet more by the spirit which had created this force, to many other countries—to Belgium and Holland, to the Palatinate, to Baden, to Switzerland, and to a great part of Italy. Everywhere the old laws of primogeniture and entail were abolished, and the principles of the French Code were adopted.

LAND LAWS OF GERMANY.

Even Prussia, and others of the German states, felt something of this impulse.   The first sign they showed was by secularising, as it was gently called, the vast possessions of the Church ; and later, when Prussia was at its lowest ebb, the legislation of Stein and Hardenberg did much to renovate her and reanimate her people, by modernising her land laws, favouring the creation of absolute owners, and substituting full ownership for feudal dependancy.

It may be worth while to dwell shortly upon the changes which occurred in Prussia,* as they were the model on which many other states have subsequently acted.   Indeed it may be said that two methods have been followed by Europe, in getting rid of the feudal land system—the French method of the Revolution, where little regard was paid to private interests, where feudal services and dues were abolished without compensation, and feudal tenures were converted into absolute ownerships ; and the Prussian method, or the legal method, by which the values of feudal rights were commuted, or a partition was made of the land occupied by the tenants, a portion being awarded to their feudal superiors in compensation for the loss of rights.

In Germany, as in France, the feudal system had not extinguished altogether the previously existing class of small proprietors.   They were indeed brought within the feudal system, and were considered as serfs ; but they continued in possession of their small holdings, and exercised the rights of property and of bequest in respect of them.   The

---

* This account of the Reform of the Land Laws in Prussia is taken mainly from Mr. Harriss-Gastrell's able paper in the " Reports on Land Tenures in Europe," laid before Parliament in 1870.

subjection of the peasants to their feudal lords was so great
that the " air makes us serfs " became a common expression.
The oppression of the serfs was carried to the utmost, and
they were not unfrequently sold to foreign governments as
soldiers ; but notwithstanding this, the class continued in
possession of their small holdings of land. The power of
the lord did not extend to the appropriation of the peasant's
lands. The lord cultivated his own demesnes, either
personally or by his bailiffs, with the aid of the services of
his feudal dependents, and by the labour of the serfs due in
respect of their separate holdings.

It appears, however, that there was from an early date a
disposition on the part of the nobility and feudal lords to
encroach upon the lands of their peasants, and gradually to
convert the latter more completely into labourers without
land of their own. We find, for instance, that in the
fifteenth and sixteenth centuries the small country towns
frequently petitioned for the better protection and
maintenance of the yeomanry and peasantry, on commercial and political grounds ; on the former, because the
nobles traded with the large commercial towns, while the
yeomanry traded with the small country towns ; and on the
latter, because it was good for the state that the yeomanry
and peasantry should not disappear and leave nothing but
nobles and labourers. The Hohenzollern princes took this
view of the case, and directed their policy to the maintenance of the peasantry. They prohibited the nobles from
annexing the peasants' lands ; and later they prohibited the
eviction of a peasant, except upon well-founded grounds, and
upon the lord of the manor replacing him by another
peasant. Frederick the Great, actuated probably by military
motives, issued severe edicts on this subject, prohibiting the
absorption of peasants' lands.

At the beginning of this century Prussia had retained
the feudal system in many of its most objectionable features.
Its subjects were divided into three classes — nobles,
townsmen, and peasants. Each class was carefully restricted by law from mingling with the others in any way.
The lands of each class were compulsorily maintained in its
possession. The nobles' lands were for the most part the
subject of unlimited entails. Freedom of commerce in land
did not exist. Though the peasants were sustained and

protected in their holdings, they were subject to the most arbitrary, capricious, and galling services and dues to their lords.

The French Revolution and the humiliating defeat of the Prussian armies by the French, brought on a crisis in this political and social system. After the treaty of Tilsit, the Prussian statesmen set to work to remodel her system, to modernise her land laws, and to abolish the remains of the feudal system. This great work was mainly accomplished by the legislation of Stein and Hardenberg. It was temporarily arrested in 1816 by the reaction which set in after the close of the French war, and was not finally accomplished till 1850, after the revolutionary rising of 1848. The effect of this legislation was to convert the feudally subjected peasant, with more or less imperfect rights of property in land, into a perfectly free peasant with absolute ownership, subject only to a temporary rent-charge for commutation of the feudal services; to convert the feudally restricted lord, with more or less perfect rights of property in his land, into a perfectly independent landowner; to relax the system of entails; to abolish all restrictions on the sale of land as between the different classes; and to establish the great principle of freedom of sale of land. The operation was assisted by the creation of Land Credit Banks, supported by loans from the state, and which in their turn lent money to the tenants, repayable by instalments spread over a term of years, for the redemption of their rents.

The result of this legislation has been that the land in Prussia is now the absolute property of a large number of owners, and that each owner is quite independent of any other owner. The law recognises no distinction between land and other property in respect of succession, and both are equally divided among the children on the death of the owner. Comparatively little land is now withdrawn from free exchange by entail. Entails are not absolutely prohibited by law; though the prohibition of them was promised by the Constitution. The law of obligatory heritage (as it is called), by which a proportion of every man's property must descend to his children (in Prussia one-third of the property must go to the children equally if there be two children, and one-half if there be more than two), tends to prevent the accumulation of very large landed properties, and the equal division of real as well as personal property on intestacy runs counter to any existing custom of primogeniture. Title to land has been made clear and almost indefeasible. The law of mortgages has been simplified; foreclosure and public sale are facilitated. By all these measures, and above all by the prevalence of absolute ownership of numerous owners, the free exchange of land has been fully attained.

The present state of Prussia as regards her land-ownership is this : exclusive of the Rhine provinces and Westphalia, it consists of 70,000,000 acres, of which about 50,000,000 acres are cultivated and 17,000,000 are forest. The land is owned by 1,300,000 proprietors, of whom about 16,000 are large proprietors with properties of over 400 acres ; 350,000 are medium-sized proprietors, and 925,000 are small proprietors. About half of the latter are wholly employed on their small holdings, and the remainder are occupied mainly as day labourers, or have other industries. The large proprietors, who own between them about 45 per cent. of the country, of which, however, a large part is forest, either farm themselves or through their bailiffs, and the relation of landlord and tenant is comparatively rare ; there are not more than 30,000 farm tenants. Of the total area not more than $\frac{1}{13}$th is withdrawn from free exchange by reason of entails ; new entails are very seldom created, and old entails are dying out.

In the Rhine provinces and Westphalia, owing to the fact that they were subjected to the French laws at the beginning of the century, the land is even more distributed ; with an area of about 11,000,000 of acres, there are said to be 1,157,000 proprietors, giving an average of ten acres to each.

Of the beneficent results of this legislation with respect to land in Prussia, extending over a period of nearly fifty years, and but recently completed, there cannot be a doubt. The universal testimony of the country is in its favour. It promotes ownership *versus* tenancy ; it aims at free exchange ; the discouragement of entail and the withdrawal of sanction to primogeniture prevent accumulation of land ; and the concurrence of all economists and statesmen is in favour of the yeomanry class as the main support of the empire. There are nearly a million owners of land living

c

wholly upon the results of their own labour ; they are said
to form the most valuable section of Prussia's population,
although not the most wealthy.   Many of them have raised
themselves from the rank of day labourers.   It is universally
admitted that the possibility of acquiring land fosters hope,
encourages energy, and never allows useful activity to
flag.

It has been thought well to dwell upon this Prussian
legislation, because it formed the model which many other
states have subsequently taken for their legislation with
respect to land.   Austria, Saxony, Hanover, Hungary, and
Denmark followed in the wake of Prussia ; and the general
principles underlying the more recent changes in Russia,
and the abolition of serfdom in that great empire, have
been to a great extent borrowed from the same source.
Generally it may be said that the French Revolution gave
the first impulse to these changes : a reaction occurred at
the close of the war in 1814, which stopped further advance,
and in some cases caused a return to the old system ; the
revolutionary movement of 1848 compelled a final change.

It is not too much, then, to say that for the last ninety
years a large part of the Continent, and for the last thirty
years nearly the whole of the Continent, has been moving
in the direction of more absolute and more distributed
ownership of land.   Its legislators have not been content
with merely abolishing primogeniture and entail ; they have
more actively thrown the weight of their laws and their
institutions in favour of individualism, and in support of
ownership as distinguished from tenancy.   The sale of
Church property and state domains has largely assisted in
this process.   In some countries, as in Sweden, old entails
are permitted to wear themselves out, but new entails
cannot be created.   In Denmark the Constitution of 1849
forbade the creation of new entails, and promised that
entailed estates should be converted into free property.
This last promise, however, has not yet been fulfilled.

In Portugal, it is reported to our Government, "that every
opportunity is seized to necessitate the transfer of land.
The extinction and dispersion of old estates ensuing from
the laws now in force have been sought for rather than
prevented ; there is a direct movement towards democratic
institutions, to which all measures of the legislature have for

some years tended. . . . Another blow dealt against the
agglomeration of landed property is the abolition of *Prasos
de Vita*—a sort of right of primogeniture which allowed
property of a certain kind to be left as an undivided
inheritance for three generations." *

Of Gallicia, it is said, the local tribunals greatly facilitate
dispersion and division of land. The Austrian civil code
of 1869 accords no preference to eldest sons ; exception is
made in favour of *majorats*, or family entails, but these
cannot be constituted without the consent of the legislature.

Even in Sicily—one of the most backward parts of
Europe—changes have been made in the same direction.
Since 1812, when the feudal tenures, which had their origin
in the Norman Conquest, were abolished, the tendency of
legislation has been to favour the alienation and division of
landed property. In 1819 entails were put an end to, and
the testamentary power of a father was limited to one-half
of his property. In 1862 a law was proposed for the
disposal of the Church lands, which amounted to one-sixth
of the landed property in the island ; by 1869 about 20,000
lots of 451,000 acres were disposed of, averaging 23 acres ;
yet we are told that, in spite of these legislative changes,
the greater part of the soil of the island is still in possession
of the few. It has not been found possible as yet to
extirpate brigandage.

RESULTS OF CHANGES OF LAND LAWS.

The methods and results of all these changes in Europe
are described at length in the series of Reports from the
representatives of this country at foreign courts, which were
laid before Parliament in 1870. They are unanimous as to
the benefits which have resulted from the changes they
report. Everywhere the production of the soil has been
increased. Industry and thrift have been stimulated.
Pauperism has been greatly reduced—in many districts
almost extinguished. Content has taken the place of chronic
discontent. The rights of property have been greatly
strengthened, and are now everywhere secure.

In the case of France it is interesting to compare the

* " Reports on Land Tenures in Europe," 1870, p. 183.

account given of its present condition by Mr. Sackville West, with the description given of it by the well-known writer, Arthur Young, immediately before the Revolution of 1789. The state of France as described by Arthur Young was most wretched; everywhere he found, on the one hand, proprietors owning immense tracts of country, heavily encumbered with debt, and which they were unable or unwilling to improve, and on the other, a vast body of poverty-stricken tenants overburthened with unjust taxation. In parts of France, however, there were, even in those days, a considerable number of small peasant owners, cultivating their own land; and Young, with his usual discrimination, pointed out the difference in the condition of these as compared with the mass of the small tenants. He said of them, " Their unremitting industry is so conspicuous and meritorious that no commendation would be too great for it. It is sufficient to prove that property in land is of all others the most active instigator to severe and incessant labour."* In another passage he said, " The property in land is of all others the most active instigator to severe and incessant labour; and this truth is of such force and extent that I know of no way so sure to carry tillage to the mountain top as by permitting the adjoining villagers to acquire it in property;" and he added the words which have become a proverb, "Give a man the secure possession of a bleak rock, and he will turn it into a garden; give him a nine years' lease of a garden, and he will turn it into a desert. The magic of property turns sand into gold."

This opinion of Arthur Young, of the influence of ownership upon production and industry, is the more important, as, while admitting the merit of small properties, he feared they would result in indefinite sub-division of the land, and in the increase of population to an extent which the soil of France could not support. " The population flowing from this division," he said, "would be the multiplication of wretchedness;" and " properties much divided would prove the greatest source of misery that could be conceived."† In this opinion he was followed by many English economists. Of these the ablest exponent was the late Mr. McCulloch, who, writing in 1823, thirty years after

* Arthur Young's " Travels in France," Vol. I., p. 407.
† Ib., p. 408.

the French Revolution, prophesied of France "that in half
a century it would certainly be the greatest pauper warren
in Europe, and along with Ireland have the honour of
furnishing hewers of wood and drawers of water for all other
countries in the world."*

So far from these prophecies proving true, the very
reverse has been the case, and the extension of ownership,
the bringing within the reach of all classes the opportunity
of becoming owners, the efforts made by the Government
to facilitate the connection between ownership and cultivation, and the enormous increase in the number of small
ownerships of land consequent upon the measures of the
Revolution, have not led to a great increase of the
population and to a consequent multiplication of a pauper
class. They have had the very opposite result. Production
has been greatly stimulated by the sense and security of
ownership; but the population has not increased relatively
in the same proportion ; the average condition of the people
therefore is vastly improved. Pauperism is almost unknown
in rural districts; the habits of industry and thrift are
universal. The complaint now made by many economists
is the reverse of that which was predicted by Arthur Young
and McCulloch ; they contend that the system of small
ownerships is to be condemned because it tends to check
the increase of population.

It is true that the population of France increases so
slowly that it may almost be said to be stationary. It is not
by any means certain, however, that this can be attributed
wholly to the prevalence of peasant proprietors. In Belgium
and Switzerland, countries differing widely in their commercial conditions, but agreeing in this that they have a very
large number of peasant owners, the population is by no
means stationary, and the births exceed the deaths in a proportion not far different from that of England. Let us,
however, assume for the purposes of argument that the
prevalence of peasant proprietors, and the wide distribution
of property in land, act as a restraint upon individuals in
such a manner as to reduce greatly the rate of increase of
population ; is it a great disadvantage, and a matter to be
deplored ? France is not a nation which has a genius for

* McCulloch's " Principles of Political Economy," p. 200.

emigration ; her sons love her soil too much, and care not
to face the unknown in other climes.   Without emigration,
and with the rate of progress of population that prevails in
England, France would not long supply a sufficiency for her
population.   The increase of the *prolétariat* without corre-
sponding increase of subsistence, would not be considered a
matter of satisfaction.   The prophecies of Arthur Young
and McCulloch, that her system of small cultivators would
lead to her becoming the pauper warren of Europe, and her
sons the hewers of wood and drawers of water for the rest
of Europe, have not been fulfilled ; but they make us feel
what might have been the destinies of France under a different system.   Both objections to her system of widely
distributed property—namely, that it may lead to her
becoming a pauper warren, and that it may tend to a very
slow rate of increase of population—cannot be sound ;
which of them is the most serious ?

   If the institutions of France have resulted in a self-
acting process of adapting the growth of her population to
the means of subsistence, it would seem to be not the
least merit of a system, which is based upon the wide
distribution of property, bringing home to the lowest, as well
as to the highest, the motives of restraint.

   This testimony in favour of the effects of a widely distributed ownership of land is not to be displaced by showing
that the average produce of wheat in France is considerably
below that of England.   It has already been shown by
statistics that France is not a country wholly of small
owners ; nearly half her cultivated area is farmed by tenants ;
and there are 154,000 farmers who cultivate upwards of
100 acres as compared with 92,000 tenants of the same size
in the United Kingdom.   The wheat crops in France are
mainly produced by the tenant farmers on these larger
farms.   The small owners, as a rule, do not produce wheat.
The low average production of wheat in France is due to
the soil and climate of her middle and southern provinces.
In the north, the average production is as high as in England.
No argument, therefore, can be drawn from this difference
as against small ownerships.

   Even Monsieur de Lavergne, who fully appreciates the
system of large farms, and who is not in favour of an
universal system of small proprietors, says on this point,

"Is it right to extol the large property system to the dis-
paragement of others, as has been done—to wish to extend
it everywhere and to proscribe the small? Evidently not;
for viewing the question merely from an agricultural point
of view—the only one now under consideration—general
results argue more in favour of small properties than of
large."*

The same testimony meets us from almost every part of
Europe. Of Baden, where landed property is very much
divided, Mr. Bailie reports to the Foreign Office :—

"The prevalent public opinion is that the system of
small freeholds tends to promote the greater economical
and moral prosperity of the people, to raise the average
standard of education, and to increase the national standard
of defence and taxation. It seems to be a generally established fact that the small farmers realise larger returns than
the larger farmers do from the same number of acres, and
the result is that the large properties and large farms are
disappearing, and being parcelled out among a number of
small farmers. In fact, the price of landed properties is
determined less by their intrinsic value than by the possibility of selling or letting them in small holdings."

He adds that, "the small peasant proprietors do not
differ from the larger proprietors in respect of dwellings,
clothing, mode of living, or education. There is no doubt
that since the Revolution of 1848 there has been a great
improvement in the houses of the peasants and their mode
of living, and in the cultivation of the soil; and their present
condition must on the whole be regarded as favourable, in
respect of their means and general well-being."

Of the Grand Duchy of Hesse, where two-thirds of the
land is owned by peasant cultivators, Mr. Morier says :†—
"An able-bodied pauper is a being altogether unknown. I
even found a difficulty in describing the sort of person
respecting whom I endeavoured to obtain information.

"The most vivid impression which I carried away from
the country was the equable manner in which the wealth of
the place appeared to be distributed amongst its inhabitants.
The whole population seemed to be on the same level of
material comfort and well-being. I could not bring back to

* "Économie rurale de la France," par M. L. de Lavergne, p. 109.
† "Reports on Land Tenure in Europe, 1870," Part II., p. 199.

my recollection any sight or sound denoting the presence of a squalid class, or any indication pointing to a higher or a ruling class. . . .

"When it has once reached a certain level of well-being, a peasant proprietary is a good judge of what amount of population the land will bear, and just as it increases in wealth and comfort, and in the special knowledge of the capabilities of the soil, so it becomes alive to the danger of jeopardising this prosperity by over-population."

He speaks of spontaneous and systematic emigration as the safety-valve. " The use of this regulation is best understood in the Rhine provinces, which is one of the best-cultivated and most prosperous districts in Europe. The Palatinate peasant cultivates his land more with the passion of an artist than in the plodding spirit of a mere bread-winner."

Of Lombardy, we are told that "public opinion holds that small proprietors are advantageous to our mountain soils, where the spur of ownership is required to compel production. From a social point of view the possession of freeholds may always be considered a benefit to the peasantry, and when *la petite culture* is possible it is favourable to agriculture."*

The official report from Switzerland is meagre, but of the condition of the agricultural population we have abundant evidence from numerous writers who have studied that country, and who all unite in bearing testimony to the wonderful improvements which have been made of late years, to the marvellous industry and thrift of its small pro-prietors, and to the general diffusion of wealth, of comfort, and of intelligence. The Rev. F. Barham Zincke, who has written most excellent accounts of this country, the result of many successive visits to it, says, " I saw no mansions in Switzerland, neither did I see scarcely any houses that with us would pass for cottages. What I did see was a surprising number of good comfortable small houses, which showed that the district was inhabited by a large number of well-to-do families. . . . It must be obvious that the yearly produce of these little reclaimed grass farms, in which every little patch and corner is made to support as many

* " Reports on Land Tenure in Europe."

blades of grass as the most careful cultivation can force into
existence, would not maintain in their present style of living
all the families that reside in these comfortable houses.
But the Swiss system suggests and encourages the practice
of saving ; and in most of these houses a capital fund has
been accumulated, which so aids what these small farmers
get during a year from their farms, that their families are
enabled to live with what is to them ease and comfort.

" It is an incidental and not unimportant result of this
system that it works in the direction of enabling the population to provide themselves with better houses than under
the territorial system they could rent from speculative
builders of rows of cottages run up by contract on land let
for the purpose on a ninety-nine years' lease. The comfortable little houses on the small farms throughout this district
are the property of those who are living in them. That
was the reason why they spent as much as they could spare
in constructing them well, and in making them roomy,
and, in accordance with their ideas and wants, com-
modious.

" We may infer from the general condition of the Swiss
that it is the possession of land, or the prospect of being
able to acquire it, that saves a labouring class from sinking
into a mob of pauperised drudges, and educates them into
men."*

How great is the difference between the state of the
Swiss as regards their houses and the agricultural labourers
of England as regards their cottages will hereafter appear ;
the difference between their occupiers is scarcely less.

In another passage Mr. Zincke says :—" The effort to
acquire land is the mainspring of the life of the peasants of
Switzerland. The better sort of men are all making this
effort, are all living for this purpose. It is the root of their
industry, of their painstaking, frugal, saving lives. The
opportunities there are under the Swiss system to acquire land,
give the land to those who deserve to have it. The system
acts as a winnowing process. It sifts out the idle and profli-
gate through the natural consequences of their idleness and
profligacy, and rewards the thoughtful, the self-denying, and
the hardworking through the natural consequences of their

* " A Month in Switzerland," by Rev. F. Barham Zincke.

thoughtfulness, self-denying, and hard work. It is a self-acting case of social, moral, and intellectual selection."*

It is not, however, necessary to go beyond the immediate possessions of the Crown of England for a conspicuous illustration of the results of a widely distributed ownership of land upon the production, the industry, the content, and the general well-being of a whole community. There is such a case close at hand in the Channel Islands. The people of those islands, since their union with England 800 years ago, have jealously preserved their local government and their distinctive laws. Chief among these distinctions are their land laws, which they have inherited from the common law of Normandy; these laws favour the dispersion of property, and forbid its accumulation by entail or primogeniture. The result is, that with an area no larger than hundreds of private estates in England and Ireland, the islands boast of not less than 4,000 landowners, cultivating in most cases their own property, and constituting a class of small yeomen.

The industrial results of these small yeomen are most remarkable; the island is cultivated to the highest point which it is capable of; the gross produce is extraordinary; there is a general diffusion of wealth; thrift and saving are conspicuous in every class; cottages such as we see in England and Ireland are unknown; the people are better housed than in any part of Europe; pauperism is almost unknown; everything testifies to the stimulus effected by the wide distribution of property, and by the fact that property is brought within the prospect of acquisition by every one.

The most enlightened people in the islands, equally with public opinion, attribute these results to their distinctive land laws; to the fact that they have successfully resisted the introduction of English laws, which they believe would have an opposite tendency; and they significantly allege that if these laws had been introduced some centuries ago, the island, by this time, would probably have been owned by a single individual; and their cultivators might have been in the condition of the Irish tenants. As it is, a more prosperous, loyal, and contented class does not exist under

* "A Walk in the Grisons," by Rev. F. Barham Zincke, p. 5.

the Crown of England than the small yeoman of the Channel Islands.

CHANGES OF LAW IN THE UNITED STATES.

Our colonies have dealt not less rudely with the principles of English land laws. The various States of North America retained them for many years, so long as they remained colonies, but after separation from the mother-country, commenced to amend them. By their new constitution the subject of the land laws was left to the discretion of the State legislatures. It is strong testimony to the strength of public opinion against these laws, and also to the result of the change, that every State has in succession abolished primogeniture, and has so restricted the power of settlement that what we call entail is impossible. They have universally, however, retained the freedom of willing. They have rejected the French system of compulsory division of property. They have preserved the parental authority intact. The universal custom, however, of testators is to distribute property on death equally among their children. Any preference not justified by exceptional circumstances is most rare, is condemned by public opinion, and where attempted, not unfrequently leads to the will being disputed and upset on the ground of undue influence. Land transfer is exceedingly simple and uncostly; mortgages, which are almost a necessity for the existence of small properties, are effected with the greatest ease and at a most trifling cost, and the whole process of dealing with land is assimilated to that of personal property. Any legislation which tends to the monopoly of land, or to reduce or curtail the free rights and dominions of its owners, has everywhere been repudiated.

Under this system, and under the influence of public opinion, there is no tendency to create landed estates on the English principle, and the country throughout its length and breadth is farmed by men owning their own land. Hence the multitude of owners of land. The relation of landlord and tenant of farming land is all but unknown. The general aspect of the country, especially in such States as New York, Pennsylvania, Maryland, and Ohio, would surprise those who have not been out of England. The rural districts have a more populous appearance than

even in this country. Every hundred to a hundred and
fifty acres belong to a separate owner, who has a substantial
house, and who farms the land himself. There are no large
owners. The three millions of landowners are the founda-
tion of the social system, are the cause of stability, are the
conservative element in a system otherwise profoundly
democratic, and are also the promoters of prosperity to the
numerous cities and towns. The same condition of things
is extending through the far West, hundreds of miles beyond
Chicago, and will eventually, and at no distant day, stretch
across the continent.

In a similar manner have our other Anglo-Saxon colonies
cast off the old shell of our land laws, as soon as they were
endowed with the power to legislate. They seem to have
found them an intolerable nuisance, wholly unsuited to
modern life and to the necessities of an industrial society,
of which freedom of commerce in land is the very life-
breath. These changes have universally taken the same
direction—the withdrawal of state sanction to accumulation,
or to the preference of one child over another ; the assimilation of the law with respect to all kinds of property ; the
limitation of family settlements, and the prohibition of a
family succession different from that of the state ; the
registration of titles ; the simplification of transfer.

CHANGES FAVOUR INDIVIDUALISM.

It is to be observed that these changes, alike in the old
world and in the new, have been in the same direction and
with the same object—to favour and strengthen individual
property in land and to promote its distribution. There is
not in any of the legislation referred to, the slightest trace of
communism, or of any new-fangled ideas of property in land.
No attempt has been made towards state appropriation of
land. No step has been taken to secure to the community
what is called the unearned increment. The individual
owner is everywhere invested with full, absolute, and undisputed control of the land which he owns. Freedom of contract is nowhere interfered with.

Mr. West says of France :—" Proprietary rights can
never be called in question. Whether a property consists of
one acre or one hundred, the owner is absolute in all

matters relating to possession. The legislature cannot interfere between him and the tenant on questions respecting
compensation for improvements or indemnities. . . . Tenant-
right and fixity of tenure are phrases scarcely ever heard of
in France."*

Monsieur de Laveleye says of Flanders : †—" The
Flemish tenant, though ground down by the constant rise
of rents, lives among his equals, peasants like himself, who
have tenants whom they can use just as the large landowner
does his. His father, his brother, perhaps the man himself,
possesses something like an acre of land, which he lets at
as high a rent as he can get. In the public-house, peasant
proprietors will boast of the high rents they get for their
lands, just as they might boast at having sold their pigs or
potatoes very dear. . . .

" Thus the distribution of a number of small properties
among the peasantry forms a kind of rampart and safeguard
for the holders of large estates ; and the peasant property
may without exaggeration be called the lightning conductor
that averts from society dangers which might otherwise lead
to catastrophes."

Let it not, then, be said that any legislation in the same
direction has any, the slightest, taint either of communism
or confiscation. The one great object in view is not to
destroy property, or to lessen its value and the sense of
security which it gives, but to extend its influence as one of
the strongest and best agents in promoting individual exertion, and as a spur to efforts to rise in the social scale,
which is equally powerful with the lowest as with the
highest. It proceeds, then, on the principle of individualism as opposed to any principle of socialism or communism.

If, then, a right view has been taken of the motives
which have led to all the changes already described in other
countries, and of the results attained, equally in the old
world as in the new, it must be difficult to suppose that
England can withdraw herself from the stream of modern
life, can hope to live in an atmosphere of her own, resist all
changes in her laws, and content herself with going onward
in the old groove, and under the pleasing assurance of

* " Reports on Land Tenure in Europe," Part I., p. 73.
† " Systems of Land Tenure," published by the Cobden Club, p. 273.

philosophers that land was intended as a luxury for the rich, and that no poor man need hope for a permanent interest in the soil of his country other than perhaps so much as is covered by his hearth-stone when alive, and his grave-stone when dead.

To those who argue that it is an inevitable law of nature that land should in a wealthy country become the luxury only of the rich, and that the existing state of things in England is due to this and not to our positive laws, two questions may fairly be put with reference to the condition of other countries. The one is, whether they would really desire to substitute the English system of complete separation between the three classes of landowners, farmers, and labourers, for the yeoman and peasant proprietorship which so extensively prevails elsewhere? Whether they would contemplate with pleasure the possibility, or whether they expect, that the three million farming owners of the United States, with the advancing wealth and population of that country, will gradually be merged in about one-twentieth of their number of landlords, and that the relation of landlord and tenant will be universally substituted there? Whether in France it would be better, or be desirable in any sense, that the five millions of peasant owners should be reduced to the position of tenants at will to about one-hundredth part of their number of landlords, and that the Irish system should prevail there and in the Channel Islands as well as in Ireland?

The other question is what, on the assumption that these changes are desirable and to be aimed at, should be the first steps taken with a view to this end, and with the object of facilitating and promoting the gradual accumulation of land in few hands, and the substitution of a class of large landowners with farming tenants, for the existing systems of widely-distributed landownerships?

Would not the first measures adopted with this object be that their legislatures should again give the sanction of law to primogeniture, should again give facilities for the entail of landed property, and should again revert to a system of land laws which would make the title to land obscure and complicated, and its transfer, therefore, costly and difficult? And if this be conceded, how can it be doubted that these same laws and difficulties have in this country been mainly instrumental in producing the result which we now observe ?

ORIGIN OF THE ENGLISH LAND SYSTEM.

In England, as in most parts of the Continent, there existed, prior to the feudal system, a very different state of things to that since brought about. In Saxon times England was undoubtedly a country of very numerous landowners : they consisted of " eorls," or larger owners, who held under the Crown, and " ceorls," a very numerous class, tilling the land they owned, and answering to the modern class of yeomen, "the root," as Hallam says, " of a noble plant, the free-soccage tenants, or English yeomanry, whose independence stamped with peculiar features both our constitution and our national character." These two classes owned the cultivated land ; beyond were the common lands and forests, then called " folk land," the land of the people, the property of which was vested in the village community, and where the villagers had the right to turn out their cattle, dig their turf, or cut firewood. The property laws of these people were not different from those now prevailing among our colonists. There was equal division of land upon death among the children ; the power of alienation and of willing was fully conceded ; there was a public register of all deeds affecting land ; alienation was simple and public. These distinctive features of the Anglo-Saxon land laws were swept away after the Conquest. In their place was introduced the feudal system of land tenure, with its web of relations between the sovereign, the nobles, the knights, the villeins, and the serfs. The greater part of the land of England was confiscated after the battle of Hastings, and was granted out by the Conqueror to his military chiefs. These chiefs or · lords again, on their part, granted portions of the lordships thus confided to them to their principal knights and retainers below them, to be held on the condition of military service.

Some of the Saxon landowners survived this process of confiscation, and were brought under the system as free tenants of feudal superiors subject only to military service. Much greater numbers were relegated to the position of villeins in the feudal system, a position under which they continued to cultivate their lands for their own use, but subject to dues and services, mostly of a personal or agricultural character, to their lords, and were considered to have no rights as against such superiors. Below these was the class of serfs, or slaves, without any rights of property, the mere menial servants of their lords and masters. The feudal system being of military origin, founded on conquest and maintained against internal difficulties and foreign foes by force, had necessitated the maintenance of military commands, or fiefs, in strong hands ; the principle of primogeniture, therefore, by which the fief was inherited by the eldest male descendant was also a necessity ; and equally opposed to the system was the power of alienation, without the consent at least of the superior lord.

The general state of England, then, shortly after the Conquest, was this. The country was divided into a great number of separate lordships or manors. The lord of each manor cultivated a portion of the land, entitled his demesne, by himself or by his bailiff, partly by the assistance of the villeins or small farmers of his manor, who were bound to render him service—some of so many days' labour, and others of so many days of team work—and partly by the labour of serfs or slaves. The common lands, or wastes, were appropriated in a sense by the lords, but subject to the rights of the freehold and other tenants of the manor to turn out their cattle or dig their turf there.

Other portions of the land within the manor were owned by free tenants, who owed only military service, or in many cases fixed rents, to their superior lord, and who in every other sense were independent owners of their holdings. The remaining lands of the manor were held and cultivated by the class of villeins. Many of them had originally been owners of their lands, but by commendation or confiscation they had been completely subjected to the will of their feudal lords, and had lost all rights as against them. In theory and often in practice they were completely at the mercy of their lords, "*taillable et corvéable sans merci ni miséricorde*" (subject to dues and burthens without mercy or pity), as the old lawyers describe them ; they were, however, rarely or never disturbed in the occupation of their lands. They were allowed to alienate them with the consent of their lords, and to bequeath them to their children ; and for a time at least the old Saxon principle of equal division among such children, on death of the owner without a will, was preserved. In those days the number of retainers a lord could muster was a source of power and strength to him. He had no object, then, in dispossessing the tenants of his manor, neither did he undertake for them any of the duties which pertain to the modern landlord, of building houses for his tenants or improving their land ; when, therefore, the country became more settled, lawyers began to study the Roman law, and they drew principles from it which recognised the right of such tenants to what we should now call fixity of tenure—a right to continue in possession of their holdings upon payment of the customary dues, services, rents, or fines, and no longer to be merely tenants at the will of their lord.

Certain it is, that between the time of the Conqueror and of Edward the Fourth these villeins acquired a clear and absolute right to their holdings, and as tenants on the Roll of the Manor, or copyholders, have ever since been recognised as having an interest scarcely inferior to that of freeholders. It is this . body of small owners who constituted a large proportion of the small proprietors, who at one time were the boast of this country.

Domesday Book, the most valuable record of the state of landownership and of the relation of various classes of a population which any country has ever possessed, informs us that about twenty years after the Conquest the number of lords of manors holding directly from the Crown or indirectly from some superior lord, was 9,271 ; that the number of freeholders holding under these lords of manors by military service was 13,700 ; and that the number of freemen holding from lords of manors by fixed or determined rent service, was 30,831 ; a total of 53,802 freeholders. The number of villeins, as distinguished from burgesses and serfs, and who were therefore occupiers of land in rural districts, is stated to have been 108,407. The four northern counties and Wales, comprising one-fifth of the country, were not included in *Domesday*. Adding one-fifth, then, to the number, there must at this time have been not short of 200,000 heads of families interested in the soil, either as freeholders or villeins. The relation of landlord and tenant, such as we now know it, did not exist. There is little trace

D

of land having been let on lease to farmers before the reign of Edward I. The principle of primogeniture did not in these early times apply to any property but fiefs, or lands held under fiefs by military service; it did not apply to that freehold property known as free-soccage land, which had escaped confiscation at the Conquest, nor did it apply to the property of villeins. It is clear, then, that between the date of *Domesday* and the time of Edward III. there must have been a great increase in the number of persons who had an absolute right in the soil of their native country. Certain it is, that Sir John Fortescue, writing in the time of Henry VI., about a hundred years later, spoke of the number of its freeholders being one of the chief boasts of England of his day. He added, that although there were some noblemen of great estates, yet that between these estates there were great numbers of small freeholders. The number of parish churches, the entries in old registries, and many other indications, point to the fact of England, before the Black Death, having been very thickly populated in its rural districts. And Professor Rogers, who has investigated many old records and manorial lists of the fourteenth century, has found that the land was greatly subdivided, and that most of the regular farm-servants of that time were owners of land.

It would be interesting to trace, through succeeding periods, the gradual reduction of this element of English life. Statistics are at no period to be obtained, so that anything like an accurate tracing of the decline is impossible. It is to be noticed, however, that, unlike most other countries in Europe, where the principle of primogeniture was confined to feudal fiefs and lordships of manors, or to the property of the nobility, and was not applied to the property of inferior classes, in England this principle came to be applied to every species of landed property and to all classes of landowners, however small. It was probably extended to copyhold property about the time of Henry III.

THE HISTORY OF ENTAIL.

It is, however, to the principle of entail that we must mainly ascribe the reduction and disappearance of small owners. This principle was by no means one of the earliest features of feudalism. Fiefs and lordships of manors being in the first instance connected with military duties, even the hereditary principle was not at first recognised, and was for a time resisted by the feudal superiors; but when fully recognised, every effort was made to secure the perpetuation of these functions and properties in the male line of the family. The Norman barons endeavoured to introduce this principle shortly after the Conquest, but they met with great resistance from the Crown and the Church.

The main object which the feudal chiefs had in view was to secure their fiefs and property to their successors, free from the chance of forfeiture in case of treasonable acts of their own. Conviction for treason was followed by forfeiture of property. Entail would preserve the property for the family, though the present holder might suffer forfeiture during his lifetime.

On the other hand, the sovereign, representing the principle of order and of imperial interests, as opposed to those of the feudal lords or petty local chiefs, was much concerned in maintaining the principle of forfeiture of property in case of treason, as one of the main securities against rebellion. Any reduction, therefore, of this penalty was to be resisted. A powerful ally in this instance was found in the Church. The principle of entail, if once admitted, would deprive the Church of the main source of its wealth, the gifts of land by its pious sons. The clerical lawyers therefore assisted the sovereign in his efforts to prevent the introduction of this principle, and we find that they borrowed principles from the Civil Law with great ingenuity to upset the grants which had been obtained by the nobles with the object of creating entails.

For the first 200 years after the Conquest, the nobles failed to secure their object, or to effect entails. During the whole of this time, therefore, land was practically alienable ; and no doubt this contributed greatly to the increase in the number of owners of land.

In the year 1285, however, an Act was passed which enabled perpetual entails to be created. It is worthy of notice that this statute of Edward I., known as " De Donis," an Act still on the statute book and part of the law of this country, never obtained the consent of the Commons. This vicious principle of perpetual entail speedily came into

common use, and it was not long before grave inconvenience
and mischief arose from it, and from the consequent withdrawal of a great part of the landed property of the country
from free commerce.

These evils continued without remedy for another period
of 200 years. After this long interval, the reviving power of
the Crown and the ingenuity of the lawyers combined to
upset these perpetual entails, and a method was discovered
by which the celebrated statute of Edward I. was circumvented and defeated. The process by which this was arrived
at, and carried out, was so subtle, technical, and ingenious,
that it would be impossible to explain it in popular language,
or to make it intelligible to others than lawyers and logicians.
It is sufficient to say, that by a kind of collusion between
the courts of law and the immediate holder of an entailed
property, the object of the entail could be defeated, and
landed property subject to it could be sold.

Later, the Tudor kings, Henry VII. and Henry VIII.,
succeeded in inducing Parliament to give legislative sanction
to this curious device of the lawyers, and also to deprive
entailed estates of their freedom from forfeiture in the case
of the treason of their holders. These acts again gave
great freedom to the sale of land, and though entails were
not wholly destroyed and were still valid for certain purposes, they were not effective to prevent the alienation of
land. Thenceforward for another 200 years land again
became freely alienable, and entails were practically rendered innocuous.

It may be not unworthy of notice that these 200 years,
when land was practically free from the shackles of entail,
when the holders of estates were really their owners, and
not merely the ostensible owners or temporary enjoyers of
them, were not the least memorable years of English history
or the least fruitful of great Englishmen. They embraced
the Elizabethan era, and they spanned the lives of Bacon,
Shakespeare, and Milton, of Sydney, Raleigh, and Blake;
of Cecil and Walsingham, of Hampden and Pim, of Cromwell and Vane, of Strafford and Falkland. It does not
appear that, even in those days, notwithstanding the absence
of effective entail, men had any fear of being unable to
hand down to a remote posterity the products of their fortunes in lands and houses. Burleigh, Hatfield, Longleat,

Audley End, Holland House, and Bramshill, and numerous other great mansions, were built in this period, and still survive as evidence that even in days when landowners were in full possession of their property, they did not fear to build for a long future.

The period of freedom. of land from entails .lasted from the date of the discovery of the means of eluding the Statute de Donis, in 1472, till about the time of the great Rebellion, another period of nearly 200 years; it might possibly have lasted till our own time, but for the accidental effects of that great political crisis upon the views of lawyers and landowners. It again became a great object to the owners of land to protect their properties from the possible results of their acts if convicted of treason; and at a time when almost every landowner was forced, either by inclination or public opinion, to take one side or the other in the great national struggle, there was almost equal danger of the enforcement of this forfeiture for treason, on either side, as now one party and now the other prevailed.

It is interesting to observe that the lawyers and judges who had previously favoured freedom of alienation, and had exercised all their ingenuity to prevent entails, or to find the means of eluding and breaking them, now shifted their advocacy, and lending their subtleties to the opposite principle, aided the landowners in protecting their family estates from forfeiture, and succeeded in forging the system of entail through family settlements, from which the country has ever since suffered.

The essence of the new principle then introduced was the settling of property upon an unborn person, against which the courts of law had previously struggled. The effect of thus permitting the vesting of property in the unborn was to convert the immediate possessors of properties hampered by these arrangements into mere life-holders, without any real power over the property, without power to sell, or even to lease for any period beyond their own lives, and without any power of bequest in favour of other children than the one named in the settlement. It had the great merit, however, at such a period, of preventing the forfeiture of more than the life estate in the event of the life-holder being convicted of treason.

It will be observed that this system has never received

the assent of Parliament. It has never fairly been brought under review of the legislature. It was the invention of lawyers, and was sanctioned by the courts of law, but has never been subjected to popular control.

MODERN ENTAILS.

The general object of such family entails may be briefly stated as follows:—to secure that the landed property which is the subject of them shall descend in the direct male line by the order of primogeniture, intact and undiminished, for as long a period as possible ; to prevent the holder, the tenant for life, and successive tenants for life, from alienating the property, or bequeathing it to their children in such proportion as they may think fit.

It is customary for lawyers, in representing this system, to speak of it as very limited in its operation, and as tying up estates for a comparatively short period. They say that once in every generation it is possible to break the entail, and for the persons interested to join in freeing the property, and selling or disposing of it as they think fit. It is true that when the tenant in tail, as he is called, the unborn son in whom the property is ultimately vested, after the death of his father and perhaps his grandfather, reaches the age of twenty-one, he and his father can agree together to break up the entail, and to cut off all other contingent interests or collateral claims.

In fact, however, the system is so curiously and artfully devised, that when this climax is reached, when after the lapse of years there are co-existing two or more persons in different generations, who, by agreeing together, can cut off the entail, there arises out of the very nature of the arrangement the greatest inducement to all concerned in such a family settlement to take this opportunity, not to free the estate from its cumbrous shackles, but to prolong the entail, and to make a new settlement which will carry on the entail to another unborn generation.

The late Lord St. Leonards, a powerful advocate of the system, spoke of it as "from its own nature leading to successive settlements." Although, therefore, in one sense, such settlements may appear to be limited in duration, the truer view is that they embody much of the vicious principle of perpetual entail.

This power and the consequent custom to entail land has now existed for rather more than 200 years. It is commonly admitted that about three-fourths of the landed property of the country are subject to such entails. What effect have they had upon the distribution and ownership of property? Have they been the cause of the accumulation of land in few hands? Do they tend to prevent the application of capital to the land? Have they been in the interest of the families concerned? How have they affected the position and well-being of the labouring class?

EFFECT OF ENTAILS ON NUMBER OF LANDOWNERS.

It would be most interesting to trace the number of landowners through these periods, and to show the effect of these various changes upon the distribution of land. Unfortunately, however, from the *Domesday Book* till the return of four years ago we have no certain facts and no reliable statistics whatever. It has been already shown that at a very early period there was a very large number of small proprietors. It is probable that in the time of the Edwards their number was very much greater than at the present time, notwithstanding that the area of cultivated land has been greatly increased in the interval by the enclosure of commons and the clearing of forests. There is every reason to believe that a large majority of farmers were yeomen— that is, were owners of the land they farmed; and that a very large number of the labouring class were also owners of cottages and small plots of land. The records of copyhold manors give abundant proof of this; and all the testimony of early writers is to the same effect. How far this number was reduced or affected by the prevalence of entails between 1285 and 1470 we cannot tell, nor whether the greater freedom of the next period either tended to increase their number, or to stem the reduction which had been taking place. It is certain, however, that in the time of the civil war the number of freeholders in rural districts was considerable. It is matter of history that 6,000 freeholders rode up from Buckinghamshire to Westminster to petition Parliament against the arbitrary acts of Charles I., from which Clarendon dates the commencement of the civil war. It was from the yeomen that Cromwell mainly drew his forces. It was the county freeholders that formed the main support of the parliamentary party.

Lord Macaulay, speaking of the yeomen class of 200 years ago, says that they were "an eminently manly and true-hearted race. These small proprietors, who cultivated their own fields, and enjoyed a modest competence, without affecting to have escutcheons or crests, or aspiring to sit on the bench of justice, then formed a much more important part of the nation than at present. If we may trust the best statistical writers of that age, not less than 160,000 proprietors, who, with their families, made up more than a seventh of the whole population, derived their subsistence from small freehold estates. . . . It was computed that the number of persons who occupied their own land was far greater than those who farmed the land for others. Great," he adds, "has since been the change in the rural life of England."*

There are also, in most parts of rural England, indications that in times not very remote the small squires and yeomen were much more numerous than at the present time. Great numbers of existing farmhouses have the appearance and tradition of having been the residences of owners and not of tenants. It is admitted that the yeomen class has all but disappeared from most parts of England, and that the labouring class has almost ceased to have any permanent interest or property in the soil. The number of squires has been also so reduced that in many rural districts there are very few resident gentlemen, except the clergy. Inquiry on this point has shown that in the counties of Berkshire and Dorsetshire more than half the parishes have no gentlemen of the landowning class resident within them. Of the county of Nottingham it was reported that of 245 parishes in the eastern division only sixty-five have resident squires. Everything, therefore, points to the reduction of the number of landowners of all classes, whether of the squire class, or of the yeomen class, or of the agricultural labourer.

* "History of England," by Lord Macaulay, Vol. I., p. 262.

A careful examination of the list of landowners will tend to the same conclusions. Of the 1,000 landowners of upwards of 10,000 acres each, and averaging 30,000 acres, about sixty appear to have come into this category during the last thirty years ; some few of these owners have bought out other large proprietors, but the greater part of them have been created by the extinction of many small proprietors ; and probably an examination of the list of proprietors in the next rank would show a somewhat similar result. Of those who have existed more than thirty years, a certain number have, from one cause or another, been compelled to sell portions of their properties, yet a greater number have increased their properties, either by marriage or by purchase ; and the general result of an examination of the list, must be the conviction that the number of large proprietors is steadily increasing, at the expense of the smaller proprietors, and that the average holdings of land by these large owners is also increasing. It may be worthy of notice that in the list of those who have risen into the first grade of landowners, within the last thirty years, by purchase, and not by marriage, there is not a single name distinguished for any great service to the state or to the public. The days when statesmen like the Cecils or Walpoles, or when great lawyers like the Howards, the Cokes, or the Bridgemans, or great generals such as the Marlboroughs and Wellingtons, could acquire great properties of land, and could found families in the first rank of landowners, seem to be past. The list consists almost wholly of successful merchants, manufacturers, brewers, coalowners, ironmasters, or tradesmen ; it is from these classes that families are now being founded, which it is hoped by means of entails to maintain for a long future among the landed magnates. Without wishing to depreciate the merits of such persons, or the services which they have rendered to the industry and commerce of the country, while building up their own fortunes, it may be permitted to express a doubt whether society is much interested in affording them the machinery for securing that their names shall be escorted by landed property in perpetuity.

, It will not be denied, however, that if of this class a certain number are continually pressing into the ranks of landowners, and if an equivalent number is not dropping off the list by the dispersion or division of the property, by will or by sale, the list of large owners must be continually increasing, and the number of small owners continually diminishing in greater proportion; and the time must come when the ideal of such a system will be reached, when the country will be divided among a comparatively few of the largest owners, and when small proprietors will have ceased to exist in rural districts, or beyond the immediate neighbourhood of large towns.

DANGERS OF ENTAIL.

But for one feature of entail by family settlements there cannot be a doubt that accumulation would be far greater than it has been. The one counteracting force is that they sometimes tend to defeat their own objects. The effect of the arrangement is to divest the present holder of the property of all real power over it, and to vest the remainder with full power in the eldest son when he shall attain the age of twenty-one and survive his father. If the son should not agree to re-settle the estate, as it is called, when he arrives at the age of twenty-one, or if the father should die before the son reaches this age, the property will ultimately vest in the son to do as he likes with it. The certainty of thus coming into possession of the estate leads not a few eldest sons into early extravagance; they not unfrequently fall a prey to the class of money-lenders who are always on the look-out for them, and who induce them to anticipate their inheritance by borrowing upon their expectations. A young man who begins in this way is speedily brought to the point when he has ruined his property even before he has come into possession of it, and many are the cases where family properties have been sacrificed and sold through anticipations of this kind, favoured, if not created, by the very arrangements which were intended to preserve them intact. The settler of the property, who thought to preserve the family estate for future generations of his family, and who deprived his son of the full dominion over it and of the power of free bequest, is defeated in his object, through having vested the remainder in an unborn grandson, of whom he could know nothing, and who turns out to be unworthy of the charge.

Another feature of such family arrangements and artificial attempts to maintain property in the family, in successive generations of eldest sons, is the gradually accumulating debt upon the estate. Although the estate is settled on the eldest males in succession, there must be some provision for other members of the family. Widows must be provided with annuities, younger sons and daughters cannot be left without means, portions for them must be charged on the property ; in many cases debts must be met by charges on the estate, generally by arrangement between father and son when the property is re-settled ; the result is that charges gradually accumulate, and it is well recognised that few except the very largest properties will bear the burthens of this nature for two or three successive generations, unless marriage of the heir brings accession of wealth, or unless the property improves greatly in value from some adventitious circumstance ; and it may be doubted whether in the long run more families are not ruined and brought down by such arrangements than are perpetuated and enriched by them.

The effect of these accumulating charges upon the condition of the property itself will shortly be alluded to ; meanwhile it must be pointed out that the family settlement involves evils of no small magnitude to the family itself. It deprives the parent of the greater part of his parental control over his eldest son ; the son is placed in a position independent of his father, almost superior to him, for nothing can be done to the estate without the son's consent ; however unworthy he may prove to be, the property must descend to him ; the father has no power of selection or veto ; and no doubt many a father has had reason to curse the family arrangement under which his property is settled upon one who is unworthy to succeed him.

There are other causes at work which tend to a constant reduction in the number of small owners, and which add to the inducement to persons to enrol themselves in the list of great landowners, and retard their retirement from the rank by sale or otherwise. They are, however, closely allied to that which has been already pointed out, and it is difficult to determine whether they are not effects rather than causes

of the system. Chief among them is the great political
power which has been, for the last 200 years, conceded to
the owners of landed property. One branch of the legislature has been wholly created from their ranks. A large
landed property is admittedly the necessary qualification for a
peerage; this rank is almost conceded to an owner of £20,000
a year in land. The English county representation in the
House of Commons is also wholly at the command of the
landowners. They rarely look beyond their own ranks or
beyond their own county for a representative. The owner
of a certain standard number of acres, if of the right side of
politics, is almost certain of representing his county. This
command over the county representation is mainly secured
through the tenant farmers. The local government of rural
districts is wholly in the hands of the landowners; the county
magistracy is their recognised appanage. The sports of country
life are such as almost to necessitate large properties, and
could not be so fully indulged in if there were many small
proprietors. The sense of power created by the possession
of a large estate in a rural district is also great, and is generally
opposed to the existence of small ownerships within its
range. Opportunities, therefore, are seldom neglected of
buying up smaller properties where they are likely to interfere with this power.

In the neighbourhood of large towns, where land has
attained a building value, these forces are counteracted by
the personal interest of the owners, tempted by high prices ;
special facilities have been given to the owners of settled
estates to avail themselves of this great demand for building
land. But in rural districts there is no such counteracting
influence.

While, then, on the one hand, all these forces promote
the creation and increase of large properties, on the other
hand the difficulties of title in our most complicated system
of land laws, and the consequent expense of transfer, and
the cost of our system of mortgage, tell with infinitely
greater effect upon small properties than on large, and act
as a great discouragement to their purchase or continued
existence. This is what Lord Hatherley said on this subject
in 1859, in his Address on Jurisprudence at the meeting of
the Social Science Association at Bradford :—

" Look how the limitations of your law affect the transfer

of land. It is only on account of these that you have difficulties in title; because, if it were not for the complexity of limitations, a system of registration would long since have been established which, so far as fraud and rapidity of transfer was concerned, would have freed us from any difficulty of title whatever. You have now the combined effect of fraud and the complicated investigations of title which operate in the most serious manner to prevent the free transfer of land in our community; what I wish for, and have long wished for, is a free transfer of land."*

All other experience tends to show that a cheap and simple system of registration of title and mortgages is an essential condition of the existence of small properties.

On the one hand, therefore, we have every encouragement given by law, and by political and social arrangements, to the concentration of land in few hands; and on the other, every discouragement given to its dispersion, and to dealing with it in small quantities, and by people of limited means. What wonder then that we should find the number of proprietors continually diminishing, and that England presents an exception so striking to the rest of the civilised world.

RESULTS OF THE SYSTEM IN IRELAND.

The most serious effects of the system thus described have been exhibited in Ireland; and it is well to pass them under review, for the case of Ireland is very different from that of England and far more momentous.

It has already been shown that the number of landowners in Ireland is proportionably far less than in England. The difference is even more striking than that already pointed out, if we compare the number of small proprietors in the rural districts of both countries.

The three agricultural counties, Bedfordshire, Berkshire, and Buckinghamshire, with an area of 1,173,000 acres, may be fairly compared with the Irish counties Meath, Westmeath, and Cavan, with an area of 1,360,000 acres. In the English counties there are 6,412 owners of between 1 and 50 acres. In the Irish counties, with a larger area, there are only 612 such owners.

* "Transactions of the Social Science Association, 1859," p. 66

Or if we take the mountainous districts of Northumberland and Westmoreland, with an area of 1,736,000 acres, and compare them with Galway and Mayo, whose area is 2,760,000 acres, we find in the former 3,003 owners of small properties, in the latter only 225 such owners. It appears, then, that, as compared with England, Ireland has less than one-tenth the number of small owners.

The difference between the two countries is the more remarkable as, whatever may be the case in England, it is certain that in Ireland land has not acquired an artificial value. The price of land in Ireland is very much below that of England; it does not average more than twenty-two years' purchase of the annual rental, and has only reached even this point within the last few years. At this rate money may be invested in land in Ireland to pay about 4½ per cent.

The explanation of this great difference in the number of landowners in Ireland, is to be found in the early history of that country, in the fact that it never passed through the feudal system, that it was not thoroughly conquered by England until the feudal system had already disappeared from the latter. Under the feudal system, the occupiers of land in Ireland, who held under ancient customs which gave them an interest in the soil from which they could not be dispossessed, would most probably have obtained the same recognition and fixity of tenure as did the villeins or copyholders in England. The later English law treated them on the Conquest as mere tenants at will of those who acquired by grant the land of the dispossessed lords of the soil.

In later years the position was still further aggravated by the penal laws directed against the Roman Catholics, which forbade their inheriting or acquiring land by purchase. When, added to these, we have the English land system tending to the aggregation of land, and offering every obstacle to its dispersion or easy transfer, we can well account for the paucity of landowners in Ireland; and for the fact that, even when compared with England, their number is so very limited.

None of the justifications which are claimed for the system of England apply to Ireland. The same laws and the same system has achieved results in the two countries as

different as possible. England is in the main a country of
large landowners and of large farm holdings. Ireland is a
country, proportionally of even larger landowners, but of
very small farm holdings. Of its 533,000 farm tenancies,
450,000 are of less than 50 acres, and 50,000 between 50
acres and 100 acres. It is, therefore, essentially a country
of peasant cultivators. In England the custom is for the
landowner to effect all the substantial improvements on the
farm ; to build the farmhouses and other buildings, to drain
and fence the land. In Ireland the landlord, as a general
rule, does none of these. It is the tenant who lays out
what little capital is spent in this way, even to the building
of the house. He does this under a tenancy which is rarely
more than a yearly holding.

The condition of Ireland is still more remarkable when
we consider that all experience from the Continent shows
that farming on a small scale can only answer when largely
combined with ownership ; that it is the magic of ownership
only which gives the inducement to the industry necessary
for very small farms. Being a country of small farms, it is
free from the argument that large properties are necessary
in order that farming may be carried out on a large scale.
It is equally free from the argument that large properties
are economically advantageous, as they result in capital
being invested in the land by the owner, and in tenants
being able to use the whole of their capital in farming.
Here, then, of all places in the world, one would expect to
find a large class of small owners. Apart from the recent
sales under the Irish Church Act, there are none. There
are all the conditions of a peasant proprietary, without any
proprietary rights, or any fixity of tenure. The condition of
Ireland before the famine of 1848 closely resembled the
condition of France as described by Arthur Young immediately before the Revolution of 1789. On the one hand,
a pauperised tenant class ; and on the other, great properties
encumbered to a degree which ·made the owners mere
ciphers in the hands of their creditors. This state of things
was brought to a crisis by the potato famine. The consequent emigration relieved Ireland of its plethora of cottier
tenants. The effort made by the imperial legislature was
first directed to freeing property from its encumbrances ;
and the Encumbered Estates Court was brought into exist-

ence for the purpose of cutting the knots of these tangled
interests in landed estates, and enabling them to be sold.
It was believed and hoped that the land, thus freed from its
bankrupt owners, would pass into the hands of capitalists,
who would improve its condition by expending capital in
buildings and drainage.   It is reckoned that one-fifth of
the landed property of Ireland has passed through this
Court, and has changed hands; the number of owners of
such land has probably been increased threefold.   Those,
however, who devised this measure reckoned without taking
into consideration Irish feelings and Irish customs.   With
rare exceptions, the new owners spent no more capital on
the land than did their easy-going predecessors.   When
they attempted to improve, the tenants often resented the
process.   It was an assertion of complete ownership which
did not tally with the ideas of Irish tenants, of their relations
to their landlords.   Whatever the English law might be,
the traditions, customs, and ideas of Irish tenants involved
a relation to their landlords far different from that which
holds in England; they claimed a participation in the proprietary rights, which was generally conceded to them by
custom, and which prevented the lords of the soil from
ejecting them without good cause, arbitrarily raising rents,
or appropriating, in the shape of increased rent, the value of
the tenants' improvements.   The new purchasers entered
upon their properties without any of these traditional
feelings, without any sympathy for their tenants, without
any knowledge of local customs or hereditary practices.
They too frequently applied to their new purchases the
most extreme doctrines of proprietorship ; they thought they
were entitled to raise rents to the highest rack-rental that
could be extracted, regardless of the previous history of the
estate, or of the customs of the country.

It cannot be denied that many cases of great hardship
and injustice arose to Irish tenants.   What was intended
for their benefit resulted not unfrequently in loss or ruin to
them.   The result, therefore, of the Encumbered Estates Act
was to intensify the demand for the recognition of tenant
right, and to give a great impulse to political agitation in
favour of fixity of tenure.   England at last turned an ear to
Irish grievances, and the Land Act of 1870 was framed, on
the principle of applying to the Irish land question so much

of Irish ideas as was not wholly incompatible with English doctrines.

It gave legal recognition for the first time to local customs, such as the Ulster Tenant Right, which had created a practical property in the tenant. It reversed the doctrine of English law, that improvements of all kinds are annexed absolutely to the land, and in default of actual agreement enure wholly to the benefit of the landlord. It recognised the fact that in the case of tenants of small farms there could be such a thing as an arbitrary and capricious ejectment, and it gave to the tenant who was ejected, a claim for any improvements effected, and damages for capricious ejectment. It did not, however, go the length of interfering between landlord and tenant as to the amount of rent. It left to the landlord the power of raising the rent to a point when the rent would practically swallow up the value of the tenant's improvements; but it left to the tenant the option of refusing this rent, of throwing up his farm, and of making his claim for the value of his improvements and for disturbance of the tenancy to which he would be entitled.

It is unnecessary to pursue further the question of tenant right or the relations of Irish landlords and tenants; it is, however, important to notice the impulse given by the state to the extension of proprietorship in substitution for tenancy, and to the creation of a class of peasant proprietors, where none such existed previously. The framers of the Irish Land Act, and of the Church Disestablishment Act, under the influence and impulse mainly of Mr. Bright, recognised the grave deficiency of proprietary rights in Ireland, and the expediency of endeavouring to increase the number of proprietors, and of converting where possible, by agreement or purchase, tenants into owners. This might indeed be deemed an alternative method to that of fixity of tenure demanded by the tenants. It was, at all events, though novel in its application as a remedy, in harmony with the ideas of English law and English proprietors. However unwilling Parliament might be to adopt any such plan in England, Ireland, it thought, might be an exception without raising any precedent dangerous to the principle of property.

The proposals in this direction met with no opposition in either branch of the Legislature. It is also worthy of

E

notice that the first attempt to extend proprietary rights followed the example of France and Prussia. It was the secularisation of Church property which gave the opportunity for first experimenting in this direction. It was probably felt that to sell the landed property of the Irish Church in the open market was to risk its falling into the hands of persons who might capriciously and arbitrarily raise rents; it was thought fair to offer such land in the first instance to its tenants; it was hoped that the result of increasing the number of proprietors would be a gain to the cause of property in Ireland. The Irish Church Act, therefore, directed the Commissioners charged with the sale of Church lands to give preference to the tenants, and to charge the land sold to them with the repayment of three-fourths of the purchase-money by instalments spread over thirty-two years.

The intentions of Parliament were admirably carried out by the Irish Church Commissioners. They have earned the gratitude of the Irish people by pointing the road where it is possible much further progress may hereafter be made. They might have obstructed the policy of Parliament, or they might have neglected to make it known to the tenants. They have, on the contrary, used their endeavours to make the policy of Parliament intelligible and acceptable to the tenants.

Under this operation nearly 5,000 tenants of the Church property, of the smallest class, have found one-fourth of the purchase-money for their farms, and have become absolute owners in lieu of tenants; for thirty-two years they will be responsible for annual instalments of the principal and interest of the remainder of the purchase-money, which are about equivalent to their former rent. It is in evidence that these new purchasers have paid their interest with regularity and without fail, and that many of them have already been induced to effect great improvements on their holdings, the result of the feeling of security created by absolute ownership in place of yearly tenancy.

The Irish Land Act contained provisions known as "the Bright Clauses" in the same direction, and with the same object—that of creating a proprietary class among the peasant farmers of Ireland. Under these clauses the state undertakes to lend two-thirds of the purchase-money of any farm sold to a tenant, repayable, as in the case of the Church property, by instalments spread over a term of years. The Landed Estates Court (the successor of the Encumbered Estates Court) is directed by the Act to afford facilities to tenants to purchase their holdings, when estates are sold in that Court, and various other provisions are contained with the same object. Hitherto, however, but little result has followed. In the eight years which have elapsed since the passing of the Act, not more than 100 sales have been effected to tenants in each year under its provisions—a result which, whether compared with the results of the Irish Church Act, or with the intention and wishes of the Legislature, is certainly most inadequate.

Looking back to 1848, when the Imperial Parliament devised means for encumbered landowners to sell their properties, what might not have been the result by this time, if advantage had then been taken to promote the sale of such properties to their tenants? Many thousands of tenants might have been added to the class of owners of land by this process; and who can doubt what would be the result of such an accession to the class of persons permanently interested in the soil of their native country? The opportunity has been lost; but with our experience of what has been done under the Irish Church Act and the Land Act, it is still possible in the future to do more in this direction. Who can say that, with such experience, the creation of a class of peasant proprietors in Ireland is a mere dream? What has been achieved may be but the commencement of a new policy which shall favour the spread or creation of ownership rather than tenancy. Can it be doubted that good results would follow the creation of such a class in Ireland? Who can look at the state of ownership of landed property in that island without feeling how insecure is its basis—how limited is the class of persons who are interested in its rights? What would not be the advantage to Ireland, if of its 550,000 peasant farmers, a fair proportion were owners as well as occupiers? They would be an element of security both in the political and social system. They would exercise a powerful influence in promoting industry and thrift. They would raise the standard of production. They would supply the step of the ladder by which the lowest might hope to arrive at the position of landowners.

Is it possible to suppose that such a result is beyond the reach of political effort? The success of the experiment in the sale of Church lands forbids a negative to the answer, and raises every hope for further success in a direction so full of promise to Ireland.

It will be said, perhaps, in answer to this, that the economic condition of small farms is unsound—that a greater net produce would result, and a higher rent to the landlord, if a number of these small farms were thrown into one, and their tenants, with one exception, turned into day labourers. Whether this economic result would be produced is a matter open to doubt. In the opinion of many, small owners will hold their own in production against large farms. But even if it were not so, it may be confidently asked, whether any one would contemplate with pleasure the conversion of every twenty small Irish farms of fifteen acres each into large farms of 300 acres? Is the condition of the English labourer such that the Irish small farmer would envy his lot? Which is the superior in general status in the world? Which has the pleasanter lot and the better hope for the future? Which is the best member of society? Which has the best opportunity of rising?

Whatever, however, English economists and theorists may think upon the subject of small farms *versus* large farms, and small proprietors *versus* large proprietors, it will be impossible to persuade the Irish tenants to any other than one conclusion. Their instincts and traditions are opposed to any conversion of small farmers into day labourers. There remains, therefore, the only alternative, to increase the productive power of the small farmers by offering to them the opportunity of converting themselves by purchase into owners, wherever this can be done without injury to the rights of property; and by throwing the influence, weight, and sanction of the state in favour of a widely-diffused ownership of land, as opposed to the opposite system which has been at work in Ireland since its subjection to the rule and law of England.

RESULTS OF THE SYSTEM IN ENGLAND.

The same laws with respect to inheritance and entail have led to the same general result, in England, in the

distribution of landed property, although the circumstances
of its early history were more favourable to the creation of
small proprietors, who have not wholly disappeared in some
rural districts. It is admitted, however, that even these are
destined to be merged in their larger neighbours under the
present system.

A wholly different system, however, has prevailed in
England as regards the management of landed property and
the distribution of land among the tenants. It has been
shown that Ireland is a country of peasant farmers, where
the landlords do nothing, as a general rule, towards the improvement of the farms. In comparison, England is a
country of large farms, and the custom is for all improvements to be effected by the landlord and not by the
tenant.

It must not, however, be concluded that England is
wholly a country of large farms. There are large numbers
of small holdings. According to the Agricultural Returns,
of 37,000,000 acres of land, 27,000,000 are cultivated and
improved, the rest being mountain, heath, commons, woods,
&c. The cultivated land may be thus divided into four
classes of holdings:

	Numbers.	Average in acres.	Total acreage.
Small holdings below 50 acres	333,630	12	4,181,346
Small farms from 50 to 100 acres	54,498	72	3,957,989
Medium sized farms from 100 to 300 acres	65,766	170	11,183,618
Large farms above 300 acres .	16,106	472	7,512,972
	470,000		26,835,925

The number of agricultural labourers and shepherds is
stated to be 787,897. It will be seen from this table that
England is by no means so fully the country of large farms
as it is often represented to be. About one-third of its
area is held in small holdings and small farms, numbering
about 388,000, and two-thirds in large farms, numbering
about 82,000. How many of the small farms and holdings
are owned by their cultivators we have no means of
knowing; it is believed the number is very small, and is
being gradually reduced. In lieu we have an admitted

tendency to substitute for ownership the relation of landlord and tenant.

The ideal of the English system of large proprietors and of tenants hiring the land they farm in lieu of owning it, is where the landlord, being a capitalist, is able to relieve the tenant of all expenditure of a permanent character, and to leave him the full employment of his capital in his trade of farming, in stocking and cultivating the land. This ideal involves a considerable expenditure on the part of the landlord, in building farm-houses and farm-buildings, in draining and other permanent improvements, and in building labourers' cottages. If these functions are performed by the landlord, if he has the capital to expend and does what is recognised as a duty, nothing can be better, from the economic point of view, than the condition of the property and the relation of landlord, tenant, and labourer

The farms in such a case are parcelled out in the size which is most suitable to the full development of the soil; the necessary capital of a permanent character is expended by the landlord; the capital of the tenant is set free to stock and cultivate the farm to the best advantage; the tenant, in order to pay full rent upon the capital laid out, must exert himself to the best of his efforts ; if he prove a slovenly farmer, the landlord gets rid of him.

The labourers' cottages are built with due regard to the requirements of the property. Some of them are attached to the farm for the convenience of the tenant, who wishes for full control of those labourers who are most necessary to him ; others are retained in possession of the landlord, that too much power over the labourers may not be vested in the farmer. The labourers themselves are stimulated to work by the certainty that they will lose their positions if negligent and idle.

From an economic point of view, then, the agricultural machine in which the landlord, farmer, and labourer play their separate parts, and the land, capital, and wages have their share in the produce, works to the best advantage. That there are many such cases no one can deny. That many landlords most fully recognise their duties, and act fully up to the highest ideal, cannot be doubted. Many, indeed, pinch themselves in other expenditure in order to perform their duty ; and few there are who would not do it if they could. If all estates were maintained to this ideal, there would be little to say against the system from the economic point of view; though even then there might be something to allege in favour of more distributed ownership, and more independence of individuals, especially of the labourers, than is consistent with such an ideal system.

The whole system, however, depends upon the owner of the property being able to provide the capital for permanent improvements, such as buildings, drainage, and labourers' cottages. If this capital be not forthcoming the system breaks down at its central point, on which the economic success of the whole system hinges. If the landlord cannot provide the necessary capital for these permanent improvements, no one else will do so. The farming tenant cannot be expected to do so upon any length of lease such as is ordinarily given to him, and still less can the labourer be expected to build or improve his cottage.

It has already been shown that it is of the essence of such family arrangements, known as settlements and entails, that they lead to encumbrances. The land goes to the eldest son, perhaps free from charge in the first instance ; the personality is divided among the other members of the family. In the next generation, however, the land must be charged for the benefit of other members of the family. It is also well recognised that the owner of a landed estate cannot do full justice to it unless he is able to draw upon other property for its improvement. The late Sir Robert Peel used to say that every landowner ought to have at least as much property in consols or other securities, if he wished to do his best by the land. The meaning of this is, that there is a constant drain upon the landlord for fresh outlay for improvements, or for the maintenance of previous improvements, if the machine is to be well worked.

What, however, is the condition in this respect of the average landowner? How many of them have other means in this proportion to their land? How many are unencumbered as regards their family estates? How many of them are able to do their duty by the land?

It is certain that the greater number of them are utterly unable to perform their duties. They are the ostensible and temporary owners of family estates, for the most part already heavily charged with debts, or with charges for other

members of the family, and wholly unable to expend further
sums in draining and improving, still less in building cottages, which at best give but a poor return on the outlay.
Most of them are in this false position, that as tenants
for life only of their property they cannot expend capital on
their estates without subjecting the money thus spent to the
same entail as the estates themselves. The limited owners
thus have the alternative before them, either of neglecting
their properties, or of spending money upon them, which
they would otherwise intend for their younger children, to
the ultimate benefit of their eldest sons, who are already
entitled to the estates. If such persons were absolute
owners of their property, and without other means of improvement, they would probably be induced to sell outlying
parts of the property, and invest the proceeds in draining
and improving the main portion of the estate. They would
gain in income by doing so. The investment in land, we
are told, produces an average of only two per cent.; the
produce of a sale, if spent on drainage, would entitle the
owner to raise his rents so as to pay five per cent. or more
on the outlay. But he is tenant for life only, and he can
only sell with the consent of trustees and reversioners, to
re-invest in other land, or to pay off mortgages.

Is it possible to conceive a system better calculated to
prevent capital finding its way to the land? That it has
this result can scarcely be doubted. This is what Mr. Caird
said a few years ago on the subject in his "Agricultural
Survey of England":—"Much of the land of England, a
far greater proportion of it than is generally believed, is in
the possession of tenants for life, so heavily burthened with
settlement encumbrances that they have not the means of
improving the land which they are obliged to hold. It
would be a waste of time to dilate on the public and private
disadvantages thus occasioned, for they are acknowledged
by all who have studied the subject."

A Committee of the House of Lords in 1873 upon the
Improvement of Land, reported that what had already been
accomplished in the way of drainage and other improvements was "only a fraction of what still remained to be
done."

Mr. Bailey Denton stated before this Committee, as the
result of his calculations, that out of 20,000,000 acres of

land requiring drainage in England and Ireland, only 3,000,000 had as yet been drained. Mr. Caird, before the same Committee, speaking not only of drainage, but of all kinds of improvements, estimated that only one-fifth of what required to be done was accomplished.

The improvements thus spoken of are of a remunerative kind; improvements such as drainage and farm-buildings are generally paid for by an increase of rent fully compensating for the outlay. Unfortunately, however, the building of labourers' cottages by landlords is a most unremunerative expenditure. It seldom returns more than two per cent. on the outlay, very often less. If, therefore, we find the outlay of capital for remunerative improvements very much in arrear, it is only too certain that it will be far worse in the case of cottages.

The Report of the Royal Commission of 1869, as to the condition of women and children employed in agriculture, contains the most full information on this subject. The evidence was collected by Assistant Commissioners who visited every part of the rural districts of England, and who are unanimous in their testimony.

Mr. Fraser, now Bishop of Manchester, who visited Norfolk, Essex, Gloucestershire, and Sussex, described the cottages in one district as " miserable ; " in a second as " deplorable ; " in a third as " detestable ; " in a fourth as " a disgrace to a Christian community." He said that " even where adequate in quality, they are inadequate in quantity ; and some rich landowner, 'lord of all he surveys,' having exercised his lordship by evicting so much of his population as were an eyesore, or were likely to become a burthen to him—still employing their labour, but holding himself irresponsible for their domicile—has, by a most imperfect system of compensation, built a limited number of ornamental roomy cottages, which he fills with his own immediate dependents. Out of the 300 parishes which I visited, I can only remember two where the cottage accommodation appeared to be both admirable in quality and sufficient in quantity. The majority of the cottages that exist in rural parishes are deficient in almost every requisite that should constitute a home for a Christian family in a civilised community. It is impossible," he added, "to exaggerate the ill-effects of such a state of things in every respect—physical, social, economical, moral, intellectual. Physically a ruinous, ill-drained cottage, 'cabin'd, cribbed, confined,' and overcrowded, generates any amount of disease—fevers of every type, catarrh, rheumatism—as well as intensifies to the utmost that tendency to scrofula and phthisis which, from their frequent intermarriages and their low diet, abounds so largely among the poor. Economically, the imperfect distribution of cottages deprives the farmer of a large proportion of his effective labour power ; when he gets his man, he gets him more or less enfeebled by the distance he has to travel to his work. The moral consequences are fearful to contemplate. Modesty must be an unknown virtue, decency an imaginable thing, where in one small chamber two, and sometimes three, generations are herded promiscuously, and where the whole atmosphere is sensual, and human nature is degraded into something below the level of the swine. It is a hideous picture, and the picture is drawn from the life."

As to the deficiency of cottages, he mentioned the parish of Spixworth, where "there are only three cottages to 1,200 acres, there might well be twenty-five ; at Waterdon only two cottages to 750 acres, fifteen would be no excessive supply; at Markshall only five to 830 acres, at the usual Essex rate there should be twenty-five. At Buckenham Tofts there are only two resident labourers on 650 acres ; at Didlington no more on 1,850 acres. At Sedgeford the Ecclesiastical Commissioners had an estate of 2,000 acres without a single cottage, and in this parish we hear of ten and eleven persons sleeping in a single room. At Titchwell, Magdalen College, Oxford, the chief owner and lord of the manor has not a single cottage. At White Colne, in Essex, the chief landowner has not one." " Instances," he adds, " of this kind could be accumulated *ad infinitum.*"

The Bishop recognised that a great deal had been done of late years, especially by the largest landowners. Unfortunately, however, the remedy did not rest with the wealthiest landowners. Many cottages belonged to proprietors too indigent to have any money to spare for their improvement ; some to absentee and embarrassed landowners ; some to mortgagees. Mr. Portman, another Assistant Commissioner, who reported upon Cambridgeshire and Yorkshire, said, " The opinion appeared to be universal that the bad state of the cottages and the overcrowding of the sleeping-rooms is the root of the demoralisation of both sexes." He states that "one of the principal causes is 'absenteeism,' under which I include not merely non-residence of the owner in the county where his estate is situated, but that which is equally bad—viz., non-attention to the outlying portions of that estate. On many occasions when, being struck by the poor state of the dwellings, I have inquired who is the owner, I have been told he is some one living perhaps in the county, but rarely, if ever, visiting the village or taking any heed as to the condition of the people." Of one very large property he reports, " The.tenements are wretched ; although the rents paid are small, the whole repairs have to be done by the cottagers, and so the rents become in fact very high ; and as one of them told me, ' The landlord does not care if they all tumble down.' On other portions of this estate there was a great want of cottages, many having been pulled down and scarcely a new one built." Of another parish in Wales he said, " No Irish property can present more wretched consequences of absenteeism than this. The only con- sideration the parish receives from the owners of property is the regular collection of rents." The statement of Mr. Portman as to absenteeism is important, as confirming what has been already stated as to the number of parishes without resident landowners.

Mr Edward Stanhope, late Under-Secretary at the India Office, reported also as to the general bad state of cottages, though making many exceptions, especially in Lincolnshire, the county where, it may be observed, small peasant owners most abound. Of Leicestershire he said, " The cottages must be described as generally bad." He added, " There is a strong feeling in Lincolnshire that Government should give assistance in providing cottages for the labouring class, and especially on entailed estates."

Mr. Culley, another of the Assistant-Commissioners, said, " There constantly arises to me, and, I doubt not, to my colleagues, the feeling that in speaking of that state of the cottages, I am exhibiting a dark picture, as if it was the fault of a class, many of whom are powerless to change it, and few of whom are answerable for it.

" What has led to the state of the labourers' dwellings being such as to justify me in speaking of it as a national disgrace? And why are so many landowners now powerless to deal with it? If I were to answer these questions, judging from the history of the estates I have visited, I would answer at once—the encouragement given by law to the creation of limited interests in land, and the power of entailing burthened estates. What can the poor life-tenant, especially if his estates be burthened, do towards providing good cottages for his labourers? Nine times out of ten he strives to do his duty, and suffers fully as much as the ill-housed labourers on his estates. The unhappy propensity to create limited interests, and entailed and burthened estates, tells hardest against the small properties, while if the owner lives as all the world expects him to live, there is no margin left for estate improvement, especially cottage improvement. Even on the large estates, by the time all is done for which farm tenants most loudly call, unless burthens be light, or the owner unusually self-denying, there is very little left to expend in the expensive luxury of cottage building. The case of small estates, however, is the worst, and in spite of the supposed protection of the law of entail, they are being swallowed up by their larger neighbours, or passing into the hands of men whose sole means are not invested in land."

Mr. Portman said, upon the same subject, "I would venture to suggest for your consideration whether it is not expedient that legislation should take place in such a direction as to bring into the market those tracts of encumbered land, enabling those who have capital to acquire such lands if they desire to do so, and conferring a boon on those who now possess them by giving them money to spend on such an amount of territory as they wish to concentrate round their homes, while at the same time the curse of poverty and misery will be removed from these districts whence all the profit is drawn and to which none returns. Bad cottages would, I think, then become more rare ; a portion at least of the profits would be spent on the spot, a more contented race of farmers and of labourers would be found, and the education of the people, now flagging for want of funds, would progress. Some may say that this question of the dwellings of the poor in agricultural districts is a passing question of the hour, and that it is not really so great an evil as is represented. I would answer—Go into the country and see for yourself. Use your common sense, and call to mind the effect of absenteeism on Ireland ; and say whether or not in those portions of England where poverty and misery, arising from the same cause, meet you at every step, there is not urgent reason for dealing with the evils now existing by some legislative enactment, which shall put an end to a state of apathy and indifference in many holders of encumbered estates, and open the doors for the spending of capital on lands by those who are able, in the place of those who are now unable, to do so."

It is only fair to add that it is not only upon entailed properties that cottages are bad. Some of the worst cases are to be found on land which has been bought by speculators, and where rows of cottages have been built of the most flimsy material, with insufficient accommodation, without gardens, and which are let at exorbitant rents. Most of these cases have arisen in what are called open parishes, adjoining those close parishes where, before the alteration of the law, which threw the burthen of the support of the poor upon the whole Union, it was the interest of landowners to neglect to provide cottages, or to pull down existing cottages, in order to avoid giving to the labourers a claim for settlement, which would throw the cost of maintaining them, when paupers, upon such parishes.

The Census of 1861 showed that in the previous ten years, in 821 English parishes, a decrease of houses was accompanied by an increase of population. The last census shows that this action has been stayed by the Union Chargeability Act, but there was nothing in the Act to undo the mischief which had already been effected.

Other bad cases are not rare, where cottages have been built upon patches of land cribbed from the waste of a manor, or roadside waste, and which the labouring occupiers now claim as their own ; these, however, are hardly fair cases of individual ownership.

Let it not also be said that all landowners are to blame for this state of things. Nothing could be more unfair. If they were absolute owners of their property, with power to sell or to charge their properties, as they might wish, there would indeed be ground for complaint if such a state of things were allowed to remain unredressed. But the system under which the great bulk of them hold their properties, as mere nominal owners, without real power over them, is devised with the certain result that it can never be their interest to expend money on cottages, and rarely in their power to do so.

Many efforts have been made by Parliament to find a remedy for these evils, short of interfering with entails or simplifying the transfer of land. The tenant for life (the limited owner, as he is very significantly called) had originally no power to bind his successor, either by leases or by charges on . the property for its improvement. Parliament, however, has interfered to give him these powers, subject to the approval of public bodies, who are to have regard to the interests of the reversioner.

Short leases for agricultural purposes can now be given by tenants for life. Longer leases can be given with the consent of the Court of Chancery. Charges can be made on the entailed property for certain improvements with the consent of the Inclosure Commissioners. The charge, however, must be made in such a way as to repay the principal by instalments in varying terms of years, according to the nature of the improvement. The result is that drainage generally involves an annual charge of $7\frac{1}{2}$ per cent. on the outlay—as much or more than the tenant will pay in the shape of increased rent. The building of cottages involves an annual charge which averages three times the amount of the rent which can usually be obtained for them. Sales may also be effected upon application to the courts of law, where there are no powers for this purpose contained in the settlement; but the consent of tenants for life and of reversioners must be obtained; the proceeds must be expended in paying off mortgages, or in buying other land to be settled in the same manner, and can never be expended in agricultural improvements, however necessary. These, however, are mere palliatives, and not remedies. They have failed to effect any substantial result. They tend to substitute for the real owner of the property a Government department, a state inspector, or a judicial tribunal; they entail troublesome and expensive applications to courts of law and Government officials; they involve friction and delay. From their very nature they are destined to failure.

The system, however, which needs such remedies stands condemned by their proposal, and, as the late Mr. Wren Hoskyns well said, "Wherever a series of supplementary devices is needed to meet a law at variance with the time, it indicates the undercurrent of another law struggling against worn-out barriers that will not long withstand it."

What is the other law, struggling against the worn-out system, which has thus signally failed to meet the demands of the country and the claims of the land for the outlay of capital? It is freedom of sale, the alienability of land, the free commerce of land; the principle that land shall be owned by those who can give full title for it, and who can either borrow for improvements or sell what they cannot . improve; the principle that land shall belong to the present generation, and not to an unborn generation; that land-owners shall be full masters of their own property, and not be obliged to obtain the consent of the unborn for improve-ments or sale, through the medium of Courts of Law and Government offices.

It must be here freely admitted that some of the largest properties are exceptions to this general condemnation, both in respect of farm improvements, farm buildings, and labourers' cottages. Such properties as those of the Dukes of Bedford, Devonshire, and Northumberland, and others that could be named, are models of all that conscientious and intelligent landowners should aim at. It is obvious that as there is a limit to the possible personal expenditure of families with such great fortunes, the margin which is left for improvement of their properties must be greater in pro-portion than on smaller estates; it will generally be found also that these very great landed properties are supported by great incomes from other sources, such as house property or minerals. It is often argued from such examples that the larger properties are, the better prospect there is of capital being expended on the land by their owners; and hence a conclusion that it is well to encourage the creation of large properties, and to regard with indifference the disappearance of smaller properties. The argument, however, is a dangerous one; the logical conclusion of it is, that it might be well to merge all large proprietors into one still greater proprietor—namely, the state itself. If the state were sole and supreme landlord, it might spend all the rent

in local improvements, in farm buildings and cottages; and
in such a case the whole of the rent would remain on the
land from which it is due. This is obviously a *reductio ad
absurdum*, but it suggests to us the necessity for bearing in
mind the principle on which alone private property in land
exists and can be defended.

If the English system fails in bringing to the land the
capital, which is so essential for its development, or for
building cottages so necessary for the accommodation, comfort, and even decency of the labourer, what is its effect
upon the labouring class? The failure to spend capital on
the land to them means low wages; low wages and bad
cottages combined mean a poverty-stricken life, which tells
upon the whole existence of the labourers.

It may be confidently said that the agricultural labourers
are divorced from any permanent interest, however small, in
the land, or even in the villages in which they live. With rare
exceptions, it is impossible for them to become possessed of
a plot of land or even of a cottage. The sense of property
therefore never comes home to them.

Can we wonder, then, at the thriftless, hopeless, and
aimless condition into which so large a proportion of them
have drifted? The effect of the English system upon them
may be best judged by the results in those counties in the
south where it has been longest in existence, where it is
carried out most fully, and where it is undisturbed by the
growth of any adjoining industries—such counties as Sussex
and Dorsetshire. Who can be satisfied with the condition
of the agricultural labourers in these districts? or who can
suggest any remedy consistent with the ideal of the present
system? What hope for advancement is there in their own
country? what prospect of rising from the lowest steps of
the ladder to the higher? An impassable barrier separates
the labourer from the farming class immediately above him,
and a still wider gulf from the owner of land who crowns
the social edifice. What wonder, then, that the labourers
should be thriftless and without energy; that education
only induces the best of them to leave the country districts
for other employments, and that by a process of natural
selection the average of those who remain is being gradually
deteriorated?

This condition is not the result of a harsh Poor Law,

nor of the want of charity. The Poor Law is in most agricultural districts administered with benevolence, and probably there is no other country where local endowments for the distribution of doles and charities, and where private charities, are so numerous and liberal. It is, however, confidently stated that in those parishes where charity is most frequent, where there are most endowments for the distribution of doles, where the clergy and squires, actuated by the best intentions, are most active in private charities, there the condition of the labourer is the most depressed, and the least satisfactory ; and there also is least thrift, and least. energy for self-help and independence. In too many of such parishes excessive charity has succeeded in undermining the self-help, thrift, and independence of the labourers, and has encouraged wastefulness and intemperance.

What then appears to be most needed in the agricultural districts of England is an element of independence, which can only be attained by the sense of property. Of all the means of giving this sense of property and this feeling of independence, the ownership of land, even though limited in extent, and the ownership of a house and home, with its garden, would be the most powerful and effective.

In what has been thus said, it is by no means intended to convey the expectation, promise, or, even the hope, that England, under an altered system of law, will become a country of yeoman farmers or of peasant proprietors. In the main, and for such a period as any legislator can prospectively look forward to, it would be impossible to realise either of these subjects. England will certainly continue to be, as it has been in the past, a country in which there will be many large properties. Even if all landowners should have secured to them the full power to dispose of their property, as they think fit, among their children, it may be confidently expected that the great bulk of them will continue to leave the main portion to their eldest sons ; and it will be long before any custom of a different kind grows up in a country so essentially conservative. We may look forward, however, to a considerable increase in the number of landed proprietors of all classes, and especially of small owners. Without aiming at a system of ownership such as we see in France, and other

F

countries organised on the same plan, it is not beyond reason to expect that some nearer approach may be made to the system which prevails in Germany, where, as already explained, although there are many large proprietors, there are also many small owners, where there is a large class of yeomen farmers, and where a very large proportion of the agricultural labourers are also owners of small holdings, varying from half an acre to five or six acres. Of the effect of this distributed ownership and this interest in the soil upon all classes, there cannot be doubt to any one who reads the reports from the countries where this prevails.

It is not too much to say that if landowners, who are unable to do justice to their properties, were empowered to sell, and should avail themselves of this power, in respect only of a small portion of their properties, a very great change might soon be effected in the state of landownership in England and Ireland, and the landowners themselves would be the first to benefit.

GENERAL CONCLUSIONS.

If then the arguments already adduced have any weight in them, the conclusions from them and the objects to be aimed at will not be doubtful.

These are, that the distribution of ownership of land is such that it is held in amounts far beyond the average means of its holders to perform their duties according to the ideal of the English system, in the outlay of capital on it and the building of cottages ; and that the most is not being made of the land as an incentive to individual exertion, and as the most powerful agent for the promotion of individual industry and thrift.

It has also been shown, from experience drawn from every part of the world, equally from Europe as from countries of Anglo-Saxon descent, that land is not necessarily the luxury only of the rich, and that if it should be placed within the reach of other classes, and the means be given of dealing with it in a simple and expeditious manner, it will become the luxury of a much wider class, and indeed of all classes proportionate to their means. The same experience has also been gathered from recent experiments in Ireland. It has been shown that while in every part of the civilised world efforts have been made successfully to free land from the obstructions and impediments of an obsolete feudal system, to withdraw the sanction of law to its accumulation in few hands, and to place it, as far as is consistent with the rights of property, within the reach of all classes, and to promote its ownership by the many rather than the few, in this country little or nothing has been done in this direction; all the influence of the state and of society has been in favour of the concentration of land in few hands; our laws of tenure sanction and assist this, the system of transfer fosters it. It has been shown that as a result we have a state of landownership such as is almost unique in the civilised world.

The objects to be aimed at by any legislation are not novel or destructive; they are not opposed to the rights of property, but in support of them; they savour not of communism or socialism, but are on the lines of individualism; they seek to make the best of individual property, for all its functions, and in all its actions on the social system; they are such as other countries have pursued with success; they claim that the state has some control over its own destinies, some voice in the disposition of its area, and that society is not necessarily the sport of an economic law favouring only accumulation, which, however we may disapprove it, we are powerless to resist. The objects, then, to aim at, are a wider distribution of landed property, to the extent that it shall in the main be held by those who have the means of performing their duties, and that it shall be brought within the reach of all classes of the community according to their means.

The means by which these objects may be attained may be summed up under the following heads :—

1. The withdrawal of the state sanction to the accumulation of land by the law of primogeniture.

2. The limitation of family settlements to the extent of prohibiting entails in the manner invented by Sir Orlando Bridgeman, by which property can be settled upon unborn persons, and a family law of primogeniture secured.

3. The requirement that there shall be for every property some person or persons, who shall have full power of dealing with the property by sale or otherwise.

4. The assimilation of the law relating to land and other

property, and the simplification of the law relating to land tenure, so that its transfer may become simple and inexpensive.

5. The withdrawal of all state influence and sanction in favour of accumulation of land, and the exercise of it in future in favour of a numerous proprietary of land, consistently with the full recognition of existing rights.

It can easily be shown that these measures hang together, and that the pivot of them all is the abolition of primogeniture.

(1) By the abolition of primogeniture is meant the removal of the state sanction to an arrangement by which, in the absence of a will, property in land descends to the eldest son of the intestate to the exclusion of the other children—a law which seldom operates without producing injustice. It is not contemplated that the property shall be compulsorily divided among the children against the will of the parent. The freedom of willing would be retained and preserved; and any interference with it would, it is believed, be alien to the feelings of the great majority of Englishmen. It is only possible in France and other countries because, as already shown, the custom of equal division of property is so universal and so entwined in the feelings of the people, that it is scarcely possible for them to conceive an unequal distribution, and because public opinion considers that a parent who does not provide for all his children, according to his means, is neglectful of his parental duty. Where such is the public opinion, compulsory division by law is possible; but that is very far from being the opinion of Englishmen in the existing social conditions of England, where historical and family traditions so largely affect the opinions and habits, not only of the wealthy, but of all classes, that it would be absurd to expect either that a custom of equal distribution would speedily grow up or that a law compelling it would be acceptable. An historic family has to be maintained, an ancient residence, in and about which the traditions of a family have centred, has to be preserved, the political institution of the peerage has to be regarded; these and many other causes will long sustain, and probably justify the custom of making a difference in favour of eldest sons in many families, though possibly not to the extent which is now often the case.

(2) When it shall be determined that the law itself will not sanction or invite inequality, it will follow almost as a matter of course that it must be forbidden to individuals to make a family law of succession different from that of the state. Freedom of willing will be permitted, and every person will be allowed to make what distinction he thinks right among his children or relatives; but he will not be permitted to transmit these distinctions to another unborn generation. If freedom of willing is conceded to him, he must not in his turn deprive the next generation of the same privilege. The freedom of willing is a part of the paternal authority, and no parent should be deprived of this power by an antecedent generation.

(3) The last principle being decided on, the next one becomes easy of accomplishment. The distinction in favour of an unborn person being cut off and prohibited, it follows that the present generation must have more power over the property, and the power of sale is one of the first and most important attributes of property.

(4) The last two principles are indispensible to the next—that of simplifying the transfer of land. The main difficulty in the transfer of land arises out of the complications due to the law of settlement or entail; so long as these exist, and so long as ownership may be divided between the present and the future, between the living and the unborn, it is impossible to expect or to hope for simplicity of title. Even the late Lord St. Leonards has said that "no young state ought ever to be entangled in the complication of our law of real property."

(5) But not less important than all these is it that the general influence of the state shall no longer be used in the direction of the accumulation of land. It is unnecessary to suggest where an opposite influence might be used. The action taken under the Bright clauses in Ireland has already shown how it is possible, with the unanimous consent of all parties, to assist in the conversion of tenancies into ownerships. This particular method may not be applicable to England; but an altered public opinion on the subject may justify other measures; and it need hardly be pointed out that the land held in mortmain in England and Wales amounts to 1,300,000 acres, of which no less than 500,000 belong to charities.

As a preliminary, however, to any action, it is necessary that public opinion should pronounce itself strongly on the broad question, whether it is satisfied with the present condition of landownership in this country. Public opinion may even without a change of law produce considerable effect. It may induce not a few of those who have hitherto considered that the interests of a rural district are best concerned where all the land in a parish or district is concentrated in one hand, to change their opinion, and to hold that as a matter of safety to the owners of property generally, as well as in the interest of all classes around them, it will be wise to favour the multiplication of land-owners, and to give facilities for the creation of small owners of all classes rather than continually to reduce them. Such public opinion can, however, only be formed by a full and free discussion of the subject.

Does the land of this country produce what may reasonably be expected of it by a proper outlay of capital and labour on it? Does it act to its full extent as a stimulus to industry, thrift, and prudence? Is it not expedient that land should be brought within the reach of all classes, even at the risk of losing something of its value as an article of luxury?

It has been attempted to answer these questions by arguments and illustrations drawn from the history and experience of this and other countries. It is believed that the result of all this experience is that a country is happiest, and its economical, social, and political condition most sound, where there is a numerous and varied proprietary of its land, and where no class is divorced from the soil. This state of things, it is believed, will and can only result where the trade in land is free ; that is, where the transfer of land is simple and uncostly, where each successive generation has full and unrestricted dominion over it, where the state gives no sanction or facilities to an accumulation of land for successive generations, and where the laws give equal facility for its dispersion as for its acquisition. Under such conditions, when artificial stimulus is removed, free competition will have its full effect, and will on the one hand prevent the undue subdivision of land, and on the other its too great aggregation.

LIMITATION OF ENTAILS
AND SETTLEMENTS.*

———◦◇◦———

HISTORICAL REVIEW OF ENTAILS.

It is often alleged that we owe our existing system of entail
and family settlements of land to the feudal law. Historical
research does not support this view. There are, doubtless,
many relics of feudalism still to be traced in the laws relating
to land, in the traditional feeling with regard to landed property, and in the relation of landlord and tenant. It must
be admitted, however, that the special form of entail,
through the operation of family settlements is not due to
feudalism, but to the ingenuity of the subtle lawyers of the
period of the civil war, who invented the system, with the
object rather of protecting family estates from the risks
incident to a period of civil war than of preserving them
from the alienation of the family itself.

Under the strictly feudal system established in this
country by the Conqueror, and his immediate successors, the
entail of land was possible only to a very limited degree.
Grants of land at first were not transmissible, and were continued to the heir only by favour; but the custom very
speedily grew up, under which such grants were considered
as conferring a complete right of property, and the power
of alienation, or, perhaps, rather it should be said, of sub-
infeudation, was fully conceded and exercised. It was probably to restrict this full power of alienation that a more
limited form of donation or concession was invented and
generally substituted. Grants were made by the Sovereign
or by feudal superiors, in such a form as to restrict the
descent of the property in a particular line—as, for instance,

---

* A paper read before the Social Science Association, November, 1877.

to the heirs of the body of the donee, or the heirs male of his body, with remainder over, in the event of there being no issue, the object evidently being to restrict alienation, and to secure the reversion of the property to the grantor. This was the earliest form of entail, and was probably introduced into England from France about the time of Henry II. The general feeling, however, in favour of alienation was so great, that the Courts of Law gave a most liberal interpretation to these grants, and borrowing a doctrine from the Roman law, they held that such grants were conditional, in the sense that they were granted to a man and the heirs of his body upon condition that he had such heirs ; as soon as such a person had issue born, the Courts held that the estate became absolute, in such a manner that he could alienate it, and could charge it with incumbrance, so as to bind his issue, and could forfeit it for acts of treason or felony. Under this ruling, therefore, entails were of little consequence ; they only operated where no issue was born. On the birth of a child the holder of the property could alienate it, but if he did not do so during his lifetime the property descended according to the original grant, for at that time there was no power of devising landed property by will.

This ruling of the Courts, however, gave great dissatisfaction to the nobility; it completely frustrated the purposes for which such grants had been devised and made, and, accordingly, in the year 1285, the nobility found themselves strong enough to force upon the Crown and the people a law, which upset the decision of the judges, and practically affirmed the power of making perpetual entails. The well-known statute, " De Donis Conditionalibus," was passed in the thirteenth year of Edward I. with the consent of the Barons, and without that of the Commons. This statute rejected the erroneous view of the judges, and provided that the intention of the giver should be observed according to the form of the grant. The effect of this was that estates " tail," as they have since been called, that is estates limited to a man and the heirs of his body, were made inalienable ; and as a vast number of estates were granted in this form, a strict and irrevocable entail was enforced in respect of a very large proportion of the landed property of the country. It was not long before great inconvenience and mischief arose from these strict entails, and from the inalienability of so much of the land.

Lord Coke, speaking of the statute " De Donis," said of it : —

" The true policy of the common law was overturned by this statute, which established a perpetuity by art for all those who had or would have it ; by force whereof all the possessions in England were entailed accordingly, which was the occasion and cause of divers other mischiefs ; and the same was attempted to be remedied at divers Parliaments, and divers Bills were exhibited accordingly, but they were always on one pretence or other rejected. But the truth was that the Lords and Commons, knowing that their estates in tail were not to be forfeited for felony or treason as their estates of inheritance were before the said Act, and finding that they were not answerable for the debts and incumbrances of their ancestors, and that the sales, alienations, or leases of their ancestors did not bind them, they always rejected such Bills."*

The bad effects of the statute on the country are also described in a well-known passage of Sir William Blackstone :—

" Children grew disobedient when they knew they could not be set aside ; farmers were ousted of their leases made by tenants in tail; creditors were defrauded of their debts ; innumerable latent clauses were produced to deprive purchasers of land they had bought and paid for, and treasons were encouraged, as estates tail were not liable to forfeiture longer than for the tenant's life." †

These evils lasted, however, for nearly 200 years. The Legislature constantly refused to provide a remedy. At last, however, the ingenuity of the lawyers devised a plan, by which the Statute De Donis could be circumvented, and lands so far freed from entails, as to be made alienable. They invented a fictitious and collusive method of bringing a suit, nominally by the purchaser, against the vendor of the property, and under which the court decreed a sale by a tenant in tail to be valid. This point, however, was only reached by degrees. In the first instance the judges laid down a rule that the issue of a tenant in tail could not avoid the alienation of his ancestor, provided he had a re-

* Nevil's Case, 7 Rep. 34 b.
† " Stephen's Commentaries," Vol. I., p. 239.

compense in value of the estate tail which had been alienated. Later, the doctrine was extended to the point that,
if the tenant in tail warranted assets sufficient to represent
the property proposed to be alienated, the sale would hold
good. According to Blackstone, this was nothing more
than exchanging the lands entailed for others of equal value.
At length, however, in Taltarum's case, decided in
12 Edw. IV., 1472 (Year Book, 14, 9), the Courts took a
further step. It is stated of this case that Edward IV., observing in the disputes between the Houses of York and
Lancaster how little effect attainder had upon traitors, protected by the sanctuary of entails, contrived that a case
should be brought before the Court for the purpose of evading
the Statute de Donis. Fictitious proceedings were introduced by a kind of " pia fraus," and the judges carried the
principle of recompense to the point that a nominal or fictitious recompense, descending to the issue in tail, should
be an effectual bar, not only to such issue in tail, but to all
persons in reversion or remainder. This gave rise to the
curious and cumbrous process know as " common recovery "
for disentailing estates tail. Another fictitious proceeding
called " fines " was later devised with the same object ; and
so late as 1834 these were the only modes of barring those
entails. The validity of fines was recognised by Parliament
in the 4 Hen. VII., c. 24, and thenceforward estates tail
were rapidly deprived of their other privileges. The
26 Hen VIII., c. 13, deprived estates tail of their freedom
from forfeiture for treason. The 32 Hen. VIII., c. 28, provided that leases made by tenants in tail, not tending to the
prejudice of the issue, were binding in the issue in tail.
The 33 Hen. VIII., c. 39, rendered liable all estates tail to
be charged for the payment of debts due to the king by
record or special contract.

A series· of great cases in the Courts decided that it was
not possible to deprive a tenant in tail of the power of
alienating his estates by fine or recovery ; and in the reign
of Elizabeth it was definitely settled that the privilege of
suffering a recovery was as inherent in an estate tail, as the
power of alienation in an estate in fee simple, and that any
prohibition of the exercise of that privilege was to be regarded as repugnant to the nature of the estate, and therefore void. In the subsequent reign, by the 21 James I.,

c. 19, s. 82, Commissioners of Bankruptcy were empowered to convey the fee simple of lands, of which the bankrupt was tenant in tail, to his assignees in bankruptcy.

It was many years after Taltarum's case before the lawyers again began to weave the webs by which the process of entail was to be re-established in a new form. The doctrine of Uses imported from the Continent, was ultimately the means of effecting this, and although by the Statute of Uses (1535) the Legislature endeavoured to extirpate these new-fangled rights, and to restore the directness and simplicity of the Common Law, yet the Chancery lawyers found the means of evading the statute, and by means of shifting and springing uses, which were held not to be within the statute, to create a kaleidoscopic variety of rights and interests under the same instrument.

It was some time, however, before the lawyers discovered the full means of utilising the principles on which the statute had been explained away, and of creating interests in land in favour of unborn persons; and for a long time the Courts resisted every effort made with this object.

The first effort in this direction is to be found in the well-known Chudleigh's case, in 1588, where a family settlement had been effected, not dissimilar to those which now have vogue. Through the medium of trustees, it was endeavoured to settle a property upon Sir R. Chudleigh for life, with remainder to his son Christopher Chudleigh, then living, for life, with remainder to the use of the first issue male of C. Chudleigh. Upon the death of Sir R. Chudleigh, his son Christopher Chudleigh came into possession, and after issue born sold the property; his son John Chudleigh, who was not born at the time of the settlement, afterwards contested the right to the property with the purchaser, on the ground that he was entitled to the estate under the original settlement. The Court resisted the claim. The judges were unable to reconcile with their notions of property the vesting of a property in an unborn son, and they declined to give a construction to the statute of uses which would permit this.

It is worth while to quote the judgment of Sir John Popham, as it shows the objections held in those days to what were then called perpetuities :—

"As the case is now used (he said) by means of these perpetuities (as they are called), if the exposition of the other side
shall hold good, the true heir shall not only be continually in
danger to lose his inheritance, but by them the very bowels of
nature itself shall come to be divided and as wrent in pieces;
for by reason of these the inheritants themselves cannot make
any competent provision for the advancement of their wives and
daughters or youngest sons, as every one according to the
course of nature ought to do; nor by reason of this can he
redeem himself if taken prisoner; and this will make diso-
bedience in children to their parents, when they see that they
shall have their patrimony against the will of their parents,
whereby such children oftentimes become unnatural and dissolute, of which in my time I have seen many unnatural, dangerous,
and fearful consequences, not convenient to be spoken of.

"And what is more dangerous, if a *feme putein* happen to
be in such an house who happen to have children in adultery,
these bastards shall have the land against the will of the father,
to the utter disinherison of the true heirs, and against the intent
of him who made the limitation, by which we may see the just
judgment of God upon those who attempt by human policy to
circumvent the Divine providence of God for the time to come ;
and of this also I have seen an example."

Referring to the efforts made by the judges in the time
of Edward IV. to bar estates tail by means of Common
Recoveries, he added :—

"The grave judges then saw what great trouble happened
amongst the people by reason of entails, and what insecurity
happened by means thereof to true purchasers for whose security nothing was before found but collateral warranties or
unlawful delay by voucher ; and thus did the judges of this
time look most deeply into it, whereupon it was found that
by Common Recovery with voucher these estates tail might
be barred, which hath been great cause of much quiet in the
law until this day, that now it begins to be so much troubled
with the Statute of Uses, for which also it is necessary to provide a lawful remedy."—*Chudleigh's Case*, 1 Rep., 131 b.

It will be seen, then, that the main grounds on which the
judges resisted the attempt to settle property on an unborn
eldest son were :—

1. That the owner of the property would be prevented providing for his widow and younger children in such proportion
as he should think fit.

2. That the eldest son being certain of his inheritance, and

therefore independent of his father, would not be subject to parental control.

3. That it would lead to complexity of title, and therefore to uncertainty and expense of transfer.

All these objections are equally valid against the family settlements of the present time.

Chudleigh's case, decided in the year 1588, put a stop for a time to any successful attempt to recreate entails and to vest property in unborn children. Notwithstanding this, there was an increasing tendency to recognise as valid, successive estates in persons living at the same time. The judges persuaded themselves that the transition from the allowance of one life in being to two or more contemporary lives was easy and logical, for they said, "all the candles are burning at the same time."

It was not, however, till nearly one hundred years after Chudleigh's case that the method was at last discovered of doing that which had been long aimed at by lawyers, namely, carrying on entails for another generation, and settling property after one or more tenancies for life of existing persons upon an unborn generation.

This was accomplished by Sir Orlando Bridgeman, a Royalist of great professional skill and knowledge, who had submitted to Cromwell on condition of being allowed to practise in private. Such was his reputation that "he became the oracle of both parties, his very enemies not thinking their estates secure without his advice." In a time of civil war, when now one party and now another was in the ascendancy, it was of the greatest moment to men of property to secure their estates from being forfeited for treason, and no way was so certain of this as that of settling them upon their issue, in such a manner as that forfeiture could not effect more than their own life interests.

The method which Sir Orlando devised was this:—He interposed, after the estate for life given to the parent, an interest in trustees which was to spring up whenever the estate should pass from the parent, during his lifetime, either through alienation or forfeiture, and these trustees were to hold the property during the remainder of the parent's life for the benefit of the children, or others, who might on the death of the parent become entitled to the settled property. These trustees were called trustees to preserve contingent remainders. It is not unreasonable to suppose that the judges, who for two centuries had resisted entails, and favoured alienation, were induced to make themselves parties to this flimsy artifice, through sympathy for the families whose estates were threatened by the enforcement of the treason law, in all its harshness as to forfeiture ; and it is said that Sir Orlando, when raised to the bench on the Restoration, himself assisted in giving currency to his own coinage.

By a series of decisions of the Court of Chancery it was established—

1. That the interest of trustees to preserve a contingent remainder constituted a vested estate in fee.

2. That it was a breach of trust of the trustees to join with the tenant for life in a conveyance, whereby the contingent remainder was destroyed.

Consequently, by this means, the interest of unborn children was protected against the alienation of the estate by the parent, and the law of the previous 200 years was set aside by the Court of Chancery.

Practically, the system devised by Sir Orlando, though somewhat modified and simplified in form by an Act of 1845, subsists to this day, and the form of family settlement which he invented is, with little change, that of such common use among landowners of the present day.

Subsequent decisions of the Courts have put limits to the power of entailing property upon unborn persons. It was only in 1832, that it was finally decided that the limit of an executory devise is a life, or lives in being, and twenty-one years afterwards, without reference to the infancy of any person whatever ; and a further principle has been laid down to the effect that, while property may be limited to any unborn child of any person living at the time of the deed or devise, yet it may not be limited to the unborn child of an unborn person.

These restrictions, however, made on the alleged ground that the common law abhors perpetuities, have made little or no practical change in the system devised by Sir Orlando Bridgeman. The main object then aimed at was to vest the property, included in a settlement, in an unborn son of the tenant for life, or of the last of several tenants for life, and to secure that the successive tenants for life shall not part with or forfeit the property to the detriment of such unborn son, or of other members of the family, who might be contingently entitled to it in the event of there being no issue of the tenant for life.

The result of the system is, that a property so settled is really vested, not in the immediate holder or tenant for life, with an ultimate destination over to some unborn person, but is held, as it were, in suspense, till the birth of a son, and then vests in him, subject to the life interest of his father; and the tenant for life has thus become in law and in fact a mere temporary holder, a limited owner, subject to all the disabilities which will be shortly explained.

From this short historical review of entail, it will have been observed that the eight hundred and odd number of years, which separate the present time from the Norman conquest, may be divided into four nearly equal periods,— the first, from the Conquest to the Statute de Donis (1285) was a period when landed property was to a great extent free from entail; on the birth of a child the holder of property could alienate it, though he could not devise it by will. During the next two hundred years, from the Statute de Donis till the decision of Taltarum's case (in 1472) it was possible and very usual to entail landed property in such a manner that it was impossible to break the entail or to alienate the property; by far the greater part of the land of this country became " extra commercium." From 1472 till 1650, or thereabouts, land was again to a great extent free from the trammels of entail, and although entails could be effected, they could be broken without difficulty and land was again brought into the market. During the last 200 years, a system has been in force under which entail can be effected to the extent that property can be settled upon any number of existing lives and upon the unborn issue of any existing person ; and practically under the operation of this system three-fourths of the land is in possession of persons who are only temporary limited owners, and the real owner-ship is vested in a son or grandson, whether born or unborn.

SETTLEMENTS OF PERSONALTY.

It must be observed that the law of settlement applies equally to personalty as to land, and that it is possible to include any kind of property in such arrangements. In practice, however, it is usual to settle personalty upon marriage or by will, in a very much more limited manner than is adopted in the case of the cumbrous family settlements of land.

The ordinary method of settling personalty is this; the money, whether consols, shares, or other forms of investment, is vested in trustees for the benefit of the husband and wife for life (if the settlement be upon marriage), with remainder generally to the survivor for life, and after the death of both, to the children of the marriage, in such proportion as the father or mother shall jointly appoint, or the survivor shall by deed or will appoint. If made by will (which is comparatively rare) it generally takes the same form—to a person for his life with remainder to his children as he shall by deed or will appoint. The object of these arrangements is to preserve the property for the benefit of the family, that is, for the widow and children, against the possible misadventure, speculations, or bad conduct of the husband. It must be observed, however, that what such settlements do not effect is this, they do not deprive the parents of the power of selection among their children, they almost invariably leave to the absolute discretion of the parents to decide in what proportion the money included in the settlements shall eventually be divided among the children. The property is settled upon unborn children in a sense, but it is settled in such a way as to preserve the parental authority intact; and the dominion of the parent or parents over the property settled is, subject to the judicious control of trustees, complete.

The children have also no such vested interest that they can rely with certainty upon it, or that they can raise money by pledging their future interest; their share is contingent upon their behaving properly, for it is always within the power of the parent to cut off a child, who shall not be worthy of it, from a share of the inheritance (except in the case of there being but one child of the marriage). The parental control over the children is, therefore, preserved, and the parent or parents retain that which is one of the chief boasts of Englishmen, the power of willing, restrained only to the issue of the marriage, if there be any.

The trustees in whose names the money is generally invested have complete power of dealing with the property subject to the limitations imposed by the law upon the investment of trust-property; they are invested with the legal power of alienation, and there is, therefore, always a person or persons who can deal fully with the property, be it shares, or stock, or house property.

Such settlements, therefore, though they effect the object and purpose of preventing the dissipation of property during the life or lives of persons in being, such as the parent or parents, and of securing the corpus of the property for the children of the marriage, are not open to the objections which were so deplored by Sir John Popham in Chudleigh's case, and which in earlier times led to the breaking up of the strict entails which had been created under the Statute de Donis.

Such settlements are now almost universal in the case of marriages, where there is any money which it is wished to secure for the family. They are very commonly resorted to by the trading classes, for the purpose of securing the wife and children against the vicissitudes of the husband's trade, and although they may in this respect have led occasionally to abuse, by giving facilities for the withdrawal of money from the creditors of the husband, yet as a rule they are productive of benefit to the families of such persons.

It may be said of them that they often proceed too much on the principle of distrust of the intended husband by the wife's parents, and that when a father entrusts his daughter to a man, he might equally confide in him to the extent of leaving greater freedom of dealing with the property of either or both.

It may be observed on this point that in the United States such settlements are very rare, the intended husband generally objects to having either his or his wife's property so tied up. But there are greater facilities there for the protection of the separate personalty of the wife. In most of the States, marriage does not operate as a gift of the wife's property and debts to the husband; she retains her own separate property as fully after as before marriage, and, consequently, there is not the same motive there for securing the wife's property against the possible waste by the husband. In this country, however, it is the settled practice in every marriage where there is money on either side, to protect it

G

by a marriage settlement for the benefit of the children of the marriage. Nor would there be the slightest prospect of success in making any substantial change in this arrangement, even if it were desirable to do so. The middle classes of this country would strongly resist any change which would interfere with the present arrangements of marriage settlements ; and as these settlements maintain intact the parental authority and preserve the freedom of willing among children, they are open to very few objections in proportion to the great security they offer for the future well-being of the family.

It may be noticed here that it is possible to effect the same kind of settlement in land ; and of late years, where the landed property is small, and where other property also is settled, it has been not uncommon to include the landed property in this form of settlement. This is usually done by vesting the land in trustees for the purpose of sale ; the effect of which is to invest the land with the incidents of personalty, so that in the event of intestacy, the land would be divided among the children or next of kin equally, as in the case of personalty.

SETTLEMENTS OR ENTAILS OF LAND.

Settlements of land have, ordinarily, other objects in view than those of personalty only, and are far more complicated in form and more permanent in their character. They are, in fact, entails.

The object of a settlement of land is not simply to preserve the property from being alienated or dissipated by a husband or his wife. Its main object is to preserve the landed property intact and undivided, and to make it descend to the furthest point possible in the direct line of succession from the settlor or testator. Settlements, therefore, are not confined to the case of marriages, but are effected by wills, and more often still by family arrangement when the heir to the property comes of age. As already shewn, the extreme limit of strict settlement is for lives in being and twenty-one years after; and this limit has been enforced by the Courts under the influence of a dislike to perpetuities. In fact, however, while, on the one hand, it is rare for a settlement to be framed so as to exhaust all the possibilities of entail, on the other hand, the mode adopted is such as to give every inducement to those concerned to renew the entail from time to time, and thus to tend to a perpetuity.

The simplest form of a settlement is that where a testator dies leaving his son A living, but without children ; the settlement then takes this form :—The land is given to A for life, with remainder to his first and other sons in succession in tail, with remainder, if there be no children, to the testator's second son B for life with similar remainders over to other sons. The effect of such a settlement is that, as soon as a son is born to A, an estate tail vests in him, and, on his coming of age, he and the father A together can join in getting rid of all other contingent remainders, and can either sell the estate or re-settle it in such a manner as the two shall agree upon.

The position of the father and son with reference to the property is this. The father has only a life interest in it ; the son is tenant in tail. The son cannot sell the estate without the consent of the father, though he can dispose of his own prospective and contingent interest. The father can still less deal with the property without the consent of the son. If the father should die before the son, without having made any fresh arrangement, the property will vest absolutely in the son, and, by executing a simple disentailing deed, he can convert his estate tail into a fee, get rid of all contingent remainders under the original settlement, and deal with the property as he likes. On the other hand, if the son should die before the father, the property will, upon the death of the father, descend to the grandson, if there be any, or to the second son if there be no issue of the eldest son. The eldest son, therefore, is certain to obtain possession of the property if he should survive his father ; he is, however, not entitled at law to any provision during his father's lifetime.

It ordinarily happens, therefore, that when the eldest son comes of age, the father, who is tenant for life, makes a bargain with him. He promises to make the son an adequate provision during his, the father's, lifetime ; he also enables his son to make certain provision for marriage, by charging the estate with an annuity for his widow, or with portions for the younger children ; in return for this the son agrees to join in re-settling the estate, taking in lieu of his remainder in tail a reversionary life interest after that of his father ; and the ultimate remainder in tail is then given to the unborn grandson—in other words, the entail is carried forward to another generation. In lieu of one life interest in the property, there are thenceforward two successive life interests, and no further arrangement can be made till a grandson is born and in his turn comes of age. The process of re-settling is thus described by an eminent lawyer, Mr. Joshua Williams, Q.C. :—

" Upon the majority or marriage of the son who is tenant in tail under a family settlement the estate is commonly resettled, he receiving an immediate provision, and, by his estate being reduced to a life estate with remainder to his issue in tail, parting with his prospective powers of alienation. By such a process as is here roughly described; the bulk of the family estates in this country are kept in settlement from one generation to another, the new fetter being added at that epoch at which the power of alienation arises."*

Lord St. Leonards speaks of it as follows :—

" Where there are younger children the father is always anxious to have the estate resettled on them, and their issue, in case of failure of issue of the first son. This he cannot accomplish without the concurrence of the son ; and as the son upon his establishment in life in his father's lifetime, requires an immediate provision, the father generally secures to him a provision—a provision during their joint lives as a consideration for the re-settlement of the estate in remainder upon the younger sons. *Thus are estates quickly re-settled.*" †

The bargain which thus takes place between the father as tenant for life, and the son who is tenant in tail, is often a matter of great·difficulty and delicacy.

Speaking of these arrangements, an able writer who is little favourable to the system says :—

" Take the case of an ante-nuptial settlement in which the son joins with the father. It is commonly supposed that the son acts with his eyes open, and with a special contingency of the future and of family life. But what are the real facts of the case ? Before the future owner of the land has come into possession ; before he has any experience of his property, or of what is best to do, or what he can do in regard to it ; before the

* Williams' " Principles of Real Property Law," p. 273.
† " Handy Book on Property Law," by Lord St. Leonards, p. 21.

exigencies of the future or his own real position are known to him ; before the character, number, and wants of his children are learned, or the claims of parental affection and duty can make themselves felt, and while still very much at the mercy of a predecessor desirous of posthumous greatness and power, he enters into an irrevocable disposition by which he parts with the rights of a proprietor over his future property for ever, and settles its devolution, burthened with charges, upon an unborn heir."—Cliffe Leslie, *Fraser's Magazine*, 1867.

It is believed that in most cases the heir who has consented to make this arrangement with his father on coming of age, lives to regret it ; instead of coming into the property after his father's death as an owner practically in fee, with full dominion over it, and with power of disposing of it as he thinks fit, he finds that, having at an early age been induced to convert his expectant interest into a reversionary life interest, his power over the property is limited and fettered in all directions, and that he is without any power of selling, leasing, devising, or charging it, except in such manner as was provided under the settlement.

Before, however, pointing out the economic and social evils which result from these family settlements of land, it is necessary to notice the defects of the system, even from the point of view of the settlor or testator who desires to prolong the continuance of the property in the family to the furthest possible point, undivided and inalienable.

These defects are serious, and sometimes result in defeating the very object of the settlor, and in securing the result which he has mainly in view to prevent.

1. It has been already pointed out that the general and most simple form of such settlements is to give an estate for life to a living person with remainder to his unborn son in tail. If such person dies before his son attains the age of twenty-one, the son on reaching that age becomes absolutely entitled to the property, and by executing a disentailing deed, can do what he likes with it. Again, if the son on attaining the age of twenty-one refuses to join with his father in re-settling the property, he will equally become entitled to it on his father's death, without any limitation. In either case the property comes into the absolute possession of a person of whom the settlor or

testator, generally the grandfather, knew nothing, and who
was not born at the time of the settlement; and it not
unfrequently happens that a person making such a settlement gives only a life interest to his son, whom he
can most perfectly trust, and destines the fee to a
person unborn, who turns out eventually to be very
unworthy of the property.

2. Still more serious are the dangers to the family
property which result from the certain expectation, which is
vested in the heir to the property.   From his earliest youth
he is brought up with the full knowledge that he will
succeed his father to the family estates.   The paternal
authority, therefore, is robbed of a great part of its sanction;
the son is independent of him, and to a great degree in a
superior position to his father.   On reaching the age of
twenty-one he finds himself the certain reversioner to a
family property.   There are not a few dangers to which
such young heirs of great expectation are exposed.

A special class of money-lenders devote themselves to
supplying the present wants of such heirs, and are always
on the look-out for them.   To a young man with a certain
reversion to a landed property of £10,000 per annum, a few
thousands supplied for immediate wants appear but a trifle
as compared with the income of the family property which
he is certain to inherit.   The money-lenders are too happy
to supply the present means, and to lead the victim on to
further loans.   It is not likely that the young man has
estimated the cost of raising money upon reversionary
interests, or of the burthen of insuring his life against that
of his father as security for the loan.   The interest of the
heir is contingent upon his surviving his father, and will
not be available till his father dies.   The terms, therefore,
on which he can borrow, are enormously increased by
the necessity of insuring his life against the possibility of
his dying before his father.   Debts to some amount are
probably incurred before any permanent loan is effected,
and when the time comes for settlement, he finds for the first
time how heavily he has to charge his expectations.

The charge depends mainly upon the age of the father,
but as an illustration it may be stated that if the father be
aged forty-five, and the property be worth £10,000 per
annum, the value of the reversion of the son at the age of

twenty-one, calculated at five per cent., is not more than £15,000. A debt therefore of £5,000 will swallow up one-third of the future expectations of the son; and how small such a sum as £5,000 must seem to the expectant heir to £10,000 per annum! It is in this way that many a property has been ruined, and ultimately sold or permanently burthened, and the object of the original settlor is defeated by his very efforts to prolong the continuance in the family. Sometimes it happens that the father takes advantage of the pecuniary difficulties of the son to induce him to join in the settlement of the property, making the debts of the son a present charge on it; and in some cases the savings destined for the younger children are swallowed up in the endeavour to save the property from eventual bankruptcy, caused by the early extravagance of the eldest son and heir.

3. Another and not less serious evil resulting from the present system of family settlements is the accumulation of charges to which the property is from time to time subjected. On each resettlement, advantage is taken to charge the property with portions for younger children, and often with debts of the tenant for life or the reversioner. These charges often become so large in proportion to the total income of the property, that the margin left for the support of the tenant for life is most scanty, and nothing remains for the current improvement of the estate or the proper maintenance of the buildings upon it. It is only the very great properties which can sustain these successive charges. The smaller landed properties often succumb to them, and even the larger properties are frequently so encumbered that their owners are unable to fulfil their duties to their tenants and to the land. In the end, the smaller properties are dispersed or change hands; and, but for the causes thus explained, the accumulation of land in few hands would be more rapid and conspicuous than even at present.

A case recently before the Bankruptcy Court, and which is therefore public property, will illustrate what has been above alluded to, better than any argument. A property of 16,000 acres, with a rental of as many pounds, was settled upon Lord A for life, with remainder to his son Lord B as tenant in tail. Upon the coming of age of Lord

B, the estate was re-settled. In consideration of an annuity of £1,500 per annum, the son agreed to join in the settlement, and to assent to charges which brought up the total encumbrance to £11,500 per annum, leaving a margin of £4,500, out of which the son was to receive £1,500 per annum during the father's lifetime. The son gave up his reversion in tail, and took a life interest in succession to his father, with remainder in tail to his own issue. Within a year from the re-settlement, the son, having run into debt for a few thousands, was made bankrupt; the whole of his reversionary life interest was then assigned to the creditors; and the result is, that during the lives of the father and son, and perhaps for many years after, this great estate will be in the ostensible possession of men absolutely without means, and without any motive, or probably power, to sell.

4. The consideration of such a case leads naturally to the more serious economic evils which result from the present system of land settlements.

The general effect of such settlements and entails is that the proprietors' rights and interests in the land are carved out into a series of limited estates for life and in remainder, each in succession barren of power and of motive to meet the wants, the improvements, and the discoveries of the time.

By law, and except so far as the law is modified by recent statutes, the tenant for life in possession of the land has no power over it beyond his own life; the fee in the land is vested in some persons probably unborn or under age, whose consent cannot be obtained to any disposition of the property, to any sale of part of it, to any lease of it, or to any charge for improvement involving an outlay beyond what the interest of the tenant for life would justify. Any act of the tenant for life extending beyond his own limited interest, even though to the advantage of the property of the successor, is not binding on such successor, and may be disregarded by him. Even, therefore, where the settled estate is otherwise unencumbered, it is seldom possible for the tenant for life to deal with the property freely. But further, whatever the tenant for life spends on the property for its improvement, whether on building farms, cottages, or in drainage, is at once merged in the estate, and subject to the same limitations under the settlement. The tenant for life is probably the father of a family; his only means of providing for his younger children may be by means of a limited charge upon the property under the settlement. He is, perhaps, anxious to increase the provision for the younger children by his own savings. He cannot, therefore, expend much on the improvement of the property without reducing the fund for the younger children, and increasing the value of that already predestined to his eldest son. Far worse is the case where the property is already heavily charged with debts or with charges for the relatives of his predecessors. The margin for improvement is then but small, and whatever margin there is must be saved for the younger children.

It must be admitted that many laudable efforts have been made by Parliament during the last twenty years to remedy this great evil, to facilitate the outlay of capital on lands which are subjected to family settlements, and to give greater freedom in dealing with such properties, in the interest both of the limited owners and the reversioners.

These efforts have taken two directions :—

1. Power is given to the Court of Chancery, on application of the tenant for life, to sanction leases for agricultural, mining, or building purposes, extending beyond the possible lifetime of the tenant for life.

Power is also given to the Court of Chancery to authorise the sale of settled property, subject to this,—that the purchase money shall be devoted to paying off any existing charges, or to the purchase of other lands, to be settled in the same manner.

2. Power is given to the Inclosure Commissioners to charge settled property with money expended in improvements, such as drainage and the building of farms and cottages, the principle and interest of which is to be repaid by annual instalments, varying according to the permanence of the improvement; and various companies have been formed for facilitating such charges and carrying out improvements.

Such remedies have proved to a great extent ineffectual. They involve expensive proceedings before the Courts of Law and the Inclosure Commission, and the employment of lawyers; improvements must be subject to the rigid rule of some official, and not according to the ، experience or wish of the owner of the property. They may be made available in the case of large properties managed by agents and lawyers. They are wholly unsuited to smaller properties. From their very nature they are destined to failure.

This failure cannot be better described than in the words of the Report of a Committee of the House of Lords, which inquired into the improvement of the land under these Acts in 1873. The Report, drawn up by Lord Salisbury, says :—

" The general result of the evidence is to show that, although considerable use has been made of Improvement Acts, and extensive improvements have been effected under them, the progress has not been so rapid as was desirable, and that *what has been accomplished is only a small fraction of what still remains to be done.* Mr. Bailey Denton states, as the result of his calculations, that out of 20,000,000 acres of land requiring drainage in England and Wales, only 3,000,000 have, as yet, been drained. Mr. Caird, the Enclosure Commissioner, speaking not only of drainage, but of all kinds of improvements, estimates that we have only accomplished one-fifth of what requires to be done. The case for Parliamentary consideration lies in this, that the improvement of land, in its effect upon the price of food and upon the dwellings of the poor, is a matter of public interest ; but that, as an investment, it is not sufficiently lucrative to offer much attraction to capital, and that, therefore, even slight difficulties have a powerful influence in arresting it."

" The interest at which the land companies lend is usually 4½ per cent. The sinking fund, to repay the loan in twenty-five years, together with the interest, bring up the average payment upon the effective outlay to a little more than 7 per cent. It appears that sometimes, though not in all cases, the tenants will pay to the landowner, in the form of rent, the full 7 per cent. which he pays to the company. In that case the landowner is, for twenty-five years, neither a gainer nor a loser upon the transaction. At the end of that time, if the drains are effective, he gains the whole 7 per cent. ; but this consideration is by no means a certainty.

" On the balance-sheet of cottages it is unnecessary to dwell. All witnesses agree that, apart from any land that may be attached to cottages, no pecuniary profit is to be obtained from building them.

" The average rent which they will bear, after provision for maintenance, appears not to exceed 2½ per cent. The replacement of bad cottages by good is an even less remunerative operation.

"A complaint against the existing system is directed to the function of the Enclosure Commissioners. A needless minuteness, and a rigour which refuses to bend to local requirements, are imputed to it   It is manifest, indeed, from the evidence of the Commissioners and their inspectors, that the latter claim a control so complete over the execution of works, as to leave little discretion to the landowner or his agent.   In the selection of sites, in the arrangement of plans, in the choice of materials, in the drawing up of specifications, it is no unusual thing for the inspector to take a view opposed to that of the landowner and his agent ; and whenever this contingency arises, the landowner must give way.. Mr. Parkin, an experienced solicitor says :—

"'I find, from my experience, that landowners do not like the interference of surveyors and inspectors sent from public bodies.   Control of any kind, however wise the controlling power· may be, especially when it comes from a public office, is distasteful to men in the management of private affairs ; and where the profit of an operation is small, the necessity of submitting to such control may be sufficient to deter men from undertaking it.'"

It is strange that, with such an opinion of the working of the system, the Committee should have failed to see how strongly the facts point against the principle of family settlements, and that they should have confined their recommendations to a few trifling improvements in the direction of those which had so conspicuously failed.

No result has followed from the report of the Committee, unless it be that, under the Agricultural Tenancies Act, 1875, limited owners have power, with the consent of a County Court Judge, to charge their properties with the cost of improvements effected by tenants under the operation of the Act.   The Act, however, has proved to be a dead letter, and inquiries made of County Court Judges have failed to discover a single case in which application has been made to any one of them under the Act.   The inference to be drawn from the failure of all these Acts is that they are no real remedies for the evil they were intended to cure.   They have for a time succeeded in diverting public attention, and by suggesting partial and local remedies, however insufficient, have postponed the day when the cause of the evil should be thoroughly probed.

It will probably be alleged that in family settlements

there is often a power of sale vested in trustees ; this may
be the case with the best drawn settlements of modern times,
but it is not the case with older settlements, or with settlements effected under wills or by country practitioners ; and
the power of sale is almost invariably accompanied by directions to re-invest the money in land, to be settled to the
same uses. There is certainly no power to invest the money
in permanent improvements of the remaining property, still
less in the building of cottages.

There remains to be considered the effects which entails
and family settlements of land have upon the distribution
of landed property in this country. This subject would
alone be a wide one, opening out a large field of inquiry. It
will only be possible briefly to point out these effects under
the following heads :—

1. In artificially maintaining properties intact for years
after they had been so encumbered and charged to an extent which leaves the limited owner in the position of a mere
nominal owner, without the means of improving the property ; and in the retarding of that natural process of dispersion under which many properties eventually change hands.

2. By preventing the fathers of families dividing their
landed properties among their children in such proportion
as they think fit, and compelling them to provide for their
younger children by a charge upon the property of the
eldest one.

3. By so complicating the title by permitting a variety of
interests to be carved out of the same property, as practically to render impossible any simple or cheap system of
registration.

From every point of view, then, these family entails are
open to most serious objections. They are equally
injurious to the true interests of the family as they are to
those of society. Whether we look at them from the
economic, social, or political point of view they are equally
to be condemned. The only class which derives any
benefit from them is that of the family lawyers, and even
amongst these there is a growing opinion adverse to such
arrangements. The late President of the Incorporated
Law Society, a solicitor of the highest standing, with forty
years' experience in this special class of business, thus
speaks of them :—

"It admits of question whether it is for the benefit of the country generally, or even of the owners of landed estates as a class, that entails should prevail so extensively as they do in England. This prevalence assumes that the majority of a generally educated class are improvident and incapable of doing justice to the estate and their families, and, for the sake of the spendthrifts and their families, hampers the much more numerous class, as I venture to estimate them, of the reasonably prudent proprietors and their families. Nor does the entail protect the spendthrift himself. He can, and does still, squander his life-interest ; and the estate itself, under such circumstances, is likely to be neglected. This may last for thirty years or more, and what damage may accrue during that period to those coming after him for whose benefit the entail has been created ! . . .

"A parent has no power under an ordinary entail of depriving of the estate a lunatic or proved spendthrift son in favour of a younger son or of a child of the eldest, nor can one will provide for every contingency. . . . In ordinary families *I think many of the entails created are more for the benefit of the lawyers than of their clients.* Some will call this rank heresy, but it is the result of forty years' experience in a branch of the law with which I have had the most intimate acquaintance."*

It would be difficult to add to the force of this condemnation of a system by one so well versed in it.

It has been shown that the law under which this system has grown up during the last 200 years is not the result of parliamentary discussion and legislative enactment. It is purely judge-made law ; the invention of a series of judges. The question arises, therefore, whether the time has not arrived for the legislature to interfere and to review this judge-made system, which has been shewn to be detrimental to the interests of all concerned, and prejudicial to the interests of the community in its economic, social, and political aspects.

LIMITATIONS OF ENTAIL.

To condemn the present system of entail and land settlements and to show their bad effects in all their

* Inaugural Address delivered at the Annual Provincial Meeting of the Incorporated Law Society at Oxford, October 4, 1876, by Mr. Henry Thomas Young, president of the society.

directions is a comparatively easy task to that of devising means to undo the knots which judges and lawyers have been engaged in tying during so many generations.

It has been suggested by some that the legislature should recognise the substantial difference in character between land and personalty, and should absolutely prohibit the creation of any estate in land but that of a fee simple, making illegal all successive or partial interests in it and rendering impossible all entails or settlements of land. This proposal would leave untouched the power of settling personalty, and while it would free land from the trammels of entail and settlement, would permit of the accumulation of other property through the medium of trustees, in favour of the unborn son, in whom it should be desired to concentrate the family property. It is difficult to understand how such a proposal could secure the objects in view. It would be open to easy evasion by conveyancers ; land intended to be settled would be mortgaged for its full value, or more than its full value, and the charges thus created would be settled in trust, in lieu of the land itself, or real property would be converted into personalty by directions to trustees to sell, and would be settled as is now the practice ; and although the title to land might thereby be greatly simplified and a power given over the land to the immediate holders, yet the owner would equally as now find himself trammelled by the settlement and unable to do justice to the land. It might also be argued that where the only property which a man has is land, it would be hard that he should not be permitted to deal with it as he may with the house property or with personalty.

The object in view can, it is believed, be attained, not by creating or adding to artificial distinctions between land and other property, but by assimilating the law relating to them as far as possible, and by extending to land the more simple and less complicated system which is generally in force with respect to personalty. The task of reforming the land laws, and of getting rid, as far as possible, of entails and settlements of land, is to be accomplished, not by any one supreme effort, but by a series of measures, having a common object in view, and dealing with the subject separately in these directions :—

1. Assimilating the law of inheritance of land and per-

sonalty, and, generally, so far as possible, simplifying the laws of both kinds of property.

2. Restricting the powers of settling all kinds of property, whether real or personal, upon unborn persons, and thus cutting off the main object of entails.

3. Securing that in respect of every landed property there shall be a full power of sale and leasing vested in living persons, who, without the consent of courts of law or government officers, shall be able to deal with the property.

4. The carrying out of a compulsory and local system of registration of ownership of land, which will only be possible where there is a legal owner for every property.

The first of these is, perhaps, the most important. When carried, the second would necessarily soon follow; for when the state has determined that there shall be one law of intestacy for all property, it will not long be permitted to individuals to deprive their successors of the power of willing, and to substitute, in the case of land, a family law of succession or distribution different from that of the state. It will not, also, be possible to deal completely with the law of entail until the principle of intestacy is settled.

With respect to the second and third subjects, it appears to me to be possible to deal, though perhaps not definitely, till the first is settled, at least in a manner which shall prevent most of the evils now due to the law and practice of family entail and settlement; and with this view I have introduced a Bill in the House of Commons, with the assistance of Mr. Osborne Morgan and Mr. Herschell.

It has appeared to me that the main object to keep in view in such a measure is to revert, as far as possible, to the old state of the law before Sir Orlando Bridgeman devised the plan of settling landed property upon an unborn person. On the other hand, I have been unable to overlook the fact that every marriage settlement of personalty contemplates the securing provision for the future children of the marriage, leaving, however, the power of selection of the parent or parents unfettered, and I have thought it inexpedient to make any substantial restriction upon this ordinary and most simple method of settling personalty. What has appeared to me, then, to be possible and reasonable, is to restrict the power of settling property, whether land or personalty, to what is the ordinary method of dealing with

personalty under marriage settlements. I have aimed, therefore, at prohibiting the entail or settlement of land or other
property upon an eldest unborn son, or any particular unborn child of a living person, in such a way as to prevent
the parent having the full power of dividing the property
among his children in such proportion as he may think fit.

The effect of such a restriction will not be wholly to
prevent settlements, but to compel them to take the form of
the ordinary settlements of personalty—namely, to a person
for life, with remainder to his children, as he shall appoint ;
in lieu of the present form, in the case of land, to a person
for life, with remainder to his eldest unborn son in tail, &c.

The result of this proposal, it appears to me, would be
this : when a settlor or testator finds that he cannot deprive
his son, to whom he destines the estate for life, of the power
of willing or apportioning the property among his children
in such proportion as he may think fit, he, the settlor, will,
in the great majority of cases, not think it worth while to
settle the property at all ; when he cannot secure the property
to an eldest child in an unborn generation, he will find it
better to leave the property absolutely at the disposal of his
son ; and therefore settlements will be confined, as in the
case of settlements of personalty, either to provisions for
marriage, or to cases where the testator or settlor cannot
trust the immediate object of his bounty not to dissipate the
property.

In those settlements which should continue to be made,
although we shall not have got rid of the tenant for life, the
position of such a person will be greatly altered, and most
of the evils which are now the necessary incident to such
limited owners will cease to exist. The tenant for life will,
as a rule, have full power of appointing the property in such
proportions among his children as he may think fit ; he may
create an eldest son in the next generation, if he so desire ;
if not, he may divide the property equally among his children, and divide it, or charge for their benefit, as may seem
best to him. The power of willing, which is said to be one
of the dearest privileges of Englishmen, but which is so
often destroyed in advance by some predecessor, and which
can be rarely exercised in the case of land by existing
owners of land, will not only be preserved to the utmost,
but will be greatly strengthened and extended, and will

be capable of restriction in the future only among the children.

The tenant for life, under such settlements, will no longer find any motive against the expending of money on the improvement of his property. He will not, thereby, be in danger of improving the heritage of one child at the expense of the others. He will have complete dominion over it, and he can divide or charge the improved estate as he may think fit. The father, also, will no longer be in a position inferior, or subordinate, to his son. The parental authority will be complete and absolute. The father will not have to ask the consent of the son to this or that improvement. The son will have no right to control his father in the management of the property. The eldest son, again, will have no such absolute vested interest in remainder that he can realise anything upon his expectations; while his father lives, it will be uncertain how the property will be devised. All the risks and dangers, therefore, incident to the certain expectations of the eldest son, and to the facility with which they now can borrow on their expectations, will be got rid of.

Instead of the father being a mere tenant for life, while the fee is vested in some unborn son, the position will be inverted and the practical dominion over the property will be vested in the parent, and it will rest with him whether it should go in turn to his eldest son in succession. This being the case, it appears to me that it will also be consistent with the new position to give much greater powers over the property, either to the tenant for life or to the trustees who may be appointed under the will for the benefit of him and his family. I have, therefore, inserted clauses giving full power of sale of the property and of leasing it to the tenant for life or his trustees. If it be thought these are large powers to entrust to tenants for life, it must be noticed that it will be always possible for the settlor to restrain them by the appointment of trustees for such purpose, and in the absence of such trustees it may reasonably be considered that the settlor commits this trust to the tenant for life. I have also provided that upon such sales the proceeds need not be re-invested in land, but may be invested in any of the funds open to the investment of trustees; for as the tenant for life will have power of ap-

H

pointment among his children, he may reasonably prefer to sell a portion of his property and appoint the proceeds to his younger children rather than charge the property for them.

I have also proposed that any money realised by the sale of settled property may be invested in permanent improvements, such as the building of farm-houses or of labourers' cottages, and drainage of a permanent character. Where adequate funds for this purpose are otherwise wanting, it seems only natural that the landowner should sell small outlying parts of his property in order to enable him to do justice by the remainder.

Not the least of the advantages which may result from this method will be that there will always be some definite person in whom the legal estate, for the purpose of sale, will be certainly vested. Every property will either be in absolute ownership or in settlement, and if in settlement, either the trustees or the tenant for life will have power of sale, and can therefore be registered as the owner of the property; and hence it will follow that it will be possible to have a register of landowners not less simple in this respect than that of ships or stock, and one, therefore, which can be made universally compulsory and local.

Whether these are sufficient advantages to compensate for the proposed restriction upon the power of settlement, must be for the consideration of those who believe in the expediency of such family arrangements. For my own part, I think that no powers are restricted which are not detrimental to the interests of the families which use them, and still more to the public; and my best hope is, that the restriction which I propose may lead to the disuse altogether of such settlements, except in very special cases, and to the restoration of a state of things when full dominion over landed property will be exercised and enjoyed by the living generation, who must be the best judges of what is the true interest both of their landed properties and of their families.

LAND TRANSFER.*

The Committee was appointed in the session of 1878 to inquire and report, whether any and what steps might be taken to simplify the title to land, to facilitate its transfer, and to prevent frauds on purchasers and mortgagees. In the course of this inquiry it was necessary to discuss the comparative merits of the system of registration of deeds as now in force in the counties of Middlesex and York in England, and in Ireland and Scotland, and the system of registration of titles offered by the English Land Transfer Act of 1875, and by the Irish Act of 1865. Numerous witnesses have given evidence as to the causes of the non-adoption by the public of the last two Acts, as to the possibility of improving the machinery for working them, and as to the possibility of making the registration of deeds more effective and valuable. Reference has been made to the evidence and reports of the Royal Commissions of 1854—57 and 1868—70. Lord Chancellor Cairns, who was responsible for the Act of 1875, has also been able to state his views in explanation of the objections which have been urged against it.

The two Royal Commissions above alluded to emphatically condemned the principle of registration of deeds, not only as now carried out in the registries of Middlesex and York, but subject to whatever improvements might be suggested. The Commission of 1854—7 expressed the opinion "that a register of assurances would not, of itself, operate to simplify title or facilitate (as respects the title) the transfer of land, or render less intricate the practice of conveyancing. It would not render unnecessary the retrospective investigation of the title on the occasion of each succeeding sale or mortgage. The effect of past dealings upon the title to

* A Report submitted to a Committee of the House of Commons, in 1879.

the land would remain the same as at present. No evidence of the ownership would be afforded, without examining the former transactions, as is now done. Abstracts of title would not be shortened, the forms of conveyance would not be simplified. The technicalities and anomalies of the law of real property would be confirmed, rather than lessened or relieved, by registration of assurances, unaccompanied by alterations in the general law. Those embarrassments and impediments in the sale and transfer of land, which arise from the state of the law, and the mode of showing title to land, would remain as before, if indeed the delay, trouble, and expense in transferring land would not be increased rather than diminished by the establishment of a register of deeds and assurances."

Among other permanent objections to the registration of deeds, they pointed out :—

" The vast bulk and increasing quantity of deeds and instruments, which would have to be kept, and on transfer to be searched and examined.

" That the registration of deeds would involve a specific addition to the existing burdens on the transfer of land, without diminishing, except remotely and casually, any of the existing causes of expense, tardiness, and difficulty in such transfer. That the additional expense and complication caused by requiring registration would be universal, and would extend to all landed property, and to all sales and purchases of it, large or small. The benefit, however, which the register would confer, by excluding the risk of fraud, would be exceptional and peculiar. All transactions would, in fact, be made to pay for the machinery contrived to defeat fraud in a few; were the register adapted to relieve sellers and buyers from the necessity of retrospectively investigating past titles, the benefit to landed property, and to commerce in it, would be universal, and in such a state of things there would be no harshness in throwing upon all transactions the cost and burden of registering. Unless, however, the investigation of the title retrospectively could be dispensed with, the main sources of expense would remain untouched.

" That in small transactions, which are far the most numerous, any increase in expense would be very oppressive.

"That if any of the instruments affecting the title are withheld from the register the system becomes imperfect. If memorials only are registered, the original instruments of which the memorials are given must be searched for, and copied, or abstracted; or if the instruments are once registered they must remain on the register. However occasional, or however temporary, their object, they cannot be destroyed; whether satisfied or not, they must still be kept, and being kept, they must all be examined by purchasers. Thus the machinery would be too complicated to answer the purpose, or complication would diminish the facilities of transfers and increase the chances of miscarriage. Simplicity and accuracy being the grand objects to be attained, the absence of these must lead to uncertainty, and uncertainty is insecurity, and insecurity is impediment. But how are simplicity and accuracy to be attained, if notice of deeds, by the fact of their being registered, is to be multiplied and perpetuated. Escheats, life estates and charges and incumbrances, which have been satisfied or exhausted, and other interests which have ceased to be of real importance to the title, must more or less form part of the abstract, and the purchasers and others would not be justified in disregarding them."

The Commission further condemned the existing systems of registration in Middlesex and York, on the ground that these registers are signally defective in not presenting at one view all the documentary evidence which a party investigating a title may have occasion to see; that the registers do not contain an enrolment of the deeds, but memorials of them only, and that these memorials are not required to show more than the names of the parties and the property affected; and lastly, that the efficiency and value of the registers are impaired by the general doctrine that express notice of an unregistered deed is equivalent to the registration of it.

The Royal Commission of 1869 appears to have concurred in these views. With reference to the Middlesex Registry, it stated that "all the witnesses examined before them agreed in saying that the registry causes a great increase of trouble and expense, affords no additional security or other special advantage, and ought not to be continued." It expressed entire concurrence in this opinion, and recommended that from as early a date as possible the registry should be closed, as regards the registration of deeds executed after that date.

Much evidence has been given in confirmation of this view as to the defects of a system of registration of deeds. Lord Chancellor Cairns, in expressing his concurrence in these views, has explained very fully the two different systems of registration of deeds, and the objections to either of them. They are of two kinds, he said, "blind registers" and "speaking registers." A blind register tells nothing about the property or the contents of the deeds ; it only tells that there are certain deeds in existence relating to the property, and having told that, the searcher must find, *aliunde*, what are the contents or effect of the deeds. The registers of Middlesex and York are of this nature ; they register only memorials or short abstracts of deeds, and the searchers or parties interested, having thus been warned of the existence of deeds, are referred to the originals for their contents, or they are satisfied by their search that there are no other deeds affecting the property. "The objections to such a register are, that it tells nothing as to the details of the deeds ; the inquirer is put on his guard, and he must go about among the persons who have put the deeds on the register, and inquire from them what the deeds mean, and very possibly it may turn out after all the inquiries and trouble connected with the search, that nine out of ten of the deeds are perfectly immaterial, and may be disregarded. The general result of such a system is, that while it may prevent a certain number of cases of fraud, it imposes a tax upon everybody in every transaction. A 'speaking register,' on the other hand, is that where the deeds are registered *in extenso*, and tell their own story. Such a register, however, involves the copying of every deed in duplicate, the comparing the duplicate with the original by a competent official before registration ; it involves the search of the register by a competent person, who is able to say, after reading through such deeds, whether they affect his client or not. The fee, therefore, which is paid for the registration and search, is a very small part of the expense to the public. It is doubtful also whether the publicity, which is a condition of such a system, would be submitted to."

These arguments, supported by other witnesses, conclusively show that the existing systems of registration in Middlesex, York, and Ireland are the cause of increased cost in the transfer of land, in all transactions which are subject to them; that this cost would only be increased by converting them from "blind registers" into "speaking registers;" and that any attempt to extend them to the rest of England would be strongly opposed, and would be a retrograde step.

The object which the Land Transfer Acts of 1862 had in view in enabling the registration of title was wholly distinct. In lieu of perpetuating the evidence of past transactions, its object was to give to the person appearing upon the register an indefeasible title to the property or estate, in respect of which he was registered, and to dispense with the necessity, in all future transactions, of tracing the history of previous transactions. In such case the purchaser or mortgagee would have only to look at the register itself, in which he would find recorded the owner of the property, and the existing charges upon it; and all past transactions, and all previous deeds would be matters of complete in-difference to him.

Unfortunately, the Act of 1862 very imperfectly carried out the principle of a registration of title. For such a purpose, it is now fully admitted that it is an essential condition of success, that only estates of freehold and lease-hold should be admitted upon the register, and that certain charges or mortgages should be allowed as encumbrances upon them; and that all limited interests, such as life estates, reversionary estates, &c., should not appear upon the register, but should be treated in other ways hereafter described.

Lord Westbury's Act of 1862 was framed on what is now admitted to be a defective principle. It embodied some of the bad features of a registration of assurances with the registration of title. It threw upon the registrar the judicial duty of registering the effect of any deeds affecting the registered property, with all their complications.

The same system was practically extended in 1865 to Ireland, where there are exceptional facilities for the estab-lishment of a system of registration of titles, owing to the fact that nearly all the landed property which is sold there passes through the Landed Estates Court, with the object of obtaining an indefeasible or Parliamentary title. A clause in the Act provided that all conveyances and declarations of a title executed by the Landed Estates Court, should be recorded on the register, as a matter of course, without charge, unless a requisition to the contrary, under the hand of the purchaser, should be lodged within seven days.

The working of the Act was placed under the Landed Estates Court; the duty being entrusted to the three examiners of the judges, and the registrar in turn, so that no one officer had the responsibility or the credit of the success or failure of the system, or the duty of suggesting amendments to improve it. The Court, however, appears from the first to have taken little interest in working the Act. Their first action after the passing of the Act was to print 2,000 copies of a common form of notice, for issue to parties before the Court, and who thus, by an easy process, could prevent their properties being placed upon the register.

It is also stated that the adoption of the Act has been strongly opposed by solicitors who have charge of sales and purchases; and the judges' examiner, who now, in addition to his onerous duty as examiner, has sole charge of the register, has expressed the opinion that it is a dangerous system, on the ground of the great risk of owners losing their property.

Under these circumstances, it is not to be wondered at that the Irish Act has not been largely adopted; 681 properties only have been registered under it, and the practice has been for persons buying land in the Landed Estates Court to sign the office notice, withdrawing their properties from the register. The system adopted by the Irish Act resembles that of Lord Westbury, and is therefore defective; but it is in evidence, that where adopted, it enormously simplified future transactions, and reduced their costs; the cost of transferring a registered property, under £1,000 in value, is only three guineas, including the costs of the solicitor employed in the case, or less than the cost of registering a memorial of a deed under the registry of deeds. The 681 properties registered have led to numerous transactions of transfers and mortgages; and notwithstanding the danger of insecurity alleged by the officer in charge, it does not appear that in any case, as yet, any loss has been incurred in consequence of defective registration.

In 1868, in consequence of the failure of the English Act of 1862, and the small number of properties registered under it, the second Royal Commission, already alluded to, was appointed, and in 1875 the existing Land Transfer Act was passed. The essential feature of this Act is that land for the purpose of registration is treated as Government stock, or as ships in the register of shipping. Every property put in the register must be registered in the name or names of some person or persons as the absolute owners thereof, and it is only susceptible for the purpose of registration of particular modifications ; it may be mortgaged, or it may be leased, or it may be transferred, or it may devolve on the real representative, on the death of its owner. All equitable interests are excluded from the register, and are protected by a system of inhibition or caveats, as in the case of Government stock.

If the registered property is the subject of a family settlement, with complicated provisions and reversions, but where trustees are appointed with power to sell, as in the case in most family settlements of the present day, the trustees for sale are registered as the owners ; and the beneficial owners, if their consent is necessary for the sale, are protected by inhibitions or restrictions. If there are no trustees for sale, the registrar selects persons for that purpose, or registers the tenant for life and the reversioner. Mortgages become, under this Act, the most simple transactions ; they are charges upon the property, carrying with them the power of sale in the event of non-payment of interest, and any number of successive mortgages can be effected with the same ease or security. The mortgagee obtains a certificate of mortgage, which is easily transferable. Similarly a lease of the property is capable of being registered or dealt with, either by way of mortgage or transfer, with the same ease as the property itself.

The Act provided two main methods for property coming upon the register: the one with an absolute title, after examination and certificate by the registrar, which gives an indefeasible title to the person registered, and to all future persons deriving through him ; and the other with what is called a possessory title, where a *prima facie* case is made out of possession, but where no investigation is made by the registrar of the past title. In such case the property registered must in future be dealt with in the manner prescribed by the Act, but no certificate of absolute title is given; and the title will only become indefeasible by lapse of time.

The system thus adopted, so far as absolute titles are concerned, closely resembles the system in force in the Australian Colonies, first introduced by Sir Robert Torrens. The evidence given before the Commission of 1870, and now again by Sir Robert Torrens and by Sir Arthur Blyth, the agent for South Australia, shows that the system is in universal use in those colonies, and has given great satisfaction; it has enormously reduced the cost of transfer and mortgage of land and house property. Sir Arthur Blyth, who has had great experience in loaning money upon real property, informed the Committee that so simple has become the system of mortgage, that he very rarely employed a lawyer in such transactions; they are settled in the office of the registrar without difficulty, delay, or expense, and as easily as the transfer of stock.

Sir Arthur Blyth says :—"South Australia was the first colony to adopt the system. The dealings in land in Australia are very numerous; a large proportion of the people are owners of freehold land, and as such they were constantly in the hands of the lawyers for mortgages, leases, selling, and so forth, and there was a good deal of expense attendant upon it. The Act has facilitated transfer, has enormously reduced the expenditure on transfers, and has been seized upon by the community as a great boon."

The system, he says, was strongly objected to by the legal profession, and was carried against their opposition. Its adoption was voluntary and not compulsory; but all land sold by the State was placed upon the register, and the experience thus gained, by purchasers of Crown land, of the enormous advantages of the system, especially in respect of the facility of mortgaging, soon led to the voluntary adoption of the system in the case of other properties, and it now rarely happens in this or the other Australian Colonies that land is sold without being previously placed upon the register. In respect of property granted by the Crown, before the passing of this Act, it is alleged by Sir

Robert Torrens that much of the land in New South Wales was held under very complicated and uncertain titles, owing to bad conveyancing, which made the investigation, prior to coming upon the register, difficult and expensive.

It has been alleged that a system of this kind might work well and be suitable to a new colony, but be very unsuitable for an older community like England. To whatever extent land and houses in the colonies are more frequently dealt with by way of sale or mortgage, so the facilities of transfer and the lessening of expense must be the more appreciated. Though family entails, in the English sense, may be less common, yet land and houses are very frequently there, as here, settled on marriage. It will be observed also that the great bulk of transactions in this country, especially in respect of house property, are not of the complicated character often supposed, but consist of simple transfers, leases, mortgages, and mortgages and transfers of leases. There can be no doubt that in all these transactions the benefit of a simple system of transfer and of a reduced cost of all transactions, would be equally appreciated here as in the colonies. The main difference between the colonies and this country is that the circumstances of the former, in respect of land sold by the state, enabled the system of registration of titles to be speedily tried on a large scale, which gave ample experience of the benefits to be realised by it, and which overcame all the professional and other objections to a new system.

It may be observed that so strongly does Sir R. Torrens consider the objection and obstruction of the profession of solicitors, to the introduction of such a system, and to the lessening of legal costs connected with the subsequent transfer and mortgage of land, that he recommends that the profession should receive compensation from the state based upon their previous income from this part of their practice; and he attributes the failure of the Act of 1875, and the small extent to which it has been adopted, mainly to professional opposition.

The Act of 1875 has unquestionably not been adopted to the extent that even a trial on the most limited scale has been made of it. Only forty-eight titles have come upon the register since the passing of the Act, of which very few are registered as possessory titles.

Various causes have been alleged for the failure of this Act, and for the unwillingness of the public to avail themselves of it. In the opinion of Sir Henry Thring, who drafted the Act, it was weighted with the failure of the Act of 1862, and has consequently not had that fair trial which it might have had, if its principles had been adopted in 1862, when registration of title was first adopted. The Lord Chancellor appears to concur in this view. It is alleged, however, by other witnesses, that various objections to the system adopted by the Act have deterred the legal profession and the public from availing themselves of it. Among such objections are the following :—

(*a*) That partial interests, such as life estates, reversions, &c., are imperfectly protected by caveats.

(*b*) That the expense of transferring property upon the register is considerable, even in the case of absolute titles, and that the necessity for going into a previous history of the title, and consequently of making abstracts of title, is not dispensed with.

(*c*) That the question of boundaries to properties registered with an indefeasible title is left open to dispute.

(*d*) That properties once upon the register cannot be subsequently withdrawn.

An investigation of these objections has conclusively shown, that they have been put forward by persons who have not sufficiently studied the Act ; and although they may have induced some solicitors to advise their clients not to avail themselves of the register, they are not, in fact, serious objections to the system.

(*a*) The Lord Chancellor has pointed out that the protection given to life interests and reversions is not by "caveats," but by "inhibitions," and "restrictions," which do not depend upon notices, or the chance of notices, miscarrying, but are regular orders put upon the register, and which cannot be taken off without the actual consent of the persons concerned.

(*b*) The very essence of the principle of registration of absolute titles, is to dispense with the investigation of title, antecedent to the last entry in the register, and any person who has been compelled to pay for such investigation must have been improperly charged by his lawyers.

(*c*) The importance of determining the question of

boundaries is overrated; and the exclusion was deliberately adopted in 1875, with the object of lessening the expense of putting properties on the register in the first instance.

(*d*) With respect to the power to take properties off the register, the Lord Chancellor has stated that there can be no serious objection to this, provided a fee be charged, which would deter people from acting on mere caprice.

The non-adoption by the public has been due not to the above causes, but to a combination of the following circumstances :—

(1) That the Act has inherited a certain amount of discredit due to the imperfection of the earlier Act of 1872.

(2) That the system being a new one, and likely, if adopted, to diminish very greatly the charges of solicitors in transactions connected with the transfer and mortgage of property, has not been recommended by them to their clients ; it was scarcely to be expected they would do so.

(3) That the expense of coming upon the register for the first time, either for an indefeasible title or for a possessory title, has been and is serious in proportion to any immediate benefit which the owner of the property is likely to obtain.

The expense of obtaining an indefeasible title must necessarily be considerable, as, in addition to the ordinary solicitors' costs, there must be not only the fees of the Registrar's Office, but also the professional costs of the solicitor in attending the registrar, and complying with his requisitions ; and as the registrar is responsible for giving an absolute title to the applicant, it is certain that he must be at least as careful as the most careful purchaser, before agreeing to give his certificate of title.

With respect to possessory titles, it is to be observed that the main advantage, which is to accrue from such registration, must of necessity be long deferred. An immediate cost is to be incurred by registration, in the hope that at some future period, when the title has ripened by time, the benefit of registration may be fully realised. It is certain therefore, that a very small expense will deter persons from availing themselves of the privilege of registering possessory titles.

A careful inquiry into the general system adopted by the Act of 1875, has resulted in the conclusion that although, perhaps, capable of improvement in some of its minor details, it is in the main founded on sound principles. If generally adopted, it would lead to a very great diminution in the cost of transfer of land and house property, and would especially facilitate and lessen the trouble and expense of mortgaging property. , It would also lead to greatly increased security, and would practically have all the benefits resulting from simplicity, and from dispensing with the accumulation and recording of past transactions.

The statistics of the Registry of Deeds in Middlesex show that the vast majority of deeds registered there are simple transfers, mortgages, leases, and assignments of mortgages and leases, and that the number of more complicated dealings with property in the nature of entails are comparatively very rare. Of 810 deeds registered in one week at the office, only two were conveyances by way of entail, and only four were conveyances of life interests. There were 90 conveyances in fee, 185 leases, 150 assignments of leases, 39 mortgages of freeholds, 90 mortgages of leaseholds, 160 assignments of mortgages, and 81 surrenders of mortgages. The returns of the landowners of the United Kingdom show a gross total of 1,153,816 owners, including leaseholders holding 99 years' leases. Of these, 852,932 are entered as owners of less than one acre of land, and are therefore, for the most part, owners of houses only; of the remainder, about 15,000 persons own more than 500 acres each, and about 50,000 persons own between 50 and 500 acres. Although, therefore, the extent of land subject to entail and family settlement may be great, the number of transactions of this kind, compared with more simple transactions, is probably very small; the more so as it is now the practice to treat house property, and even small landed properties, as personalty in marriage settlements and other family arrangements. The difficulties, therefore, which are alleged to exist to the carrying out of any system of registration of titles, from the prevalence of complicated arrangements and settlements of land, are greatly overrated ; and the benefit which would result from the establishment of a simple, effective, and cheap system of registration of titles would be quite as great in this country in respect of house property, and almost as great in respect of land, as in the Australian Colonies ; and if the system adopted by the Act of 1875 could be tried on a scale sufficient to make its advantages known to the public, it would be generally accepted, as has been the case in those colonies.

There is no reason, therefore, for abandoning the hope that means may be devised of inducing the public to adopt the system on a scale sufficient to accord it a fair trial. It is not sufficient that an Act of this nature should be well drawn, and that the working of it should be entrusted to an able lawyer. It is further necessary that the efforts of the Government should be directed to facilitate its adoption, and to commend it to the public; and that the working of it should be committed to men able to push the system from a business point of view, as well as to cope with its legal difficulties.

Sufficient attention has not been paid to the question of fees. The Lord Chancellor has expressed the opinion that the fees are infinitely too high at present; he believes that if it be considered that the state has an interest in having the system of land title adopted, a case would be made out for lowering the fees or dispensing with the fees, and he has no doubt that in such case the system of putting land on the register would be much resorted to.

In the case of possessory titles, where little or no responsibility is thrown upon the registrar, and where the benefit which will accrue from registration will be realised only after the lapse of time, there can be no reason whatever for charging a more than nominal fee for the first entry upon the register, and the *ad valorem* fee should be dispensed with.

It has been suggested by an eminent solicitor, a member of the late Royal Commission (Mr. W. J. Farrer), that an inducement might be held out to solicitors to place their clients' titles upon the register, by fixing the charges for their professional work in connection therewith at an *ad valorem* scale, which would render it their interest to make the business as short as possible, and at the same time relieve them from the present method of charge, which the outside world does not at present understand; and he has suggested a scale of charges with this object. The proposal is well worthy of consideration, and should be entertained as part of the business management of the system which is essential to its success in its early stage.

To whatever extent the system owes its non-success

to the fear of professional loss by its general adoption, this difficulty might be remedied or lessened by fixing professional charges in connection with it, at such a rate as would make it the interest both of the legal adviser and his client to adopt it.

In the case of Ireland, it is greatly to be regretted that advantage was not taken of the opportunity of the recent sales of the property of the Disestablished Church of Ireland to its tenants, to try the system on a comparatively large scale. Upwards of 5,000 tenants have bought their holdings, and as the state will practically remain in the position of mortgagees of such properties for 32 years, it might reasonably have made it a condition of the loans that the proprietor should be placed on the Register of Titles.

The same remark applies to the case of properties sold to tenants under the Irish Land Act (1870), which, however, have not as yet been numerous. In all these cases the properties have been withdrawn, as a matter of course, from the Register of Titles, although it is admitted that in the case of such small properties the advantage of registration would be far greater than in the case of large properties.

In the case of an extension of the principle of the Bright Clauses of the Irish Land Act, the Committee are of opinion that the state may reasonably require, that where loans are made to facilitate such purchases, the properties shall be registered.

There is a general concurrence of opinion that to ensure a permanent success of the principle of registration of title, it must be applied locally, and be accompanied by a cadastral map of the country on which the registered property may be identified. One of the difficulties of starting the system is, that it is not worth while to establish numerous local registry offices for a system, the adoption of which is voluntary, and which may not for some time be extensively adopted ; while, on the other hand, a single central registry office is not convenient for transactions at a distance, especially in respect of small properties.

In this view special exertion should be made to introduce the system, in the first instance, in London and its neighbourhood, where the registry office is already established, and where it is necessarily local and within easy reach of any person wishing to deal with property, and where the Ordnance Survey on the 25-inch scale is complete. It is admitted by almost every witness that the existing system of registration of deeds in Middlesex is, in its present condition, perfectly useless, and involves a considerable charge upon the transfer and mortgage of property, with no benefit to those who register. Of the four registrars prescribed by the Act only one is now in existence, and his post is virtually a sinecure. The difference between the fees received and the salaries of the working staff represents an annual sum of no less than £8,000. It was recommended by the Royal Commission of 1870 that this registry should cease.

In the hands of an able administrator, this registry might, without difficulty, be turned into a registry of titles ; and very little persuasion would be sufficient to induce persons to register possessory titles which would ripen in the future into indefeasible titles, rather than continue to pay for what is admitted to be of no value. It is worthy of consideration whether the registration of possessory titles might not be made compulsory in this district in substitution for the registration of deeds, which, by the provision giving to registered deeds priority over unregistered dreds, is now virtually compulsory ; at all events in this district, the one system might be substituted for the other without difficulty. The Middlesex Registry of Deeds should be combined with the Registry of Titles Office with this object.

It is by the adoption of such measures, that the system of registration of titles may be gradually introduced ; and it is in this direction, rather than in the direction of the registration of deeds, that any decided improvement is likely to be made in the direction of simplifying and cheapening the transfer and dealing with land and house property in this country.

It has been urged by numerous witnesses that the same rule should be applied to freehold property on the death of its owner as is now the case with leasehold property—viz., that it should vest in the personal representative of the deceased, for the purpose of administration, either according to the terms of the will of the deceased, or, if he should die intestate, according to the law of descent of real property. Such a change of the law would undoubtedly tend to reduce the difficulty of tracing titles, and would also facilitate the

I

registration of titles by relieving the registrar of responsibility in the case of transfer on death of the registered owner.

Other changes of law have been urged, especially with reference to the limitation of entail and the repeal of the Statute of Uses. These changes, however, involve other considerations which are not within the scope of the present inquiry; but they would undoubtedly simplify and cheapen the transfer and other dealings with land, and would remove many of the difficulties which have been urged to the system of registration of titles.

The above Report was not accepted by the Committee. By a majority of seven to five, the Committee adopted a Report in favour of making universal a system of registration of deeds, as distinguished from that of titles.

THE BRIGHT CLAUSES OF THE IRISH LAND ACT, 1870.*

THE Committee was appointed in the middle of the Session of 1877, to inquire into the working and results of that part of the Irish Land Act, 1870, which had for its object the promotion of the purchase of land in Ireland by its occupying tenants, and to report whether any further facilities should be afforded for this purpose.

The Committee have to report an almost unanimous concurrence of opinion as to the expediency of giving greater facilities for the creation of a class of proprietors cultivating their own farms in Ireland. It is admitted that Ireland is almost wholly deficient in such a class; it is believed that its social, political, and economic condition would be greatly improved and strengthened if a numerous class of such persons existed; that better contentment would be spread through the country, and greater inducements be given to industry and thrift.

A Return, prepared at the instance of the Government in 1870 with a view to legislation on the land question, and subsequently laid before Parliament, showed that in the whole of Ireland (exclusive of town districts), with an area of over 20 millions of acres, there were (including a number of duplicate entries) 19,294 owners of land of above one acre in extent, of whom 3,827 only were owners of between one acre and fifty acres, with a total of 81,862 acres, giving an average of 21 acres to each such owner, showing that less than 1-250th part of Ireland is in the ownership of persons possessing less than 50 acres of agricultural land. The agricultural statistics show that of 592,590 farm holdings in

* A Report proposed to the Select Committee of the House of Commons, on the Bright Clauses of the Irish Land Act, 1870, by its Chairman.

Ireland 498,000 are between one and 50 acres. The cases, therefore, of occupiers farming their own lands are most rare — so rare, that it has been stated in evidence that the very term of "freehold" is unknown to the bulk of them, and those who have become purchasers of their farms from the Church Commissioners often continue to speak of the interest and repayment of instalments as their rent, and of their title deeds as their leases.

Comparing this state of things with England, which, like Ireland, is a country, in the main, of large landed properties, but, unlike Ireland, is a country where large farms prevail, the difference in the number of small ownerships of land is remarkable. Dr. Hancock has pointed out that, comparing districts of the two countries as nearly similar as possible in their conditions, there are for every one owner of land of between one acre and 50 in Ireland, ten such owners in England.

If we compare Ireland with any other country in Europe where small peasant farming prevails, the difference is still more remarkable. In France more than half the land is in the occupation of its owners, and nearly two-thirds of the land is owned by persons having less than 75 acres of land, who are numbered by many millions. In Switzerland, Baden, and the Rhine Provinces the proportion of owners is even greater. In Belgium one-third to one-half the land is owned by the cultivators of its soil. In Prussia, Austria, Bavaria, Holland, Denmark, and Sweden, where there is a greater proportion of large properties, the number of small owners cultivating their own land is very great, and nearly one-half the labouring class own small holdings of land averaging about five acres in extent.

In all these States much has been done during the last 100 years to increase the number of owners of land, either by revolutionary measures, as in France, after 1789, or by facilitating the conversion of feudal tenancies into ownerships by purchase, assisted by the State, through the intervention of credit banks, as in Prussia, or by direct loans to the tenants, as in Bavaria, Wurtemburg, and Austria, where losses were purposely incurred by the State for this object. In most of these countries also legislation has encouraged the multiplication of ownerships by simplifying and cheapening the transfer of land, by establishing local registries of land, by facilitating mortgages, by prohibiting or limiting entails, and by assimilating the law of inheritance of real and personal property.

In Ireland, the class of small owners, apart from recent efforts of the Legislature to create them, can hardly be said to exist. The difference is the more remarkable as Ireland is essentially a country of small farmers, and the Legislation of the Continent, already referred to, was based on the principle that peasant farming is most successful, if not only successful, when combined with ownership, or with such security of tenure, as gives the greatest inducement to the cultivator to expend his labours on permanent improvements.

The small number of owners of land in Ireland is alleged to be due to the following causes :—

(1) The confiscations of land which took place at various periods of English conquest, and especially in the seventeenth century, which substituted the English system of absolute ownership over vast districts for the old Irish tenures, under which ownership was divided between the chiefs and the dependent occupiers, and absolute ownership was not fully recognised.

(2) The penal laws which, during the last century, prohibited the Roman Catholic population owning land in fee, and therefore shut out the bulk of the population from the possibility of becoming owners.

(3) The extent to which land has been entailed and encumbered with settlements and charges, by which means the greater part of it has been withdrawn from the market, or, when sold, was encumbered with charges or annuities, which prevented its sub-division.

(4) The cumbrous and costly system of transfer and mortgage of land, which tells specially against small owners.

The establishment of the Encumbered Estates Court in 1849, by which encumbered landowners or incumbrancers were enabled to petition the Court for the sale of landed properties, did something to free land in Ireland from such difficulties. It was expected that purchasers would come in and buy with capital sufficient to improve the land, and to supply the deficiencies of its previous owners. Estates sold in the Court were broken up into smaller properties, but not in such a manner as to facilitate purchase by the occupying tenants. A large extent of land found its way into the hands of smaller capitalists, but often of persons who were not more able to expend capital on improvements than the encumbered owners from whom they bought, but who were more intent on exacting the highest possible rent, and who entered on the position of landlords without any previous relation to the tenantry or the neighbourhood, and without the family traditions or the customary forbearance, under which the tenants had acquired interests which could not justly be disregarded. The introduction of a class of speculative purchasers or land jobbers, who not unfrequently raised their rents ·to a point which absorbed the recognised or legitimate tenant's interests, gave rise to much alarm, and has everywhere added much to the desire of the tenants, on the change of ownership of the land they occupy, or on its sale in the Landed Estates Court, to become the owners of their holdings by purchase.

It was doubtless this feeling which contributed to the necessity for passing the Irish Land Act of 1870, and which induced the Government of that day to make its two proposals to Parliament with the object of facilitating the purchase of their holdings by tenant farmers ; and it is to be observed that both these proposals passed through Parliament without a single objection in either of the two Houses.

The first of these was that under the Church Disestablishment Act, 1869. This Act directed the Church Temporalities Commission, in disposing of the landed property of the Church, to give to the occupying tenants thereof the preference of purchase at a fair market value. It empowered them to assist the tenants in the purchase by leaving three-fourths of the purchase-money on mortgage at 4 per cent., payable by instalments spread over thirty-two years. The property consisted of glebes and episcopal estates to the extent of 108,000 acres, in the occupation of 8,432 tenants, paying an aggregate rent of £95,430, giving an average of thirteen acres each. The greater part of the property was glebe land, situate chiefly in Ulster ; the episcopal property was spread over all parts of Ireland.

It is stated by Mr. Murrough O'Brien, the valuator employed by the Commission, that the Church glebes were, for the most part, in poor condition, below the average in value of the adjoining properties, let in small holdings, and more highly rented than is customary on large estates. The evidence shows that the Commissioners, while securing a full value for the property, have, by judicious arrangements, and by explaining the matter to the tenants, fully carried out the intentions of Parliament. In their Report of 1874 they say, " When we first commenced to offer the Church lands for sale to the tenants occupying them, they were not generally prepared to take advantage of the offers. Few were aware of the privileges conferred on them by the Act. As a class they were poor and ignorant, and offers of sale were often misconstrued ; many of them thought that the purchase-money demanded would only secure a lease for ever, and that the rent would still be payable. The intentions and effect of the Act are now fully appreciated." And in 1875 they say, " The agricultural tenants are almost universally anxious to purchase their farms, and when they do not accept the offers of sale, it is generally from inability to pay in cash even one-fourth of the purchase-money as now required by the Act."

Of the 8,432 holdings, 5,243 were sold to the tenants up to the end of 1877 ; of the residue, properties with 1,006 tenants, who had not been able to purchase themselves, have been sold to the public, leaving properties with about 2,200 holdings undealt with, of which a portion will probably still be sold to the tenants. Of the 5,243 tenants who bought, a certain number, estimated at about 800, unable probably to find the balance of the purchase-money themselves, assigned their right to some neighbouring landowner or local capitalist or solicitor, who bought in their names; but in these cases the tenants generally received some consideration, obtaining a lease of more or less length at the old rent, and not unfrequently receiving a perpetuity lease.

A deduction must also be made of some 500 cases of mere house properties or labourers' cabins; but making these deductions, there still remain about 4,000 cases in which agricultural tenants, holding from three to four acres to fifty or sixty acres, have by this process become owners.

The number would have been greater had not the Commissioners laid down the rule that they would not advance any of the purchase money by way of mortgage on properties sold for £50 and under, or more than half the purchase money upon properties valued from £50 to £100, and the difficulty of the purchase of their holdings was thus greatly enhanced to the very small tenants.

It may be worth while here to illustrate the transaction by the case of a tenant paying a yearly rent of £10. If the purchase money was £230, or twenty-three years' purchase (the average price at which the land was offered to the tenants), the tenant was expected to pay down one-fourth, or £57 10s.; the remainder was left on mortgage, repayable by half-yearly instalments of £4 15s., spread over thirty-two years. The new owner, therefore, has to pay £9 10s. per annum, or within 10s. of his previous rent, and at the end of thirty-two years his farm will be free, and absolutely his own. No restriction was placed by the Commissioners upon alienation; the new owner, therefore, could give security for any further advance that might be made to him from other quarters; and some of the tenants availed themselves of this power, and borrowed a portion of the balance of the purchase money; others obtained portions of the purchase money from relatives in service, or from friends in America.

A return handed in by Mr. O'Brien of four sample cases of glebes sold to tenants will show the various ways in which the tenants obtained money for completing their purchases. In one glebe, where twenty-one tenants bought their holdings for £3,500, the amount paid in cash to the Commissioners was £1,560; of this £430 was borrowed elsewhere; in three cases money was sent from America; in three others, children in service assisted in the purchase. It is worthy of notice that the costs of the purchase (which in this case was effected through the Landed Estates Court) were £367, or 11 per cent. on the purchase money, and nearly equal to the total sum borrowed by the tenants. Money was not unfrequently raised by the sale of cattle and other stock, or was provided out of money destined as marriage portions for the children. A report made by the Chairman of the Committee, after personally visiting a glebe not far from Newry, which had been sold to the tenants, will further illustrate the nature of the transaction, and the efforts made by the tenants to find the balance of the purchase money. "In every case visited," the chairman says, "it is clear that great benefit has resulted from the purchase. Ownership has been a spur to increased industry and thrift. In many it has prompted improvements."

The price obtained by the Commissioners for the land thus sold to the tenants averaged twenty-three and three-quarter years' purchase of the rental, which is slightly higher than the average price obtained for land in Ulster sold in the Landed Estates Court during the last two years, and from two to three years' purchase higher than the land sold in other parts of Ireland by the same court.

After selling portions of the glebe lands and other Church properties to the tenants, there remained residues of what appeared to be very undesirable property, honeycombed, as it were, by the small freeholds, and dispersed about in an inconvenient manner. The Commissioners believed there would be great difficulty in selling these residues, but have found an unexpected demand for them. For those portions of them already sold the price realised has averaged twenty-two and three-quarters years' purchase of the rental, which was somewhat higher than the price at which the same land was offered to the tenants. They have sold 1,006 tenancies to 123 purchasers. The land thus sold was in a decidedly inferior condition to that sold to other tenants. Hence the lower average price at which it was offered to the tenants and sold to the public.

The Commissoners report that the new purchasers have paid the interest and instalments of capital with great regularity, and that out of the whole number only forty are in arrear, and their collector anticipates no difficulty in obtaining the rent in these cases. They also state in their last report that improvements are being generally effected in the building of houses, and in draining and reclaiming land. Mr. Murrough O'Brien has stated as the general result of his own observations, that the sales to the tenants have made them more contented with their position, and have tended to make them more industrious.

Mr. Vernon, from personal observation, gives the same opinion :—" In my opinion the result has been extremely satisfactory in every way, both as to the tenant's industry and as to his contentment, and as to his attachment to law and order. I think in every way it has had a favourable influence wherever it has been acted upon."

In their report of 1876 the Commissioners attribute the general success of creating a class of small proprietors out of a body of poor tenant farmers to two causes : " The first and principal is, of course, the advantageous terms on which the purchase money of the holdings is payable. The privilege to pay only one-fourth of the price in cash, whilst three-fourths may remain on mortgage, is a most valuable boon ; indeed, without some such arrangement, purchases by small farmers would be impracticable. The second cause is, in our opinion, that the farmer has not been obliged to take the initiative in opening negotiations for the purchase of his farm, nor afterwards to conduct any correspondence on the subject. Everything has been made easy to him. He has not been obliged to encounter that real calamity for an illiterate man, writing a letter. A fair price has been put upon his farm ; full printed explanations and instructions accompanied the offer which was sent to him. He has had only to write, or get written for him, from one to six words on a printed form supplied to him, to sign his name or affix his mark ; to provide within three months one-fourth of the purchase money, and the thing was done. He was transformed, without trouble to himself, from a rent-paying tenant into a landed proprietor. A simple form of conveyance and ·mortgage was settled and printed by an authority, and the cost of the transaction was thus reduced to a minimum." It will be observed that the Church Commissioners stand to the new purchasers in the simple relation of mortgagees and mortgagors under the general law of the land ; and there is no prohibition of alienation or of sub-letting ; but that sub-division of the holding would be unlawful without the consent of the Commissioners.

The Committee have adverted at length to the results of this part of the Irish Church Disestablishment Act, because it was the first of the two experiments made by Parliament directly with the object of converting tenancies into ownerships, and because the substantial success attained points out in so many respects the course which may be pursued in the future with the same object.

The other experiment made in this direction was that under the Irish Land Act, 1870, which is more immediately the subject of the inquiry of the Committee. Two methods were proposed in the Act to effect this purpose : (1) By giving inducements and facilities to landlords (whether limited owners or owners in fee) to enter into agreements with their tenants for the sale or purchase of holdings through the medium of the Landed Estates Court. (2) By directing the Landed Estates Court, in the case of the sale of landed property in the usual course in the Court, to afford, by the formation of lots for sale, or otherwise, all reasonable facilities to occupying tenants desirous of purchasing their holdings, so far as should be consistent with the interests of the owners of the properties thus dealt with.   .

In both cases the Board of Works of Ireland was authorised to advance, by way of mortgage on the land thus sold to tenants, two-thirds of the value of the land, repayable by equal half-yearly instalments spread over a period of 35 years, at the rate of £5 for every £100 so advanced, a rate which makes the interest three and a half per cent. The terms, therefore, are, in respect of the rate of interest, more favourable than those of the Church Commissioners, namely, three and a half per cent. in lieu of four per cent., but the proportion to be advanced on mortgage was less—namely, two-thirds of the value of the land, in lieu of three-fourths of the purchase money. There are also stringent provisions against the purchasing tenants mortgaging, alienating, assigning, charging, sub-dividing, or sub-letting their holdings, without the consent of the Board of Works, while any part of the annuities remain unpaid ; any such act is to operate as an absolute forfeiture of the land to the Board of Works. By the Amending Act of 1872 a sale was substituted for forfeiture.

Under the first process contemplated by the Act, where the vendors are tenants for life, or limited owners, the Landed Estates Court is empowered to distribute the purchase money in repayment of charges upon the land, in accordance with priorities, or the purchase money may be lodged in court for investment in other land, subject to the same trusts, and pending such purchase, might be invested in consols. The land sold to the tenants under this part of the Act is to be free from incumbrances, except rights of way, easements, and other charges specified in the Act. The Treasury was directed to prescribe the fees to be charged in respect of such sales, and the Court is empowered to apportion rents, charges, and covenants, &c., in respect of land thus sold.

This part of the Act has been almost a total failure. In six years there have been only 35 sales to tenants, of which two only were by tenants for life. The reason given for this failure is the great cost of passing such sales through the Landed Estates Court. Mr. M'Donnell, one of the examiners of the court, says : "A single tenancy will not bear the cost of the investigation of title ; an owner is offered £2,000 for a tenant's farm ; he would have to pay £200 as the cost of showing title to it. The lowest cost for passing a property through the court is £100, and there would be in addition the personal costs of both parties outside the court." Mr. Lynch, the registrar of the court, agrees in the opinion that the failure is due to this ; he says that there are few owners of estates who are anxious to part with a small portion of their estates, and that there are very few estates which have not incumbrances upon them, and that there is difficulty in paying off these incumbrances according to their priority, or in getting their consent to the sale. He adds, " You must pay off the first incumbrancer, whose incumbrance will exactly exhaust the amount of the purchase money, and who would be satisfied to take the same in discharge of his incumbrance. It is necessary to make a title to the whole estate, and to settle a schedule of incumbrances for the whole estate, for a charge which affects one part, as a rule affects the whole. The owner has to take exactly the same proceedings in a sale under these clauses as under the ordinary vendor and vendee clauses of the Act." The costs also are very much the costs of an ordinary sale. The Treasury settled the percentage fees for sale under this part of the Act at the same rate as under the principal Act. No effort, therefore, appears to have been made to reduce the costs of small transactions. The sums received for the sale of lands under this part, if not paid away in discharging incumbrances, must be invested in consols, subject to the trusts of the settlement. It is obvious, therefore, that it would not be a profitable operation to a landowner to incur costs in selling land to a tenant at twenty-three to twenty-five years' purchase of the rental, and to invest the proceeds in consols paying three and a quarter per cent.

Under these conditions the failure of this part of the Act is only what was to be expected. In 1872 a supplemental Act was passed, enabling the Board of Works to make advances to tenants purchasing by agreement from their landlords, upon being satisfied as to the title, without the necessity of passing the property through the Landed Estates Court.

Under this Act forty-seven purchases by tenants have been effected in respect of fifteen different properties. The Board of Works appear to have laid down the rule, very early after the passing of the Act, that they would entertain no proposal under it, except where title was derived from the Landed Estates Court, on the ground that their solicitor had not sufficient staff to go through the titles which would come before him, and see if incumbrances were cleared off, and so forth. In consequence, therefore, of this decision very few applications have been made under this supplemental Act; and those, whose titles were not derived through the Landed Estates Court, were at once rejected, except in the case of some sales by one of the City companies where the title was notoriously good. It is stated that the Board of Works refused to advance where property was sold under the direction of the English Court of Chancery.

It is clear, then, that this supplemental Act has also failed for the same reason as Part 2 of the Land Act— namely, the expense of proving title, and the difficulty caused by incumbrances.

There remains to consider the operation of Clause 46 of the Act, which directed the Landed Estates Court to give facilities to tenants desirous of purchasing their holdings by making lots, or otherwise, so far as this could be done without detriment to the interests of the owner of the estate, and directed them to hear applications on behalf of the tenants from the Board of Works in this respect.

During the six years, 1871 to 1876 inclusive, since the Land Act was passed, landed property to the value of £5,872,000 has been sold by the Landed Estates Court in the usual course of their business, and it is stated that nearly all the landed property now sold in Ireland passes through this court. Some small deduction must be made from this in respect of demesne lands not in occupation of tenants. The rental of the land in occupation of tenants was about £230,000, and it is probable that this, on the average, represented 11,500 separate holdings or occupations.

During the six years ending 1876, 523 of these tenants were able to buy their holdings, and to avail themselves of the Government advance, making, with the eighty-two cases previously mentioned, 605 holdings, of which the purchase-money was £598,000, and the Government advance £338,000. It will be seen, then, that about five per cent. of the number of holdings sold in the court, and one-tenth in value of the property sold, was purchased by the tenants; the difference in the proportion is explained by the fact, that purchases by tenants have been principally of farms above the average size. Of the 605 holdings sold 84 were of 100 acres and over; 109 were from 50 to 100 acres; 128 from 30 to 50; 90 from 20 to 30 acres; 54 from 15 to 12; and 49 under 10 acres; and the average about 40 acres. Of these 605 holdings 359 were bought in aggregate lots, seventy-one in number, and were subsequently sub-divided, of which fifty were portions of the estate of Lord Waterford, sold in 1871; 164 were bought in separate lots in the ordinary sales of the Court. The purchases by combinations of tenants were confined mainly to the case of the Waterford tenants, and have lately almost wholly ceased. The sales to tenants are, therefore, practically confined to those cases where they have the opportunity of bidding separately for their own holdings; whether they have this opportunity depends upon the discretion of the examiners of the Court, whose duty it is to determine the lots in which the properties sold in the Court are put up for auction.

The practice of the Court is stated as follows by Mr. M'Donnell: "Notice is given to the tenants before the settlement of lots, informing them that if any of them are desirous of purchasing their holdings, they must attend before the examiner on a certain day with a proposal for the purchase, containing an undertaking to pay for the same, after which no proposal for the sub-division of a lot will be entertained ; and in the event of such proposal being accepted, regard will be had to the same on the settlement of lots." No information is given in the notice as to the terms upon which the Government advance will be made ; it merely gives them the opportunity of appearing before the examiner themselves, or by attorney, if they wish to purchase. When the examiners settle the lots, they hear the applications from the tenants, and, after reference to the agents for the vendors, decide in what lots the property will be put up.

The main difficulty opposed to the working of this part of the Act has been, that the owners of property sold in the Court have been unwilling to run the risk, by selling to some of their tenants, of having a residue left on their hands unsold ; and the examiners and the judges have been unwilling to act against the wishes of the persons having the conduct of the sale, and to exercise the discretion vested in them by the Act, of directing the property to be put up in lots so as to suit the tenants who are anxious to buy.

Those tenants who have been able to bid separately for their holdings have given prices decidedly above the average price of other land sold in the Court. The one examiner has only consented to put up tenants' holdings separately upon their undertaking to bid an upset price, which has generally been about twenty-five years' purchase of the rental, or nearly three years' purchase above the average price of land in Ireland ; the tenants, therefore, have gone to the sale with the disadvantage of having possibly to bid higher than their offer, but in no case to obtain the property for less. The other examiner has never agreed to put up a separate holding for sale in this way, but he has excepted such holdings from the sale by auction where the owner and tenant could agree upon a price.

It is clear from this practice that the sale of a property, or part of a property, to the tenant, has depended upon all, or nearly all of the tenants being in a position to buy ; and if even a small minority have been unable to do so, the sale to the other tenants has been practically rendered impossible. Under these circumstances, therefore, it is not matter for surprise that the sales to tenants have been very few in number, and that great numbers of tenants, who were anxious and ready to buy, have been disappointed in not having had the opportunity of doing so.

The inherent and main difficulties in the way of sales to the tenants have been increased by other circumstances arising out of defects of the Act, or the practice of the departments which are concerned in administering it.

(1) No sufficient notice has been given to the tenants of properties sold in the Landed Estates Court, explaining to them the objects of the Act, and the nature of the facilities offered by the Government. For more than two years after the passing of the Act no notice whatever was issued to tenants by the Landed Estates Court, and when finally a notice was decided on, it has conveyed very little information to them. The tenants were invited to appear before the examiner; this involved either a personal appearance or the employment of a solicitor, with the very great uncertainty of having ultimately the opportunity of bidding for their holdings. Judging from the experience of the Church Commissioners of the ignorance of small tenants, their want of business knowledge, and their reluctance to employ legal assistance, this alone must have prevented many who would otherwise have been able to buy, if properly informed.

(2) The Board of Works, by the direction of the Treasury (to whom every point of detail in working the Act was referred by the Board), laid down in the first instance, as the measure of value of the property on which advance was to be made to the tenant purchaser, not the price which was given by him in the Landed Estates Court, or the upset price put upon the holding by the officials of that Court, but twenty-four years' purchase of the official tenement valuation, upon which valuation two-thirds, or sixteen years' purchase of the tenement valuation, would be advanced by the Board. The tenement valuation, however, is notoriously below the rental value of property in Ireland, and is unequally assessed in different parts of the country. The amount advanced to tenants on this basis seldom exceeded more than half the purchase money, and gave rise to great complaints on the part of those who had bought, expecting to obtain two-thirds of the amount of the purchase money from the Board. Subsequently, the Treasury agreed to

advance up to twenty years' purchase of the tenement valuation ; this being still objected to as insufficient, they later agreed to a special reference to the Commissioners of Valuation, and to a special valuation of the property at the expense of the tenant. Where this has been adopted the Board has been enabled to advance two-thirds of the purchase money, but the process has involved delay, uncertainty, and expense, to the tenant. Tenants are unwilling to incur the expense of a special valuation, and are stated to have been suspicious that it would entail an increase of taxation. If the valuation took place before the sale, the tenant might not have the opportunity of bidding; if after the sale, the tenant was uncertain in making his bid whether he 'would obtain the full two-thirds from the Treasury. Mr. Stack, the Chief Clerk of the Board of Works, states that tenants have been in the habit of coming to the office to inquire as to the amount of the advance, and were most dissatisfied when they found what was the maximum of the Board. A tenant often said to him, " I have so much of the purchase-money, and if the Board would give me so much more, I would feel warranted in going before the examiner and making an offer." Fully one-half of the applicants went away dissatisfied with the conditions. The evidence shows the importance of even a small difference in the amount of the advance in facilitating such transactions.

(3) Another difficulty not unfrequently occurred where a portion of the holding was sub-let. The Act of 1870 contained an absolute prohibition against sub-letting any part of the holdings on which advances have been made by the Board. The Amending Act of 1872 provided that where any part of a holding charged with the payment of an annuity to the Board of Works should be sub-let to' agricultural labourers, *bona-fide* required for the cultivation of such holdings, for cottages or gardens not exceeding half an acre in each case, such letting should not be deemed to be a forfeiture. It has since been held by the judges of the Landed Estates Court that this Amending Act defines the exceptions which may be made in the case of the original advance ; and if any portion of the holding be sublet, except within the terms of this Act, they refuse to make a charging order. As it not unfrequently happens that

J

small portions of a holding are sub-let to relatives of the
tenant, or to other persons not employed on the farm, this
has operated to deter purchasers in many cases. It has
also been held that it was not lawful for the Board to
make an advance upon that portion of the property not
sub-let, excluding from the security the portion sub-let to
tenants.

(4) The 46th section of the Act of 1870 clearly intended
that the Board of Works should represent the tenants desirous of purchasing their holdings before the Landed
Estates Court, and should make any applications that
might be necessary on their behalf for the lotting of the
property to be sold, in such a manner as to give them the
opportunity of buying, thus intending to relieve the tenants
of the necessity of employing lawyers, and of the expense
and trouble of such transactions. In fact, however, the
Board of Works has never acted in this manner for tenants,
and the tenants have been left to incur this expense, and
to make such applications without assistance.

(5) Another difficulty has been found where charges or
annuities existed upon properties from which the separate
holdings could not be freed, so as to admit of a prior mortgage to the Board of Works. The practice of the two
judges of the Landed Estates Court has been somewhat
different on this point. Where there was ample security
for such charge or annuity, apart from the holding proposed
to be sold to the tenant, one of the judges has been in the
habit of making an order charging the holding in favour of
the Board of Works, thus giving to such charge priority
over the annuity. The other judge, however, has not considered that he has power to do so, and has refused to
make such charging order, however ample the remaining
security. In the opinion of the Examiner of the Court,
such action would be equivalent to " picking pockets."
The refusal to make the charging order has prevented the
tenants purchasing in a certain number of cases.

(6) The costs incurred by the tenant purchasers have
been very high. As already shown in the case of a property of the Church Commissioners sold through the
Landed Estates Court, the average cost to the tenant was 11
per cent. on the purchase money, and in those cases where
the purchase money was under £150 the costs amounted

to over 18 per cent., equal to four years' additional purchase of the rental.

(7) The cost both to vendors and purchasers has been greatly increased by the necessity of determining the easements and rights-of-way affecting the property, and defining them in the deed of transfer. This involved a fresh reference to the Ordnance Department for survey of the property, and has been the cause of delay and expense. Part II. of the Act directs the sale of land to tenants to be subject to existing rights-of-way and easements, but clause 46, not being in this part of the Act, has been subject to the usual practice of the Court. It is admitted by all the witnesses that much delay, trouble, and expense would be saved to tenant purchasers by amending the Act in this respect.

(8) The working of the Act has been further limited by the construction given to the 47th clause, which enables the Treasury, where four-fifths of the tenants of a property agree to purchase their holdings, to advance one-half of the purchase money of the remainder upon the same terms to any other purchaser not a tenant. This has been held to apply to the whole of the property only, and not to a lot containing several holdings sold in the Landed Estates Court.

(9) The clauses prohibiting the alienation or charging of properties sold to tenants and mortgaged to the Board of Works, have also limited the purchases by tenants. Tenant purchasers have been unable to give security upon their holdings for any sums which they might be able to borrow from other sources, so as to make up the balance of the purchase money.

It has been shown that in many cases the tenants of the Church property (where no such prohibition against alienation existed) borrowed from other quarters a portion of the balance of the purchase money, giving a second charge upon their farms for the same. This course is not open to tenants purchasing under the Land Act, and if they borrow at all, it must be on personal security. It is stated that the tenants' interest in their farms is always of considerable value, and that tenants frequently borrow on this security. On purchasing the farm, their tenants' interest merges in the fee ; and the prohibition against alienating or charging prevents them from borrowing even on their tenants' interest, thus limiting greatly the existing borrowing powers of the new owners, and putting them under a serious disability.   There seems to be no good reason for thus prohibiting them from borrowing; the power of borrowing in no way detracts from the value of the security to the State.

(10) The Treasury has carried the principle of prohibition of alienation to such an extent that they hold that a devise by will, even to a son, without the previous consent of the Board of Works, operates as a forfeiture ; still more so the devise to any other person.   This is stated by Mr. Stack to have given such great dissatisfaction, that many tenants who have bought are now talking of paying off their loans as soon as they can in order to be free, while others, when informed of this prohibition, have been deterred from availing themselves of the facilities offered by the Act.

In reviewing the work effected under the Land Act, the conclusion cannot be avoided that it has been inadequate and disappointing; that it has not sufficed even for an experiment on the most moderate scale ; and that it is calculated rather to excite disappointment in the minds of those for whose benefit it was intended than to effect any sensible change in the condition of the ownership of land. At the present rate of progress it cannot be expected that more than 100 tenants in each year will avail themselves of the facilities offered for becoming owners, a number so small that it will produce no effect, and nearly 20 years would elapse from the passing of the Land Act before the sum proposed to be loaned by the State for this purpose would be expended, and even if amendments be made in the Act, and in the practice of the departments upon the points referred to, the increase in the number of purchases will, it is admitted, be inconsiderable.

The results of the experiment of the Church Act and of the Land Act, so far as it has operated, fully warrant Parliament in going further in the same direction, and in endeavouring to make effective and workable, clauses which have been shown to fail almost wholly in their purpose. Without the intervention and aid of the State, it is improbable, if not impossible, in the present state of the land laws, that any number of small owners of agricultural land will come into existence. The excuse of State intervention for this purpose is, that for centuries all the influence of the law has been in the opposite direction, and that a state of things has resulted which makes the natural creation of small ownerships almost impossible.

The desire for ownership of land by the farming tenants of Ireland cannot be better illustrated than by the high price given for tenant-right throughout the greater part of Ulster, and in many other parts of Ireland where it is conceded. The tenant-right of land, fully rented, fetches in the market from 15 to 25 years' purchase of the rental, and in parts of Donegal, as much as 40 to 70 times the rental.

Major Dalton has given to the Committee a good example of the effect of this qualified ownership, or interest in the land on the part of the occupiers. He is agent for two adjoining landed properties, the one in the county of Cavan, and the other in the adjoining county of Meath. The rents of the two properties average about the same ; in the former tenant-right is recognised, and the tenants are permitted to sell their tenant-right subject to the landlord's approval ; and it has averaged eighteen years' purchase of the improved rental, that is on the re-valuation which always takes place on a change of occupation ; on the other property tenant-right has never been permitted or recognised. On the former estate, where tenant-right exists, the tenantry are in a more thriving condition than in the latter ; and, in the opinion of Major Dalton, the interest thus conceded to the tenants has been an incentive to industry and thrift, and has given a status to the occupiers, who feel invested with a *quasi* property in the land.

The same result has generally followed in Ulster, and accounts, in the opinion of many, for the greater industry and contentment of that province. The great sums thus given for the mere right of occupation, often far beyond the value of tenants' improvements, show that, under a system of simple transfer of land, and a more distributed ownership, great prices would be given for the freeholds of farms. The sale of a freehold farm, without an occupying tenant, is at present a rare occurrence. When it takes place the price is very high, for it includes not only the price which the free-hold, if let to a tenant, would fetch, but also the tenant's interest. The Church Commissioners have sold a certain number of small freeholds in hand (*i.e.*, without tenants), and the prices realised have been exceedingly high, averaging more than 50 per cent. above the price at which they would have been sold subject to a tenant's interest; and almost every witness has stated that land without a tenant, in any part of Ireland, will sell for a price greatly beyond what it will command if in the occupation of a tenant. The importance of this fact will be seen later: meanwhile it is worthy of observation, as showing the price which small freeholds are likely to command from the farming classes of Ireland.

Of the numerous witnesses examined, including the land agents for some of the largest properties in Ireland, and whose interests, therefore, might be supposed to be opposed to any general substitution of ownership for small tenancies, the great majority are in favour of giving greater facilities for the creation of a class of small owners. Mr. Vernon, agent for the properties of the Marquis of Bath and the Earl of Pembroke, and Governor of the Bank of Ireland, speaks in the strongest terms of the importance to the proprietary class in Ireland of greatly increasing their numbers. After dwelling upon the great disproportion between the number of owners and tenants, he says, that an increase in the number of the former would give stability to the state, and would, in the true and highest sense of the term, be a conservative measure.

Major Dalton, agent for the Marquis of Headfort's estates, is strongly in favour of creating a peasant proprietary in Ireland. " I think," he says, " it would be a most con-servative measure, not using the words in a political sense, but as giving the occupiers of land that which they have not got now, namely, an attachment to the constitution under which they live ;" and he quotes a passage from a speech made by the late Bishop of Lichfield to the following effect : " In New Zealand, the English, Scotch, and Irish people live together on the best terms. The qualities of each class blend together for the improvement of all. No dispute as to tenant-right can arise, because every tenant has the right of purchasing the land he holds at a fixed price. Under these circumstances, the tenants, instead of being lazy and drunken, strain every nerve to become owners of the land they occupy. In this way it happens that the most irregular people of the Irish become steady and industrious, acquiring property, and losing all their wandering habits; and it becomes impossible to distinguish between the comparative value of the Irish and Scotch elements."

Mr. Hussey, one of the leading land agents in the south of Ireland, has spoken to the same effect : " An increase in the number of small owners of land would give us a class of jurors which we do not possess in Ireland at the present time, who are not connected with property as tenants, and would check the agitation which is going on continually for taking possession of the landowners' property and giving it to the tenant class."

Sir William Gregory, formerly Member for Galway County, says : " I have always considered that in a country like Ireland, where the land is possessed by landowners, the great majority of whom differ in blood and in language in some respects, and in religion, from the cultivators of the soil, it would be about one of the most conservative, or the most conservative policy possible, to fix upon the soil a large number of the people of the country itself. I believe that in every man, who is thus placed upon the soil as owner of his land, you have as it were a special constable on the side of law and order, and I have always looked forward to the measure as one which would bring at once the people of the country more in harmony with the landlords, and be for the general interest of the country."

Mr. Justice Flanagan says : " I am sure it would add to the stability of the institutions of this country if there were a considerable infusion of tenant-proprietors in the country, provided always, you took care that the possession of the land in the hands of the tenant-proprietor were not severed from what I may call the ownership of the land." Professor Baldwin says : " Considering the state of Ireland, I should say the most important result of creating small owners would be this : each small proprietor would be a centre of loyalty, and the more of these centres of loyalty you create, the better for the state."

Many other witnesses have given evidence to the same effect ; the almost solitary exception has been the evidence of Mr. Olpherts, a landowner in Donegal, whose district is one of the poorest in Ireland, and where the holdings are very small. This gentleman is of opinion that it would be positively injurious to the occupiers that they should become the owners of their holdings : " My impression is, that they cannot do without a landlord over them in some form or other ; they must have a landlord to consult ; they must have a landlord to stand in front of them when they get into difficulties, in order to assist them, and they must have a landlord to secure them in their holdings." The tenant-right in his district has risen to a very high amount, averaging from 30 to 70 years' purchase of the rental, and in-coming tenants often pay double what the landlord can obtain for the fee-simple. It has been raised to this point, he says, by people coming home from America, and who like to come back to the place they went from, and who, finding it very difficult to get land where they can settle, will give anything to get into their own locality again. The tenant-right is fully recognised by himself and his neighbours. Mr. Olpherts admits that the tenant-right is useful in some respects ; if the tenant gets into difficulties he can sell out, and will have the means of getting out of the country : it also gives him a sense of security. " It is evident such a man holding under tenant-right is as much an owner as I am, because I cannot put him out ; it would cost me more than it is worth." " Therefore, there is no reason for granting him the remaining portion of the ownership ? " —" None whatever."

Sir Frederick Heygate, a considerable landowner in Londonderry, while admitting the want in Ireland of a middle class, and believing that it would be for the interest of the country that there should be a more numerous class of owners of land, is of opinion that this class should consist rather of farmers of the more prosperous class, and with from thirty to fifty acres, sufficient to maintain a pair of horses, than of the smaller class of tenants ; he fears that the result of facilitating ownership among the small farmers would be to promote sub-division of land, and the building and sub-letting of cottages of a bad description. He fears also the effect of a bad harvest in reducing the condition of the small owners, and that Government would find it very un-popular to enforce payment of the interest and instalments by such persons, or to sell them up. He thinks, therefore, that if the Government should make loans, it should not do so in the case of holdings below a certain size, because it would otherwise get a class of people who, he thinks, would not secure the prosperity of the country.   His opinion is to some extent shared in by Mr. Ball Greene, the head of the Valuation Office in Ireland, and by Mr. Bence Jones, a landowner in the County of Cork.

Sir F. Heygate, however, has most frankly admitted that it would not be possible to draw a line, and that the attempt to do so would be fatal to the whole scheme.   Mr. Ball Greene also does not see his way to draw a line, and admits that it would be unjust to do so.   Mr. Bence Jones equally does not appear to contemplate drawing a line ; he uses the objection rather as an argument against plunging hastily into any scheme.   He admits that the present scheme as worked by the Landed Estates Court is a failure, and says he would be glad to see the experiment tried on a larger · scale ; he thinks that if 1,000 tenants were converted into owners in each year for the next ten years, that might give a fair trial of such an experiment.

With these exceptions, all the witnesses before the Committee have expressed the opinion that it is quite as important to facilitate the creation of the smaller class of landowners as of the large class, or, as Major Dalton has put it, " It is not proposed to create more small tenants than now exist, but simply to elevate in the social scale those who are now on the land."

Of the 592,000 tenant farmers in Ireland, 423,000 hold less than thirty acres of land.   The great bulk of the purchasers of the Church property were tenants of this class ; the average holdings in Ulster are also of this class.   In the opinion of Mr. Murrough O'Brien it is even more important that ownership should be encouraged among the smaller tenants than among the larger.   Speaking of small farmers, averaging about ten acres each, he says, " I think that lots of this sort are just as suitable for sale, and that the small farmers are most desirable members of society to encourage.   It makes them orderly, and it gives men labouring in England or America a home to come back to."   Speaking of holdings of about five acres, he said, " For one thing, it is the best mode of housing the labouring population ; it does not pay the landlord to build houses for them, and it is a matter of experience, that when they have the opportunity, they, not all at once, but from time to time, invest their little savings of money and labour in building themselves houses and improving their little plots of land.   The holders of these small plots do not also require so much capital in proportion as those with larger holdings.   The labour of the man and his family is his capital, and is sufficient for the cultivation of a small farm."   He adds : " I think the fact of the tenants having only a yearly tenure is the reason why the Irish are the worst housed nation in civilised Europe.   Of course, where the farms are very small, some of them being hardly worthy of being called farms, but rather agricultural labourers' holdings, on those it would never pay the owner to build houses suitable for the occupants.

"In my opinion, there is no objection to small plots being sold as freehold any more than large plots ; in fact, I think that there would be more small farmers desirous of being freeholders than large farmers, because a large farmer has a trade ; he wants his capital to trade with, and it does not always suit him to invest in land ; whereas, as far as my experience of small holders goes, they are most anxious to become freeholders.

"The capital chiefly required for working a small farm, say of five acres or less, which could hardly be called a farm, is the tenants' labour.   I can see no objection to encouraging the making of small freeholders like that, or even smaller.   The tenant need not necessarily be a labourer ; he may be a tradesman, as many such small farmers are, and it is his pride to spend the savings of his time and labour in making his house more comfortable, and in setting out gardens and orchards, as many farmers do now upon the security of their tenant-right."

Major Dalton has given evidence to the same effect :— " There are a good many tenants on Lord Headfort's estate holding from one to five acres.   They are rather labouring men than farmers.   They live chiefly by labour.   Now these are men whom I should like to fix upon the soil ; I think it, is one way of dealing with the most perplexing question of all, perhaps—namely, the labourers question, and how to house them.   It costs the farmers much to build cottages, and, moreover, thatch is getting more expensive every year ; they do not like to waste it on the roofs of their cabins.

Then, on the other hand, landlords cannot do it on a very large scale, except upon the land which they have in their hands; they are not rich enough; but if you give the labourer a property in his small allotment or holding, I think he would be very likely to do it himself, and I know instances where they have done it." Any attempt to exclude such a class from any facilities offered by the state would, in his opinion, be impolitic and most invidious. "I think that it would be fatal to the measure, from a conservative point of view, at all events, because it would create so much disaffection that I would rather do nothing."

Mr. Henderson, of Belfast, has spoken to the same effect :—" Judging by the analogy of the Ulster tenant-right, the small holdings bring a higher price, and the people are often as comfortable in the small holdings as in the larger."

Mr. Vernon says :—" If you look for high farming, or scientific farmers, you would never dream of *petite culture ;* you would never establish small farms, you would have large farms ; but in Ireland we deal with facts as we find them, and the fact is that the country is in the possession of small occupiers, whom the Legislature, rightly or wrongly, declines to disturb. Therefore it appears to me that the only question that arises now is, whether land held by a small holder as a tenant, having the superintendence, and, perhaps, the assistance of his landlord, will not be better cultivated than land in possession of a man of the same calibre, but having no control over him at all. My answer to that would be this, that I think it is true to human nature that the right of ownership ought quite to make up for the other." When asked by Sir John Leslie this question :—" Supposing that a farmer, one of those who happened to live on a large estate, had to purchase his holding, and should be called upon to find the money, would he not draw that money, to a certain extent, from that which he should put into the ground?" Mr. Vernon replied :—" No doubt he would in a certain degree, but, on the other hand, look to the operation of what takes place in your own county [Monaghan]; you will see there that the man will give nearly the value of the fee of the land for possession of it, yet in some way or other will thrive. We see in the north of Ireland they give large sums for tenant-right, and after that we see them cultivating better than they do in the south of Ireland, where they give nothing." ·

Professor Baldwin says that there are many parts of Ireland which cannot be cultivated, except by spade labour, which are so rough and stony that a plough cannot be used. At Glasnevin there are three model farms, one of six acres, cultivated entirely by spade labour, another of twenty-five acres, which is managed as an example for the bulk of working farms, and a large farm in which high farming is practised. His experience, he says, is that the average of produce decreases as the size of the farm increases, and that under spade labour the land produces more. He considers that ownership is an essential condition to a small farm being properly worked, and that small occupiers are much more objectionable than small owners, on both social and economic grounds, and even more so for political reasons. He is, therefore, opposed to any artificial line being drawn by the state for discouraging owners holding below a certain amount of land. He would trust to the operation of the ordinary economic laws, if properly set in motion, to work out what is best for the interest of the country, and under which the thrifty would buy out the unthrifty, and he thinks that the natural operation of consolidation of farms would be set on foot, where it is really and economically sound.

The same opinion has been given by many other witnesses. It is stated that there is no longer the same tendency to sub-divide holdings that there was before the famine of 1846. Mr. O'Brien says : " I think the sub-division which took place formerly, of which I have no knowledge except from reading, arose from this : that the tenants sub-divided and misused land which was not their own ; they had little or no interest in it, and they did not care how they misused it ; now when tenants invest in land, and more especially when they have a permanent interest in it, I think they are much more likely (contrasting my experience with what I have read of in the past) to use it judiciously and wisely, and to make their possessions of the greatest advantage to themselves and the country. I think that farmers in Ireland are just as unlikely as anywhere else to sub-divide their farms in a manner which would be injurious to their property ; they are quite aware of the disadvantages of a farm being left among a whole family of children ; they generally make wills, even where they have nothing to leave but a yearly tenancy, and they would be much more likely to make wills when they have freeholds to leave.

" There is also a much higher standard of living than there was formerly ; moreover, the younger men of the families go to other countries. It is a thing which has been said to me over and over again when I have visited farms in Ireland, that the whole family cannot expect to live upon the land ; the sons and daughters go to America or to England. There are, therefore, three distinct causes to render sub-division less likely than it was formerly ; first, that the tenant will be the owner of the land, and have a permanent interest in it ; secondly, the higher standard of living ; and thirdly, that the young people are more in the habit of going to America and elsewhere."

Mr. O'Hagan also concurs in the view that the habit of sub-division has greatly gone out, and that there need be no fear on this score. He thinks, however, that so long as the state stands in the relation of mortgagee of the properties created by the facilities given, it should insist upon the property not being sub-divided. " I think," he says, " it would be quite wise that it should have that power, and, besides, that it is right of the state to require it. I think it would work beneficially in this way : that it would, for a certain time, at all events, tend to keep up the habit, which has very considerably grown, of there being no sub-division." " This would maintain the property undivided for thirty-four years, the length of the annuity, and in that time I would hope that the habits of the people would have so altered that the excessive sub-division of former years, which really resulted to a great degree from the improvidence which came from utter destitution, would not then exist."

Major Dalton entertains no fear on this score :—" Of course it would take place in some cases, but I have found from my own experience, which is a tolerably long one now, that the wish for sub-division is dying out altogether on the Headfort estates ; the tendency is rather the other way, towards the consolidation of farms, which is generally brought about by emigration. Before the famine the tendency to sub-division existed to a very great extent, but since then the opening afforded in the Colonies and the United States has exercised what I may call a centrifugal force upon the home population, and instead of sub-dividing the holding among the family, one of the sons retains the farm, and the others emigrate or adopt other employments. Of course sub-division would take place in some cases, but then the neighbouring tenant would buy the property of the man who was going away, and in that way it would tend rather to increase the size of the holding than otherwise."

Upon the evidence given on these important questions, the Committee are of opinion that it would be neither politic nor just to make any distinction in the class of tenants to whom facilities to purchase their holdings should be given by the state; and that, granting there exists in Ireland an immense number of small tenants, holding land of various extent below thirty acres, some of whom are small farmers living wholly by their land, others are agricultural labourers living mainly by their labour away from their holdings, and others are in part supported or assisted by other members of their family working in the towns, at sea, or in service, it is equally important that all these classes should be brought within the range of the stimulus to industry and thrift caused by the feeling of security which ownership alone can give, and which would also raise their status in society, and make them more contented and loyal members of the state.

Provided the freedom of willing be left without interference, there is no reason to fear the future sub-division of the small holdings, which may be brought into existence by the facilities given by the state. The question may be safely left to the ordinary laws of supply and demand. Under a free system, with a simple and cheap system of transfer, the thrifty will buy out the unthrifty, and if there be a tendency to sub-divide in some cases, there will be the opposite tendency to consolidate in others, and the two forces may be left to balance one another. So long, however, as the state retains a mortgage on the property, it should have the ordinary right of a mortgagee of insisting upon the holding remaining in its integral state as security for the money advanced, and this will practically prevent sub-division or sub-letting for a period of thirty-five years.

It is clear, however, from the evidence which has been given by the officers of the Landed Estates Court and others, that even if such amendments be made in the Act, and in the practice of the departments concerned in administering it, as have been suggested, no great increase will be effected in the sales to tenants. The difficulty of the residues will still remain. It will still be seldom that tenants will have the opportunity of bidding separately for their holdings, and the examiners and the judges of the Landed Estates Court will still feel it difficult to act in opposition to the vendors of properties, or to exercise the discretion which was given to them by the Land Act, of putting up properties for sale in lots suitable for the tenants to buy. Judge Flanagan, one of the judges of the Landed Estates Court, says :—" The 46th section of the Irish Land Act is one which, in my opinion, it is almost impossible to work. I mean to work in the sense of enabling tenants to become purchasers of their holding to any considerable amount. It has imposed upon the Landed Estates Court a duty which it is almost impossible to work out."

Various plans have been suggested by witnesses for the purpose of overcoming this difficulty, and for extending the operation of the Land Act in the creation of small ownerships. Mr. Vernon, after pointing out that it is impossible to expect any substantial result from the clauses of the Land Act as now drawn, and that the duty imposed upon the Landed Estates Court, of selling preferentially to the tenants of land coming before them, is abnormal to their true functions, and puts them in a false position, has said :—" Assuming that the Legislature desires to create a peasant proprietary, or a body of small proprietors, I think that whoever sells the property to the tenants must be in the position that the Church Temporalities Commissioners were put into ; that is to say, they must have the absolute power. I think the property should vest in the state before it is conveyed to the tenant, and that the state should deal with the land as between itself and the tenant. I do not think it will ever work otherwise. I think you must vest the property in the state ; that means presumably in some Commission appointed by the state. I think that where an estate is for sale in the Landed Estates Court, it should be the duty of that Commission to send down a proper officer to report upon the value of the property, and upon the conditions under which it is held, and to see all the tenants and learn from them what price they are prepared to give, if any, for their lots. If the tenants say, "We will not buy," then this imaginary Commission withdraws its action altogether, and leaves them to pass under the ordinary rules of sale to any purchaser who may be found. If, on the other hand, as I think will be found to be the case, the tenants declare to buy, then, let it be for that Commission to see what price they will give. Add to that some fair commission which shall cover the expenses of the transaction, and then let them become buyers in the open market from the vendor. They would then be in this position, that they would be able to offer the full value for the land. The vendor, consequently, would not be damnified in any way. The Landed Estates Court would have no conflicting duty at all; they would sell to the Commission precisely as they would to the outside public. I think that such a Commission would be able to offer a full, fair price to any seller for his property, and could, without damage to anybody except, perhaps, to the state, that has to pay the money in the first instance, sell, and raise a class of owners which never can be raised in any other way."

It is the opinion of Mr. Vernon that the Commission thus appointed and invested with these duties should be independent both of the Landed Estates Court, the Office of Works, and of the Imperial Treasury; that it should be entrusted with funds for the purpose of buying properties in the first instance and re-selling them to the tenants ; and that it should have a wide discretion as to the method of carrying out the details of such a plan, and not, therefore, be subject to the constant control of the Treasury.

In this view he has suggested that, inasmuch as the use of imperial funds would necessarily imply imperial control, an effort should be made to find an Irish fund suitable for the purpose, and he points to the surplus of the Irish Church funds as a fund which might be made applicable to the purpose. It is stated by the Church Temporalities Commission, in their report of 1877, that the available surplus in 1880, when their functions cease, will amount to about six millions. " I think," said Mr. Vernon, " there ought to be no loss to the public ; I think you have the funds available for it. You have a fund in Ireland which you do not know what to do with. Some people want to send it to the lunatics ; some here, and some there ; I suggest making a tenant proprietary with it. I think the measure would be more effectually worked if the funds could be drawn from an Irish source."

Under such a scheme, the Commissioners, having ascertained what proportion of tenants of a particular property are in a position to buy, and what margin of price would be offered by such tenants, and having formed an opinion whether the transaction could be carried out without loss, would buy the property either in the open market or privately, from the owners; and having then become owners of the property, would sell to those tenants willing to buy, and dispose of the residue at the best price to be obtained in the market. It is the opinion of Mr. Vernon that the residue would in this way be reduced to a minimum, and that the possible loss upon the re-sale of the residue would be recouped by the higher price obtained from the individual tenants.

Mr. Vernon contemplates, therefore, that no loss would be sustained by the funds of the Church temporarily used for this purpose. The funds of the Church would be invested in loans to the tenant-purchasers, and would ultimately be repaid with interest, in the same manner as the money lent by the state, or as that now advanced by the Church Commissioners to the tenant-purchasers of the Church glebes. In lieu of using imperial funds for the purpose, an Irish fund would be available, and therefore a wider discretion could be allowed to the Commission, who would no longer be subject to imperial control, though still subject to imperial audit.

The Commissioners appointed with this object would only act where they find that a certain proportion of the tenants of a particular property are prepared to purchase, and where they are of opinion that the residue could be disposed of so as to involve no loss by the transaction ; and it is part of the suggestion of Mr. Vernon that the proportion to be advanced by way of mortgage to the tenant purchasers should be the same as in the case of the Church Commission—viz., three-fourths—and that the prohibition against alienation should be removed, thus enabling those tenants who are unable to produce the balance of the purchase money to borrow, if they can obtain credit.

K

The scheme thus propounded by Mr. Vernon for getting over the many difficulties by which the intention of Parliament, as indicated by the Clauses of the Land Act, has been attended, has received the support of other witnesses who have given evidence before the Committee, such as Major Dalton and Mr. O'Hagan.

Mr. Justice Flanagan has also given an approval to the principle contained in Mr. Vernon's proposal. He says :— " My view is, that you will never have sales to tenants in any number until practically you adopt what I may call Mr. Vernon's suggestion ; that is to say, you must sever altogether the duties of the Court as selling on behalf of the owner from the duties of the Court as selling to the tenants. . . You must have, as Mr. Vernon has put it, some persons who would, in the interests of the tenants, be prepared to come forward and buy ' *in globo* ' from the owner of the property which he offers for sale, and then that body, call it what you like, should, under the powers to be given to them, re-distribute that property, and then sell it back to the tenants, if they had satisfied themselves by previous inquiry that such transaction would be a beneficial or a safe one on their part to undertake." He considers such a method equally in the interest of the owners of property as of their tenants :—" In my opinion, it is the only way in which you can protect the interests of owners of property, and it is the only chance you have of selling largely to tenants."

With this object, Judge Flanagan proposes that all the jurisdiction which the Landed Estates Court has under the Land Act for facilitating the creation of small proprietors should be worked by one of the judges instead of two, as at present ; that a body should be made up of one of the judges of the Court, with the assistance of one of the Commissioners of the Board of Works, or of the Valuation Office, and some other person of great knowledge in the management of landed property in Ireland, and that this body should have the power of making all preliminary investigation in the case of any property for sale in the Court ; of ascertaining whether there are a great many tenants who wish to purchase or not ; and whether, having regard to the number of those who wish to buy, and the amount of the residue the tenants of which could not buy, it would be a desirable transaction for them to enter upon; and that they should then have the power of purchasing the property, either by private contract or at the auction, and, having done so, should re-distribute the estate by sale among the tenants.

The judge proceeds to point out that this process would leave a certain amount of residues to be dealt with, for there would generally be a certain number of tenants who would be unable or unwilling to purchase. He proposes to deal with these residues by giving power to the Court to give to their tenants fee-farm grants or perpetuity leases, at such an increased rent as might appear to them reasonable; and that, having done so, they should sell their fee-farm rents by auction. " My reason," he adds, " for suggesting that is this : —I think that in dealing with these residues the difficulty is not so much selling the residues as really protecting the tenants of the residues, because where there are residues of this kind, and these residues are put up by public auction for sale, and bought, you get a class of purchasers and land-lords whom I look upon as about the greatest curse you can inflict upon the country. I think the small landlords are, as a rule, the most tyrannical class ; I hardly know what term to use ; they look upon it purely as a mercantile transaction in the extreme sense of the term ; their whole object in going in to buy these small residues being to extract from the un-fortunate small tenants, who have thus lost the protection of their former landlords, the very highest penny which by possibility they can extract from those tenants. I think that unless you protected the tenants of the residues by giving them fee-farm grants, in that way you would be doing an amount of injury which, in my opinion, would be simply in-calculable. I fully believe that as the purchasers of these small residues (for I am pre-supposing that they would be comparatively small and undesirable, as being detached plots) you would get little shopkeepers who had made £200 or £300 in trade, and by lending money at usurious rate ; 'gombeens ' we call them in the west : in every townland there is a man we call a 'gombeen,' and when a tenant gets into difficulties, he lends his money at a most usurious rate. These men would become the landlords of the tenants ; and I say, deliberately, that a greater curse cannot be inflicted upon the tenantry of Ireland than a system of selling pro-perty which would leave the residuary tenants in their power ;

they are the most merciless, the most avaricious, and the worst class of landlords that can by possibility be put over an unfortunate class of tenants."

The evidence of Judge Flanagan as to the difficulties which have prevented the operation of the Act, is especially valuable, as pointing to the expediency of giving such general power of purchase to a Commission or department with the object of removing these difficulties. As an illustration, the difficulty caused by jointures, annuities, or rent-charges, with which so many properties are burthened, and which would prevent such properties being divided for sale among the tenants, could only be disposed of by the purchase of Government annuities out of the proceeds of the sale to the tenants.

The judge further points out that, looking to the amount of property annually sold in the Landed Estates Court, there is no reason to expect that even if his and Mr. Vernon's proposals be carried out, the sales to tenants would be so numerous as to effect a revolution in the ownership of land in Ireland. It would have the effect of making a substantial addition to the number of small owners in Ireland ; but it would be a reform in this direction, and not a revolution.

The judge has also explained at length the obstacle to transactions under the other part of the Land Act, especially in the case of tenants for life, or limited owners who may be anxious to effect sales to their tenants ; he suggests that such limited owners should have power to grant perpetuity leases to these tenants, either at an increased rent or at the same rent, upon payment of a fine, to be approved by the Court in the interest of the reversioners, and he believes that many landowners would be glad to avail themselves of such a power.

The proposal of Mr. Vernon is not substantially different from a scheme which was put forward by a committee of influential Irishmen in 1868, before the disestablishment of the Irish Church, and before the Land Act was under consideration. The committee consisted, among others, of Judge Lawson, Judge Flanagan, Mr. Law, M.P. (the present Attorney-General), Mr. John O'Hagan, Q.C., Mr. M'Donnell, the Examiner of the Landed Estates Court, Mr. Dix Hutton, and others. The scheme, which is to be found in the Appendix to the Evidence of the Committee, proposed the use of the funds of the then Established Church for the purpose of creating a peasant proprietary.   It proposed the appointment of a Commission, who should be empowered to buy landed properties as ordinary purchasers, in the open market, either on sales in the Landed Estates Court, or by private contract, such properties to be re-sold to the tenants, or to be granted on fee-farm leases for ever to the tenants upon payment of a small fine, or at a somewhat increased rent, thus giving three alternative methods of dealing with the tenants of such properties.   It was stated in the scheme that, "the possibility of effecting the operation with ease and advantage to both tenants and owners must depend on the advances being made at a low rate of interest.   This is demonstrated by the large and long-continued experience of Prussia, and the other leading States of Germany, where the Governments used their financial credit to facilitate the conversion of occupiers into owners."

On the other hand, Mr. Baldwin, Chief Inspector of Agricultural Schools in Ireland, who has had considerable experience of the agricultural tenants in all parts of Ireland, is of opinion that a considerable proportion of them would find difficulty in advancing even one-fourth of the purchase money without either selling some of the stock on the farm, which would be injurious to it, or without borrowing money from local solicitors, which would encumber them with debt at the first start as owners.   He recommends that the State should advance the whole of the purchase money, within reasonable limits as to value, repayable by instalments, at 3½ per cent.   On being further questioned as to this, he added that it would not be desirable that the interest and repayments of capital to the state should exceed the rent previously paid to the landlord. The effect of this limitation would be, that if the present period of 35 years for the repayment of the principal be retained, the advance ·by the state could not exceed 20 years' purchase of the rental. Mr. Baldwin, however, further suggests, that if the purchase-money exceeds 20 years' purchase of the rental, the term of repayment of the advance should be extended, so ·that the interest and instalments should not exceed the previous rent.

The following table will explain this proposal :—

Rent.	Purchase Money.	Interest at 3¼ per Cent.	Sinking Fund.	Years of Sinking Fund and payable off at 3¼ per Cent.
£10	£200	£7·	£3·	35
10	210	7·37	2·65	37
10	220	7·7	2·3	39
10	230	8·05	1·95	44
10	240·	8·4	1·6	49
10	250	8·75	1·25	55
10	260	9·10	0·90	63
10	270	9·45	0·45	82
10	280	9·80	0·20	Upwards of 100 years.

This table shows how readily the plan of a Government loan, repayable by instalments spread over a term of years, lends itself to any scheme for converting tenancies into ownerships, and how great is the boon of such loans.

It is probable that if the State were prepared to extend the repayment of the loan over fifty-five years, and to advance up to the point when the interest and instalments equal the previous rent, which would enable twenty-five years' purchase of the rental to be given, nearly every estate offered for sale in the Landed Estates Court could be purchased on these terms, and the tenants would at once, and without any effort on their part, be converted into owners, subject to the payment of sums equal to their previous rent, payable for a term of fifty-five years. The tenants of a property thus purchased would be treated upon the same terms as the landowners, who redeem the tithe rent-charge upon their properties, were dealt with under the Church Disestablishment Act, 1869.

The objections to such a scheme are, that it would involve no exertion on the part of the tenants; that the period of repayment of the loan would be a very lengthy one, equal to the average of two generations; that in the meantime the relation between the State and the new owner would be very much that of landlord and tenant. There is an advantage in the shorter period of repayment in this, that every year a sensible portion of the principal is repaid, and every year, therefore, the interest of the new owner becomes greater, and the security of the State or lender safer; every year the owner will feel that he is rising more and more to the position of an unincumbered owner. If, through bad management, the owner should fall into difficulties after a few years, the farm would in the meantime have acquired a substantial value, over and above the tenant's interest, and public opinion would fully justify the insistance by the State, or by the Commission, of the payment of the instalments, or the sale of the property under process of law. It is of importance, therefore, to retain the shorter period of thirty-four years, as the term over which the repayments of the advance are to be spread. It has been suggested that if a famine such as that of 1846 were to recur, and the State were to find itself in relation of mortgagee to a large number of small owners, there would be great difficulty in collecting the interest. If such a calamity were to occur, involving the whole of the cultivators of the soil in one common misfortune, it would, perhaps, be necessary for the State to show consideration to the owners indebted to them, but this could easily be effected by spreading the repayments over a longer period of time, so as to recoup the State for any temporary loss.

The proportion of the advance to be made by the State is evidently of considerable importance. It has been stated by numerous witnesses that the difference between the three-fourths of the purchase money conceded to the Church tenants, and the two-thirds, as provided by the Land Act, has prevented many purchases being effected under the latter Act. The Land Act, when originally introduced in the House of Commons, proposed that three-fourths of the value might be advanced by the Board of Works, and the proportion was cut down to two-thirds in Committee. A general impression has prevailed in Ireland that three-fourths would be advanced, and great disappointment has often resulted on finding that the proportion is no more than two-thirds, and that even this is cut down by the principle on which the Board of Works estimates the value of the property at little more than one-half. Mr. Stack, of the Board of Works, who has been much consulted by tenants applying for information of the Board as to the terms of advance, has reported that great numbers of tenants have been obliged to abandon the idea of purchase on finding that the proportion to be advanced was so much less than they expected.

Mr. Hussey, an agent for very large properties in Cork, has also pointed out that the difference in the advance, of between two-thirds and three-fourths of the purchase money, has had great effect in deterring transactions. He is of opinion that the State could, with perfect safety, advance even so much as four-fifths of the purchase money. He puts the tenant's interest as worth, at the very lowest estimate, five years' purchase of the rental, and assuming that the property sells for twenty-five years' purchase of the rental with a tenant, it would sell for thirty years' purchase without a tenant, and he thinks that this is perfect security for a sum equal to twenty years' purchase of the rental; this would amount to four-fifths of the purchase money given by the tenant.

It is evident that just in proportion as the advance made by the State is increased, so the sale of the whole of a property to the tenants is facilitated, and the difficulty of the residue is diminished. The advance by the State may, with safety, be increased in all cases to three-fourths of the purchase money; and a discretion may be given to the body entrusted with the work, in exceptional cases, to advance even beyond this, with the object of facilitating the disposal of residues, and of enabling the purchase of a whole property or lot to be effected by the tenants; provided always, however, that the interest and instalments do not exceed the amount of the rent previously paid, or the fair annual letting value of the holding.

It has been already shown that in the case of the Church property where twenty-three years' purchase was given by the purchasing tenants, the interest and instalments at four per cent. upon three-fourths of the purchase money, or seventeen years' purchase, equalled the previous rent. Under the more favourable terms as regards the rate of interest of the Land Act, the Office of Works would be able to advance twenty years' purchase of the rental, or four-fifths of the purchase money on twenty-five years' purchase, and the interest and instalments payable annually would still be no more than the previous rent.

With reference, however, to these financial proposals, much must depend upon the discretion of those who have ultimately to deal with the subject. In review of the many difficulties which have occurred in working the Act in the past, and the various suggestions which have been made for its amendment and extension, there can be no doubt as to the expediency of concentrating in one body, whether a Commission or an existing depart-ment, all the functions, financial, legal, and administrative, which are now distributed between the Landed Estates Court, the Office of Works, and the Treasury. Between the proposal of Judge Flanagan of a re-constituted Landed Estates Court, and the association, with one of its judges, of two other officers with special qualifications, and of Mr. Vernon's proposal for a new Commission, there is no difference in principle. There are obvious advantages in utilising an existing department. On the other hand, it is difficult to understand how the Judge of the Landed Estates Court can act in one branch of the Court in the interest of the owners of property, and in the other, in the interest of the tenants.

Both schemes involve such department or commission being entrusted with funds for carrying out the purchase and re-sale of properties, and for both it has been urged, as a condition of success, that such a body should be entrusted with a wide discretion, and be freed as far as possible from the control of the Treasury. This would best be secured by obtaining such funds from some fresh source ; and it is in this view that the proposal to allow the surplus funds of the Disestablished Church of Ireland to be temporarily in-vested in loans to tenants purchasing, and in the purchase of properties for the purpose of prompt re-sale, commends itself to attention ; an application which would not interfere with the disposal at any subsequent time by Parliament of the income arising from such surplus fund. If an Irish fund could be made available for the general purpose of extending ownership among the occupying farmers of Ireland, great advantage would result. It would bring under one executive body functions which are now dis-tributed between the Landed Estates Court, the Board of Works, and the Imperial Treasury. It would also be of much advantage that the funds thus to be disposed of should be, while ample, limited and specific, and it would give great weight to the action of the Commission in in-

sisting upon repayment, that the funds were Irish and that
any diminution of them would be to the detriment of purely
Irish interests. With respect to the scheme of purchase and
re-sale, it might be that such a process would not often be
necessary. The Landed Estates Court would still, as here-
tofore, on the sale of properties, break them up into lots,
with the object of obtaining the best price for the owners ;
it would not be necessary, therefore, for the Commission
to deal with the tenants of a whole estate, but only with
the tenants of a particular lot.

If the experience of the Church Commissioners is to be
relied on, the sale of residues, when properly conducted, would
realise a fair price, and a proof of this by a few transactions
would probably induce vendors in the Landed Estates
Court more readily to listen to offers on behalf of the
tenants who are prepared to buy at full prices. It is probable, therefore, that the Commission would not frequently
be called upon to purchase properties with a view to
the re-sale to the tenants, but the power and means of
doing so would greatly add to the general success of their
operations.

In the cases, however, of properties or lots subject to
rent-charges, annuities, or jointures, sales to the tenants, as
already explained, can scarcely be expected in any other
manner. It should be a condition to such purchase and
re-sale that the transaction should be carried out without loss
to the fund employed. The contracts with the purchasing
tenants might be so arranged as to make the amount of their
annuities dependent on the sum obtained for the residues,
so as to provide against possible loss.

Apart, however, from the question as to the funds which
may be made available for the purpose above indicated, it
would be wise to appoint a Commission (for a period, say of
10 years), for the purpose of effecting the objects of the Land
Act in facilitating the creation of small proprietors of land in
Ireland. The work must necessarily be tentative. The Commission would gradually feel its way. It would put itself in
relation with tenants of properties about to be sold. It
would advise them fully as to the intentions of the Legislature, and as to the nature of the advance. It would represent their interests in the Landed Estates Court. It
would conduct negotiations for them with the owners of

property. It would deal with residues in the manner proposed by Judge Flanagan. It would relieve tenant purchasers of law costs, and act as receiver of the interest and repayments of principal after the advance is made. It would be in a position to advise the Government from time to time as to the difficulties which may arise in carrying out the scheme, and the best means of removing them. It would, through its solicitor, examine titles of properties offered to them for sale to tenants without the expense of going through the Landed Estates Court. It would work in the direction suggested by many of the witnesses, of dealing with the subject of settled estates by enabling the limited owners thereof to convert their tenants into perpetuity tenants, on payment of a fine or at a small increase of rent. The Commission might have power to consent to such operations so as to bind the remainder-men of such entailed properties ; though the Committee are not of opinion that the creation of perpetuity tenants offers the same advantages as that of freeholders, subject to instalment mortgages. In the case of instalment mortgages it would be well that the occupiers should be allowed to pay off at any time parts of the debts due, so as to give them every encouragement to save with this object.

It is most neccessary, before concluding, to call attention to the evidence of Dr. Hancock as to the further measures which are necessary for the continued existence of a small proprietary when called into existence—such measures as were undoubtedly contemplated when the Irish Land Act was proposed to Parliament, for simplifying and lessening the cost of transfer of land, for creating local registries, and otherwise facilitating the mortgaging and dealing with land—measures, also, for simplifying the inheritance and devise of land, and for freeing it from the complication of settlements. These measures form no part of the present inquiry, but it is certain that just in proportion as the present state of the law in these respects has tended to prevent the existence of small owners in the past, so will it speedily undo the work which it is proposed to effect in creating small owners through the intervention of state aid. It is above all important that small owners should be able to deal freely with their property, without being overwhelmed with law costs.

The subject, therefore, is eminently and urgently deserving the attention of the Legislature.

The following, then, are the conclusions resulting from the enquiry:—

1st. That, in the present state of landownership in Ireland, it is most desirable that facilities should be given by the State for the conversion of tenancies into ownerships, by purchase ; that the increase of small owners would tend to give stability to the social system, would spread content-ment and loyalty, and would give a spur to industry and thrift.

2nd. That the experiment which has already taken place in this direction, in the sale of the Church property to its occupying tenants, is eminently satisfactory, and shows that there is a great desire on the part of tenants to become owners by purchase, especially at the time when the land they occupy is changing hands, and there is a prospect of their being handed over to new landlords.

3rd. That, as now framed and worked, the clauses of the Land Act, 1870, having this object in view are wholly inadequate for the purpose, and are the cause of much disappointment, and that little better result is to be expected from them by such minor amendments as have been suggested, which will leave the administration of them divided between the Landed Estates Court, the Board of Works, and the Treasury.

4th. That it is desirable that a special Commission be constituted for a term of ten years, for the purpose of carrying out these objects, and that it should be entrusted with funds, by way of loan, for the purpose, and, if possible, from an Irish source.

5th. That a wide discretion should be given to the Commission, for the purpose of effecting the object in view, whether by granting loans to purchasing tenants, repayable by instalments, or by the purchase and re-sale to tenants of properties or lots where a large proportion of such tenants are willing and able to buy, and where a minority are unable to do so, or by granting perpetuity leases, with a view to the disposal of such residues as recommended by Judge Flanagan.

6th. That the Commission should also be empowered to assent to the granting of perpetuity leases by the limited owners of entailed estates to their tenants, upon payment of a fine, or at such increased rent as may be reasonable, having regard to the interests of the reversioners.

7th. That the proportion of the purchase money to be advanced on loan to tenants purchasing their holdings be increased, subject to the approval of the Commission, to three-fourths of the value of such holdings, with a discretion to the Commission to exceed this proportion in special cases, with a view to complete the sale of the whole property to the tenants, so that the instalments payable annually shall not exceed the previous rent or annual letting value.

8th. That the restrictions against alienation, charging and devising of holdings subject to such annuities, be repealed, but that the prohibition against sub-division and sub-letting be rigorously maintained so long as the charge remains.

9th. That the Church Temporalities Commissioners be empowered to grant perpetuity leases at fair rents to such of the residuary tenants of the Church property as are unable to purchase their holdings.

10th. That the law of transfer of land be re-considered specially with reference to its effect upon the transactions in small holdings.

———————

The above Report, proposed by the Chairman, was not accepted by the Committee; by a majority of one, a Report, proposed by Mr. David Plunket, was substituted for it, but was afterwards amended, so as practically to conform to the above conclusions.

APPENDIX.

REPORT,

To the Statistical Society of Ireland,

Of a Visit to Church Lands sold or under offer to the Tenants, in the Autumn of 1877.

By the advice of Mr. Murrough O'Brien, the valuator employed by the Irish Church Temporalities Commission, I selected for my visit two properties distant about six and twelve miles from Newry, one of which was sold four years ago to the tenants, and the other of which, owing to some technical difficulties, is only now about to be offered to its tenants.
The object of my visit was that I might personally judge of the motives which the tenants had or have in view in effecting the purchase, and of the results, so far as they could be ascertained by ocular proof and by conversation with the new owners.
I.—The first consisted of about 250 statute acres, distributed in twenty-one small farms, with an average rent of £1 4s, per acre. All the tenants of this property bought at rates of about twenty-four years' purchase of the rental. The property is in a purely agricultural district; the land light and undulating; the tenants are small farmers of about average condition.
The following are the notes of my conversations with the new owners.
(1) A B farms twenty acres, for which he paid the Church Commissioners £516, the whole of which he paid down. He spent some years of his life as an engineer in the merchant service; later at Liverpool as a marine store dealer. A few years ago he inherited the tenant's interest of a small farm of eight acres, and subsequently bought the tenant's interest of an adjoining farm of twelve acres, for which he paid £350, or thirty times the rent. Since his purchase of the fee from the Commissioners he has built a range of superior farm buildings, at a cost of £500, tiled the floor of his house, put in an excellent kitchen range, and had drained and reclaimed a part of his land. He

would not have done this, he said, but for the security of ownership. There was general satisfaction, he told me, among his neighbours at having become owners. Those, however, who had to borrow the balance of the purchase money, beyond the amount left on loan by the Commissioners, had a hard struggle. A neighbouring lawyer lent them money at five per cent., which they were paying off by degrees, and they could not lay out money on improvements until these debts were discharged. Those who had not borrowed were making improvements. He himself works harder now than ever before, for he likes the life. His wife would rather be in Liverpool.

(2) Farm of two and a half acres, rented at £2 15s., bought for £77, of which the tenant paid down £39. This he borrowed in small sums from different persons—giving £1 for the use of £10 for ten months ; 10s. to a sister for £11 for a year, and so on. Has repaid most of it, and will soon be free. Is a labouring man, working at wages for the clergyman, to whom he has let a part of his land for grazing ; his wife does washing, and uses the remainder of the land for drying clothes. They are well pleased to have the land for their own ; expect to have it free before they die. Wife said : " It all seems like winning (saving) now ; we never could save before."

(3) Tenant bought his little farm of five and a half acres for £164. Is ninety-two years of age ; has nine sons and two daughters. Seven sons at sea ; one of them, sailing out of Newry, gave the money for purchase, and last year gave more to build an additional farm building ; has a neat slated cottage ; gate piers, and iron gates to fields. A son, aged forty, who was for some time in hospital at New York and Dublin, far gone in consumption, told me he had every comfort and all the care he needed at home.

(4) Farm of seventeen acres, rented at £27, bought by tenant for £648, of which he paid down £226 ; saved this at sea— " many a salt wave went over his head for it." Since his purchase he paid £87 for building materials, has converted his thatched cottage into a two-storied slated house ; would have rebuilt the house in any case, but would have had no security unless he bought, and is well pleased to be the owner ; has seven little girls, too young to help him, and lives wholly by his labour on the farm.

(5) Tenant bought ten acres for £273, of which he paid down £75, but borrowed this from friends. Wife says her husband is an able seaman in a vessel trading between Liverpool and Rotterdam ; borrowed the money lest they should be turned out of the farm. Four months ago her eldest son, " a fine quiet boy of twenty-five," died ; he used to work on the farm. She now finds it hard to struggle on, her second son being only thirteen. No improvements effected ; but they hope to pay off the debt.

(6) Tenant, a widow, bought nine and a-half acres for £314, of which she paid down £79. Family consists of mother, two daughters, and a boy of fifteen. The eldest daughter, a fine, able young woman, full of spirits, says they borrowed £75 at six per cent. All but £15 has now been repaid. She works on the farm, and the family have no means of living except from it. A brother in Liverpool sent a few pounds towards the price. " How do they manage?" I asked. " Well, just cooling and supping." Last year they had a good bit of flax, and paid off £10. " Why did they buy ? " " Every one said, if ye don't yez 'ill be thrown out, and may go lie behind a hedge." House is thatched, clean, neat and comfortable.

(7) Farm, fifty-one acres, bought by tenant for £1,583, which he paid in full. Is now farmed by the son ; the father lives in an adjoining property.

(8) Tenant bought the farm of fifteen acres for £421, of which he paid down £106 ; leaves the remainder on mortgage. Purchaser died, leaving farm to his son, but in charge of his widow. Son, aged fifteen, is at sea ; will soon be able to help his mother out of his earnings. Father, a Scotchman, was tenant of a farm of ninety-five acres in Fermanagh ; sold the tenant-right of it for £600, and bought this farm. Widow says he preferred being the owner of a small farm to being tenant of a larger farm. Since they came they have greatly improved the house.

(9) Farm of eighteen acres, bought for £508, of which £128 paid down. Purchaser died three years ago, leaving farm to his widow for life, and then to his youngest son. Other house property was to be sold ; £300 to go to his eldest son, and remainder to second son. Property sold for less than was expected, and only sufficed for eldest son's portion. Widow is laying by for second son. " Please God, when she has done this, she will pay off the debt to the Commissioners." She is well pleased with the purchase of the farm. It enables them to be independent, and to save. She added that those who had to borrow from other quarters have had a hard struggle.

It might be dangerous to draw conclusions from this limited number of cases on one property, were it not that they confirmed in every respect the evidence which was laid before the Committee of the House of Commons. In every case it was clear that great benefit had resulted from the purchase. Ownership has been a spur to increased industry and thrift. In many, it has prompted improvements. If it has not had this effect in all, it is because the first obligation has been to pay off the money borrowed from other sources than the Commissioners. It has lifted the family in the social scale—from the position of tenants, dependent on the good will of a landlord, who might be changed at any moment, to that of owners. It has caused a hard struggle in not a few cases ; but these struggles will not be without their result. The money paid off the land remains in the value of the farm, as a nest-egg for the family. The increased industry and thrift of a few years required to pay off the loans will establish a habit for the future ; and the freehold and tenant-right of the farm together will always fetch a high price in the market.

It will be seen that many of the families I visited are in part supported by contributions from one or more members of the family at sea. In this respect the district is, perhaps, fortunate, from its proximity to Newry, where such employment can be easily found. I have, however, always contended that small landowners are not necessarily to be expected to derive the whole of their sustenance from the land. Some members of the family may obtain employment elsewhere, and contribute to the maintenance of the family home. The system thus working in with other employments, the home is maintained, to which, in bad times, sickness, or in old age, the absent members will return. I feel confident that many of the older people I saw would in England have been in the workhouse.

Under the English system the nine small farms I visited, amounting to 150 acres, would be thrown into one. In lieu of nine families such as I have described, there would be one farmer's family, four or five families of labouring men, each with perhaps a quarter of an acre of garden. The farmer and his family would be somewhat above those I visited in social status, but little above them in intelligence. The labouring men would be infinitely below them—without any hope of bettering themselves, without any sense of property, without any prospect in old age but parish relief. Even if the net produce of the latter system, looked at from the food-producing point of view, be greater—a point of some difficulty to determine— there would be few, I think, bold enough to advocate its substitution.

In a few years the sums payable to the Church Commissioners for interest and return of capital will cease, and the owners or their families will be free from anything in the shape of rent. Charges will perhaps accrue for other members of the family, when death of the owner occurs ; but how infinitely pleasanter to pay the interest of such obligations to relatives, with the power of paying off the principal by thrift and industry than to pay the rent. The main difference, however, will be that every pennyworth of labour invested in the land will remain the property of the family, without the smallest danger of being swept away by increase of rent. Who can doubt the benefit resulting from such a change?

II.—The second glebe which I visited is of very different character. It consists of 298 acres of light, and, in part, very poor land, held by twenty-seven tenants, and also of a barren

L

and rocky mountain of 500 acres, held in common by them, and on which each tenant has the right of turning out cattle and sheep without stint. It lies in a mountain glen, rising to six hundred feet above the sea, is difficult of access, and the rough road down the centre is not unfrequently a mountain torrent. The tenants' holdings are divided into two parts—the one in the lower part of the glebe, where the soil is comparatively good ; the other in the upper part, where the land is miserably poor, and has been reclaimed from rock and bog with infinite difficulty.

The holdings have not yet been offered to the tenants, but will shortly be so. The average rents are under £5. It may be presumed that the purchase money in each case will scarcely exceed £100 ; in many cases will be below that sum.

I saw and conversed with most of the tenants. I found them, without exception, anxious to buy, but doubting whether they could find the balance of the purchase money. The following are the notes of cases which appear to be worthy of record :—

(1) Rent, £5 17s. Farm consists of two plots, about a mile apart. House thatched, walls good, roof bad. Tenant has thirty sheep on the mountain. Wanted to know if he bought the farm and paid one-fourth of the purchase money, whether he would still have to pay rent? Would strive to buy, and would sell some of his sheep for the purpose. Intended to have slated his house : "the sheep would have fitted him well for that."

(2) Rent, £4 6s. Tenant forty-four years old. Returned from America a few years ago with some money : did so at request of his father and mother, since dead. Spent his savings in building a slated house—a neat, tidy, two-roomed cottage. Has no money in hand now. A brother in America might help him to find the purchase money. " The town," he said " will be apt to borrow rather than let a landlord over them: will put themselves to great straits to do so. It will do me no great good in my time ; but I'd like to buy for my children." Doesn't live here as well as he did in America, but has no intention of leaving the place.

(3) Farm sixteen acres ; rent, £4 14s. One half the farm is the rough and rugged bank of a mountain stream, of little value. Has a comfortable slated house, built by his father, who reclaimed all the available land on the farm. His farm is two miles from the country road, and six hundred feet above the sea. The road is kept in repair by the tenants—often at great expense, on account of the mountain torrents. A son in Liverpool helps him sometimes out of his wages. Has five sons and three daughters at work or in service in England. They often came to him for a month's holiday. Intends to buy, and is encouraging his neighbours to do so.

(4) Slated cottage and half an acre at the highest point of the glen, on the edge of the mountain. Tenant a poor woman, with one illegitimate daughter, aged fifteen. Daughter was knitting and mother preparing to spin when we called. The neighbours say she was betrayed under promise of marriage, and that she is now a most respectable, industrious woman; works hard among the neighbours. She is anxious, like the others, to buy, but has no money or stock of any kind. Couldn't buy even if she got her place for £5.

Though this property differs from the previous one in many respects, yet it has this in common, that the tenants exhibit the same desire to obtain possession of the land, and the same dread of a new landlord, who may, perhaps, buy merely as a speculation, in the hopes of screwing up the rents by a few pounds. There is the same feature, that the tenants are largely dependent on other resources, on wages of other members of the family, or on other work; and there is evidence of the same inter-dependence between the rural family home and the wage-earning members in the centres of human industry, which is promoted so much by the facility of communication.

I cannot but come to the conclusion that society is as much interested in these smaller and poorer tenants becoming owners as it is in the case of their somewhat better-conditioned neighbours on the other property.

Looking at the condition of these tenants, and the difficulty of making them understand the nature of the offers made to them by the Church Commissioners, I am the more surprised at the success of the Commissioners in effecting sales to so large a proportion of their tenants; nor am I less persuaded of the difficulties which must necessarily attend and prevent the sales to such people in the Landed Estates Court.

One point only of criticism I have to make on the action of the Church Commission. Their present terms are somewhat more hard upon the tenants in small holdings than upon those with larger holdings. If the purchase money is less than £100, the Church Commissioners will only advance one-half the purchase money, by way of mortgage; and if less than £50, they will make no such advance. After seeing the poor tenants in the mountain glen I have spoken of, I cannot but come to the conclusion that it would be wise and just to treat the lowest class upon even more liberal terms than those above them.

For such small holdings the tenant-right in respect of the house bears a higher proportion than in larger holdings. The security of the Commissioners is therefore better, and the Act of last Session, giving equitable jurisdiction to the County Courts, removes any difficulty which existed against lending money to such small owners. The small owners find it also more difficult to borrow elsewhere. I would venture to hope, then, that this difference of treatment may be removed. I am certain that, as it stands, the rule presses very hardly upon the small tenants I visited.

In conclusion, I have only to add that I would willingly have visited other properties sold to the tenants had the time at my disposal permitted. I had promised a visit to Cavan, to some property of Lord Gosford's, sold in the Landed Estates Court to the tenants, but my correspondent in that district informs me that the purchases were only effected last year, and that the tenants have scarcely had time to realise their new position. " Some of the most shrewd of them," he says, " are big with the hopes of their future. One of them said he believed that in fifteen years he will have every acre on his farm worth the average of every two acres at present." Another correspondent, writing about some church property in the same county, says of the tenants :—" Not a few have had to borrow money to effect their purchase, but by renewed energy and increased industry which they bring to their work, conscious that no one can take from them the fruits of their toil, I am certain that even these will in a few years pay off their liabilities and become contented and prosperous. Those who had means to purchase their hold-ings, and had sufficient capital to work their farms, are already becoming independent. Some have expended large sums of money on buildings and on other improvements on the farms. I am certain that if they were still tenants at will, not one sixpence of the money would have been expended."

These statements only confirm the evidence given before the Committee, and my own observations. They are striking testi-monies to the truth of Arthur Young's statement, that property in land is, of all others, the most active instigator to severe and incessant labour ; and to the conclusion of all the experience of Europe, that it is only when combined with ownership of the soil that small farming can be expected to achieve good results.

On the 2nd of May, 1879, I called the attention of the House of Com-mons to the Evidence in Report of the Committee on the Purchase Clauses of the Irish Land Act, 1870 ; and moved the following Resolution, that—

" In view of the importance of a considerable addition to the number of owners of land in Ireland among the class of persons cultivating its soil, it is expedient that Legislation should be adopted without further delay, for increasing the facilities proposed with this object by the Irish Land Act of 1870, and for securing to the tenants of land offered for sale the opportunity of purchase, consistently with the interests of the owners thereof."

The motion was in the first instance opposed by the then Irish Secretary, Mr. Lowther, but was ultimately accepted by the Government and unanimously agreed to by the House.

THE LAND SYSTEM OF THE CHANNEL ISLANDS.*

A VISIT to the Channel Islands in the course of the spring of 1879 afforded an opportunity long desired of verifying the accounts which Mr. Barham Zincke and others have given of the small yeomen proprietors of these isles. Their condition presents so many contrasts to that of the small tenant farmers of the United Kingdom, and especially of Ireland, that it will be worth while, at a time when attention is specially directed to such subjects, to explain and account for it. In doing so it is necessary to say a few words upon the history of the islanders ; for their condition is the result of a well-sustained historic tradition, and is due not a little to the fact, that while they have been conspicuous for their loyalty and attachment to their connection with England, they have resisted with equal persistency and success any attempt to interfere with their local self-government, or to introduce among them the principles of the English system of the tenure and inheritance of land. Their two qualities of loyalty to England and attachment to their own island customs have, in fact, mutually sustained one another. For their loyalty to the Crown has induced successive Sovereigns of England to guarantee and preserve their special privileges and local institutions, and the fidelity with which these charters have been observed for many centuries has confirmed the islanders in their attachment to England.

It is not easy to account for the fact that when the Duchy of Normandy was lost by the Sovereign of England, these islands were retained. Moored off the coast of France, and within the great bay caused by the projecting provinces of Normandy and Brittany, they seem to be marked out by

* An article published in the *Fortnightly Review*, October, 1879.

nature as dependencies of that country; and to those Frenchmen who regard territorial arrangements from the point of view of scientific frontiers, or geographical annexations, or even from that of nationality, it must be somewhat galling that these islands should not be subject to French rule. Originally part of the Duchy of Normandy, as founded by Duke Rollo, they were the special appanage of its Dukes, and were identical in race, religion, language and law with the Norman people. The islanders still make it a boast that their relations with England commenced in conquest on their part, that they took their share in the Norman invasion of England, and that their connection with their Sovereigns dates from a period before the Dukes of Normandy became Kings of England. Their separation from Normandy took place when King John lost his possessions on the Continent. It has often been observed with surprise how little resistance the Normans on the mainland, notwithstanding their hatred of the French, offered to the invasion of Philip Augustus, when executing the sentence of deposition from the Dukedom declared against John for the murder of his nephew, Arthur, and indeed what little effort the English King himself made to retain his provinces on the mainland.

Far different was it when the Channel Islands were threatened. After overrunning and subduing Normandy on the mainland, the French King landed a force in Jersey. Here, however, his troops met with a vigorous resistance. Twice they were driven back. John himself shook off his lethargy, and showed energy and spirit. He hastened to the islands; he fortified the weak places which had been invaded by the French; he rewarded the people for their gallant conduct; he gave them numerous privileges and immunities; he freed them from all foreign dependency; matters which in the last resort had been carried to the Exchequer in Normandy, he directed in future to be brought before himself and his Council in England; all other matters he left to be determined by the local courts in the two principal islands. He gave a charter to the islanders which has ever since been the security for their self-government and other privileges.

This charter exempted the islanders from taxation without their consent; it secured to them the privilege of free trade with England, the right of importing into England all articles of island manufacture and growth free of duty; it established local legislatures for Jersey and Guernsey; their bailiffs were to be appointed by the Crown, but twelve Jurats elected by the inhabitants of each island were intrusted with jurisdiction in all matters, civil and criminal; above all, it secured them from the encroachments of English law, and recognised and maintained their own customs and laws.

It is probable that John's charter merely confirmed, so far as the judicial authorities of the islands were concerned, the previously existing state of things. The elective judges, or Jurats, existed in many parts of France, as in Aquitaine and Bayonne. The separation, however, of the islands from Normandy placed them in a peculiar and to some extent independent position. They belonged to the Crown, but they formed no part of the realm ; they were not represented in the Parliament of England. It was necessary to secure to them their new relation to the Sovereign, and it is this which they have ever retained. The customary law of Normandy continued to be the law of the islands, and to this day forms the basis of their laws, modified from time to time by ordinances of the Crown in Council, to which the assent of the island legislatures has been obtained ; and it is to the customs of Normandy that the people still owe their system of land tenure, their laws of descent of property, and every other distinguishing feature of their law.

From the time of John, almost every successive King of England gave fresh charters to the islands, confirming their privileges, securing to them immunity from English law, and recognising their local self-government. In all these charters reference is made to the loyalty of the islanders to their Sovereigns, and to the dangers they had undergone. Thus the charter of Edward III. runs :—

"We, remembering with pleasure how constantly and courageously our faithful and beloved subjects, the inhabitants of Jersey, Guernsey, Alderney, and Sark have always hitherto continued faithful to us and our ancestors, the Kings of England, and how many dangers they have undergone, and what great charges they have been put to for the preservation of our rights and dignities therein ; being, therefore, willing to honour them with our gracious favour, &c. &c."

And the charter of Edward IV. runs :—

"We, therefore, calling to mind how valiantly, courageously, and constantly the said people and community of the Island of Jersey have adhered to us and our ancestors, and how many losses and dangers they have sustained for the defence of the said island and the recovery of our castle of Mount Orgueil, have of our grace, &c."

and the charters of Henry VII., Queen Elizabeth, and the four Stuart Kings, run in almost the same words.

That the inhabitants of the islands had well earned these praises and favours, no one who reads their early history can doubt. Attacks were constantly made upon them by the French, and were as often repulsed, more often without the aid of British forces than with it. Frequently, however, the French obtained temporary successes, and were able to get possession of Castle Cornet, in Guernsey, or other strongholds, but they never succeeded in long retaining their hold ; more often they contented themselves with ravaging the islands and driving their inhabitants into their strongholds. So great was the misery caused by these constant wars, that an understanding was at last arrived at between the English and French Kings that the islands should be considered as neutral territory, even when there should be war between the two countries.

On the application of Edward IV., and apparently with the consent of the French King, and of the Duke of Brittany, a Bull was issued by Pope Sixtus IV., in 1483, by which all who should in any way molest the inhabitants of the Channel Islands were *ipso facto* excommunicated ; and for many years, by virtue of this Bull, the islands enjoyed a kind of privileged neutrality during the wars between England and France. Merchant vessels belonging to the islands and taken by French cruisers were released by the French prize courts, and French vessels trading to Jersey were similarly released by the English courts. In the charter of Elizabeth it is specially mentioned as a privilege of the islands, that they had a right to trade with France during time of war, and that French traders coming to the islands should be exempt from capture while in sight of the islands. The privilege, however, gradually dropped out of practice, and William III., in declaring war against France, specially withdrew this exemption from hostile capture of French property while in the Channel Islands.

It is worthy of notice that twice only during their long connection with England has there been any serious danger to the islands of subjection to France, and on both occasions through treachery under very similar circumstances. When Henry VI. was at the lowest ebb of his fortunes, in 1461, his brave consort, Margaret of Anjou, crossing the Channel, sought help from the French Court ; an agreement was made through her that, in consideration of assistance to be given to Henry, the Channel Islands should be given up to France, to be holden in future independently of the Crown of England. In pursuance of this arrangement, the Count de Maulevrier landed with 2,000 men in England to assist Henry ; and, on the other hand, a French force was sent to Jersey, where, by orders of Queen Margaret, the Castle of Mount Orgueil surrendered to it. The French force then succeeded in reducing about half the island ; the other half resisted under the leadership of Philip de Carteret, Seigneur of St. Ouen. The French retained their hold upon the island for no less than six years, at the end of which Sir Robert Harléston, Vice-Admiral of England, arrived in Jersey with a fleet, and, co-operating with the loyal inhabitants, laid siege to the castle, and after nineteen weeks compelled its surrender, and drove the French forces from the island.

The other occasion was in 1646, when Charles I. was in the hands of the Parliamentary forces. His queen, Henrietta Maria, and Lord Jermyn, the Governor of Jersey, appear to have commenced an intrigue with the government of France for the sale of the Channel Islands. The negotiation did not proceed far ; for on news being received in Jersey of what was being attempted, the greatest indignation was manifested. It was determined by the inhabitants to give up the islands to the Parliamentary Government, and with their aid to resist any invasion of the French, rather than be handed over to their ancient enemy. Lord Clarendon gives an Act of Association signed by himself, then Sir Edward Hyde, and acting in Jersey as one of the Council of the Prince of Wales, by Lord Capel, Sir R. Hopton, and Sir Edward de Carteret, engaging themselves to oppose the alienation of the islands to France.* The blame of the attempted transaction is

* "Lord Clarendon's Papers," vol. ii., p. 279.

thrown, in this document, upon Lord Jermyn, the Governor; but it was evident that he was merely the agent of the Queen, or, perhaps, even of the Prince of Wales. The proposed sale of the islands was the more unjustifiable, as Jersey at least had shown the greatest loyalty to the royal cause. When the civil war broke out, the two islands had taken opposite sides. Guernsey, impelled probably to the popular cause by its more pronounced Presbyterianism and by its abhorrence of Episcopacy, declared for the Parliament; Jersey, although it had also embraced Protestantism, was more mindful of the privileges which it had always enjoyed, and of its special relations to the Sovereigns of England; it had suffered no grievances from the arbitrary acts of Charles I.; the powers of the Star Chamber had not extended to the islands. It remained true, therefore, to the royal cause, and in 1645 the Jersey States issued a proclamation announcing their continued adhesion to the King.

In the course of this document they say—

"Tout le monde scait assez que ceste Isle est ung reste du Duché de Normandie, que les ancestres de sa Majesté possédoient ancienment devant que de passer en Angleterre. . . . On n'a jamais considéré ceste Isle comme partie du royaume d'Angleterre, et on ne lui peut attacher sans lui oster le plus ancien et le plus avantageux de tous ses priviléges, de sorte qu'il n'est besoin que nous nous meslions dans les affaires et les différents des Anglois. Il nous suffit de savoir que nos lois et nos libertés (qui sont différentes des leurs) ne nous permettent de prendre les armes contre nos princes."

In the following year, 1647, the Prince of Wales found refuge in Jersey, arriving here from the Scilly Islands; and here, on the execution of Charles I., he was proclaimed King. He again visited the island shortly after his proclamation as King, and resided there some months. The island remained in his hands for some years after, under the governorship of Sir George de Carteret. During this time the island was the centre of activity for the Royalists; numerous privateers were fitted out to cruise against the commerce of England; they struck terror over the whole Channel; they interrupted trade, and seriously interfered with Cromwell's operations in Ireland by capturing vessels carrying stores for his army. The gains from this source enabled the Royalists to maintain a numerous garrison; and it was not till 1652 that Cromwell found time to direct a force against the nest of Royalists. A fleet was fitted out under Blake, and a force was landed on the island in spite of a vigorous opposition; after a protracted siege, Fort Elizabeth, at St. Helier, was taken, and the island was brought under the power of the Commonwealth. The loyalty of the people, however, was fully acknowledged by Charles II. on his restoration, and a renewal of their privileges and immunities was secured to them by fresh charters, both from himself and his brother James II.

It is worthy of note, however, that Jersey did not dissociate itself from England on the occasion of the revolution of 1688. James II. appears to have roused the same dislike and distrust here as elsewhere. He had sent Papists to Jersey, who filled Elizabeth Castle with soldiers of the same faith; and when he fled from England the people of Jersey were under great alarm that this garrison of Papists would hand over the fortress to the French. To guard against this the magistrates persuaded the Governor to admit inhabitants of the island to mount guard in the castle in equal numbers with its garrison; and consequently, when William III. was proclaimed King in England, the change of government was effected in the islands without trouble.

Thenceforward the history of these islands is uneventful, and is not to be distinguished from that of England. So completely have they been identified with England, and so hopeless has appeared to the French the task of permanently securing them by conquest, that, although so near to their coasts, and although so great the loss inflicted on French commerce by privateers fitted out there, during all the wars that have occurred between the two countries since 1688, there was only one occasion when a serious effort was made to take possession of them.

In 1781 a considerable force was embarked at Granville, under command of Baron de Rullecourt. A portion of this, consisting of 700 men, landed in Jersey, in spite of very tempestuous weather, and marched across the island to St Helier. Here they surprised the Deputy-Governor, Major Corbet, compelled him to capitulate the fortress, and to send an order to the troops in other parts of the island to deliver up their arms. Major Pearson, in command of the 95th Regiment, refused to obey these orders; he summoned the militia of the island, and with their aid he attacked the French force in the market-place of St. Helier, and completely routed them. Both Rullecourt and Pearson were killed in the action.

From the earliest times the inhabitants have been trained to arms ; and even in times of peace every male in Jersey between the ages of eighteen and sixty-five must serve in the militia, and muster with this force for drill during six days in the year. A very respectable force of nearly 3,000 men is thus organised in Jersey, and a proportional force in Guernsey. A British regiment usually quartered in the islands serves as a nucleus ; and it may be confidently stated that thus armed the islands will successfully resist any force which may reasonably be expected to attack them at the commencement of a war. They have not the less been the subject of constant panics at the War Office. They bristle with forts and armaments. In Guernsey and Alderney alone no fewer than 550 guns have been mounted within the last twenty-five years. They are already, however, out of date, and would be utterly useless against ironclads and more recent artillery. The real defences of the islands are the loyalty of their people, and their determination to resist any attack till aid can be sent them, and the command of the sea by the British fleet. Without command of the sea, it would be impossible to hold the islands ; with command of the sea it is equally easy to prevent the French from maintaining any force there, even if they should temporarily obtain possession of them.

Looking back, then, at the history of the islands, we cannot fail to be struck on the one hand by the loyalty shown by their inhabitants to their Sovereigns and to their connection with England, and on the other by the good faith which the Government of England has observed towards the islanders in leaving to them their local government, their own laws and institutions, in conceding to them immunity from English law, and yet allowing to them all the privileges of the empire.

It is to be remarked that the governments and laws of the two islands are quite distinct and independent of one another. Each has gone its own way from the time of King John to the present ; there is no connection between them save that of the Crown. They have each retained, however, the principles of the old Norman law, and in the main their constitutions and governments are identical. In each island there is a Lieutenant-Governor, generally a military officer, in command of the forces, and with certain limited civil powers as representing the Queen; there is a Bailiff, a civil administrative officer, appointed by the Crown, who presides over the Royal Court and the States. In both, the States are composed in part of representatives elected for a term by the inhabitants, in part by the Jurats or judges, who also are elected by the inhabitants for life, and in part by the rectors of the various parishes; for the Church of England is very firmly established by law. By strict law Orders of the Queen in Council, and probably also Acts of the British Parliament, which specially mention the islands, prevail even without the consent of the Island States; but the long-observed custom, sanctioned by repeated charters, has been to consult the islanders through their States before passing such Orders.

When an Act of the Imperial Parliament is passed, which in the opinion of the Home Secretary should be extended to the Channel Islands, the practice is to send a copy of it to the Lieutenant-Governors, with the request that it may be submitted to the States, with a view to a subsequent Order in Council; but not unfrequently, through remissness, an Order in Council is passed in England without such previous consent of the States, and when this occurs, the island authorities, jealous of their privileges, find it their duty to discover some defect in the Order, and return it with the request that it may be amended, after obtaining the approval of the States. In this way the privileges of the islands and the rights of the Crown are maintained without serious conflict.

By degrees, an assimilation has taken place of the island law to that of England, in respect of most of the modern requirements of government and administration. In respect, however, of their land laws, the tenure of property, and the law of inheritance or bequest, their laws remain much the same as they were before their separation from Normandy. To find the full explanation of these laws we must still have recourse to treatises on the customary law of Normandy before the French Revolution.

It should be recollected that the customary law of

Normandy applied only to the common people ; there were also the feudal laws, which regulated the descent of property, and other privileges of the nobility. In Normandy these feudal laws had a wide application ; the feudal manors were numerous and important ; the nobility were powerful and wealthy. They had their laws of primogeniture and of entail, their manorial courts, and numerous privileges exempting them from taxation ; these were swept away by the Revolution of 1789 ; but many of these laws, which in this country are considered to be the special offspring of the Revolution, were in fact the customary laws of the common people throughout the greater part of France, and affected all those who were not of the privileged classes. Thus it was with Normandy, and the common law of this province was that also of the Channel Islands. The feudal laws have also left their trace in the Islands, though a slight one. There were feudal manors in Norman times, and a class of nobles ; but when the separation took place, most of the nobles having property on the mainland threw in their lot with the French, and their manors in the islands were confiscated by King John. There remained only four important manors in private hands which retained, and retain to this day, the privileges of primogeniture and other feudal rights.

Thus it happened that the islands practically escaped from the feudal system, and were subject only to the customary law of Normandy. This customary law, in respect of property, is not very different in principle from the law made universal in France by the great code which goes by the name of the Code Napoleon, but which in fact was mainly the work of the revolutionary government. The island law aims at division of landed property, and is opposed to its accumulation. On the death of the owner of land, his property must be divided among the children in a certain proportion, and there is no power of disposing of it by will, if there be children. The eldest son has, however, a certain slight advantage ; he gets the principal house and two acres of land. The remainder is divided in the proportion of three-fifths equally among the sons, and two-fifths equally among the daughters ; but with a further provision that a daughter's share is not to be larger than a son's share. The widow, however, receives the income of one-third for her life ; and as her right of dower to all landed property belonging to her husband at the time of marriage is indefeasible, the necessity for marriage settlements is avoided. Till the year 1851 no land could be subject to a testamentary devise, but a law was then passed permitting the devise of land, which has been acquired by the testator, provided he has no children, and in respect of inherited land, provided there be no descendants of the original purchaser. Under these restrictions it is obvious that bequests of landed property must be very few. In respect of personalty, the rule even more closely approximates to the French law. If there be a widow and children, the testator may dispose only of one-third of his personalty by will. One-third goes to the widow, the remainder equally to the children. If there be no children the testator may dispose of one-half of his personalty ; the remainder is divided equally among the next of kin.

Entails are not permitted, just as in Normandy they were prohibited except to the nobility. There was a time in the history of the islands when public opinion seemed inclined to favour the introduction of entail. In the year 1617 there appears to have been great distress in the islands, due to the decay of the stocking trade ; the Jersey States petitioned the Crown to the effect that the island was much weakened by means of the continual partition of lands among co-heirs, and they prayed the King to grant them liberty to entail their lands, rents, and tenements upon their heirs, to remain impartible, for the better maintenance and continuance of their houses. An Order in Council was accordingly passed authorising the Governor, Bailiff, and Jurats to give patents to all persons who should desire it, to entail so much of their lands and rents to remain impartible as they should think fit, provided that the greatest entail was not to exceed the annual value of one hundred quarters of wheat. Under this law a certain number of estates were entailed ; but apparently not in such a way as to prevent their being alienated or encumbered, and the practice has long ago fallen into disuse. When in 1850 the law was passed authorising devises of real estate, subject to the limitations already described, it prohibited the creation of successive estates for life.

There are other peculiarities of law or custom which are worthy of notice, and some of which facilitate the creation or maintenance of small ownerships. There is a curious system under which land can be charged with the payment of "rentes." The owner or purchaser may burthen his property with rents up to three-fourths of its value. These rents are a permanent charge upon the property. The non-payment of them justifies the rent-holder in selling the property. He cannot, however, call in the principal, neither can the owner of the property pay off the rents directly, but he may discharge his property of them by substituting rents on other property (which he may buy in the market), and the holder is bound to take such substituted rents, provided they are of the same value and security. These rents are treated as real property. They have the advantage that they offer the means of investing small sums in the purchase of real property, without the inconvenience of their being liable to be paid off like a mortgage. The debtor, on the other hand, instead of being obliged to wait until he has accumulated a sum sufficient to pay off his mortgage, may disencumber himself of the debt by buying and assigning to his creditor small sums of rent as low as £8 to £10 at a time. The Jersey freeholder who has bought subject to rents, has the advantage of being independent of the rent-holders as long as he can pay his rent. On the other hand, an English mortgagee can call in his mortgage, often to the great inconvenience, and even distress, of the mort-gagor. By law, in Jersey, a purchaser must pay one-fourth of his purchase money in cash, but may leave the remainder as a charge on the property in rents. This facilitates the disposal of real property, by extending the sphere of com-petition and enabling many to become freeholders who could not under a different order of things. Most of the freeholds in Jersey are more or less encumbered with these rents ; but if the owner is an industrious man, he pays them yearly, gradually reduces their quantity, and instead of being liable to be turned out of his farm, as in England, has all the security and all the status and incentive to improve his land of a freeholder. There are, however, disadvantages connected with this system, the chief of which is that the rents may be split into mere fractions, and that the expense of collection becomes heavy ; there are proposals now before the Jersey States for amending the law.

Another and much more doubtful law is that which is

called " Retraite lignaner," under which, where the owner of land, in Guernsey, sells his inheritance (not his acquired property), the next of kin, or, upon his neglect, the next after, and so on to the seventh degree of kinship, may, at any time within ten years, redeem the inheritance, on paying down the full sum for which it was sold, with all the charges. If the inheritance be sold by decree of the Court for payment of debts, the next of kin has but a year and a day to make his claim, and if he neglects to do so within this time he is excluded from his retreat. The case is the same if the purchaser registers his deed, and as all property deeds are registered, this practically limits the custom of retreat to a year and a day. This custom, together with another, which renders the purchaser of land liable in certain cases for debts incurred by previous vendors, makes the purchase of property by strangers a difficult and hazardous operation ; but as between islanders who know the previous history of each little property, there is little danger. The costs of transfer are inconsiderable, and the system of registration of deeds and rents greatly facilitates it.

Another old custom, descended from Norman times, is also interesting, though it does not bear upon the question of the tenure of land. The " Clameur de Haro," or the appeal to Rollo, is attributed to Duke Rollo of Normandy, who gave to his people a personal appeal to himself and his successors, in certain cases of wrong. To this day, in the islands, if there be a question of encroachment on the right of property, such as the wrongful building of a wall or the removal of a boundary, the custom is that the injured person may make his appeal to Rollo on the spot, by falling on his knees in the presence of witnesses and exclaiming in the prescribed words, " Haro, Haro, à l'aide, mon Prince, on me fait tort! "—Haro being the abbreviation of the words "Ah, Rollo ! " On this invocation, the workmen employed on the work are bound to cease, and cannot proceed with it, until the Royal Court has investigated the matter and pronounced judgment. If the person thus appealing is found on inquiry to be in the wrong, he is fined by the court for having, without just grounds, called on the name of Rollo. A notable case of this Clameur de Haro occurred in Normandy at the funeral of William the Conqueror, and accounts for the scene so graphically told by

M

Mr. Freeman, though he does not connect the incident with the peculiar custom or right of appeal. In order to provide a site for the great Abbey of St. Stephen, at Caen, the Conqueror had taken the property of several persons, one of whom complained that he had not been compensated for his interest. The son of this person, Ascelin, observing that the grave of William was dug on the very spot where his father's house had been situated, went boldly into the assembly collected at the grave for the funeral, and making his appeal to Rollo, forbad further proceedings until his claim of right was decided. He addressed the company in these words :—

" He who has oppressed kingdoms by his army has been my oppressor also, and has kept me under a continual fear of death. Since I have outlived him who injured me, I mean not to acquit him now he is dead. The ground wherein you are going to lay this man is mine ; and I affirm that none may in future bury their dead in ground which belongs to another. If after he is gone, force and violence are still used to detain my right from me, I appeal to Rollo, the founder and father of our nation, who though dead lives in his laws. I take refuge in these laws, owning no authority above them." *

This brave speech, delivered in presence of the Conqueror's son, Prince Henry, afterwards Henry I., wrought its effect. Compensation was immediately given to Ascelin for the value of the ground occupied by the grave, a further sum was promised for the remainder, and the opposition ceasing, the dead king was duly buried. Mr. Freeman thinks it improbable that William should have wrongfully taken the land ; it was not his character to commit acts of mere robbery ; but there may have been a dispute of right, and Ascelin having made his appeal to Rollo according to custom, the funeral could not have been proceeded with ; it may well have been, then, that it was found more convenient to compensate him on the spot than to delay proceedings, and disappoint those who had come for the ceremony.

Reverting to the laws affecting the tenure of land, it will be seen that they greatly favour the distribution and division of property. Practically, the principle of compulsory

---

* I have taken the speech as given by Paulus Æmilius, which differs from that in Mr. Freeman's account, taken from Ordericus Vitalis, and which seems to me to lose the point by omitting the appeal to Rollo.

heritage, which prevails throughout a great part of the Continent of Europe, and under which land must be apportioned among the children, prevails also in the Channel Islands, subject to a very slight advantage in favour of the eldest son.

The islands have been saved from the introduction of the feudal law upon any such scale as to have any practical effect. They have also resisted any attempt to introduce the English system, with all its intricacies of family entail, successive remainders, vested and contingent, and its executory devises, and have avoided the multitude of perplexities which arise from them. The people of the islands are devoted to their system of land tenure. They attribute to it the fact that property is distributed so widely, and they assign it as the cause for the universal thrift and industry and saving habits of the people, which have led to such remarkable results in the aggregate wealth and prosperity of the islands. .

In the *Falle's History of Jersey*, edited by the Rev. Edward Durell, which gives the best account of the special customs of the island, the following passage occurs, which fairly represents the prevalent view in Jersey upon this subject :—

" If the descent of property had been regulated here as in England, the island would long ago have become the property of a few powerful families, which would have left no intermediate class between the large landlord and the dependent rack-renter. It is to the land laws that we owe the substantial Jersey freeholders, who are at once the boast and the protection of the country. . . . Under this system the country has flourished. Perhaps no population anywhere possesses collectively a greater aggregate of wealth ; at the same time that there is scarcely any other place where a population of equal numbers could show so few very splendid fortunes. The system corrects itself. Where the shares are small the younger children do not think of farming them, but sell them to the elder brother for money or rents, and go into business. It is, therefore, so far from being correct that estates are reduced almost to nothing, that very few indeed could be found which are materially reduced by partitions, and none whose relative agricultural produce is affected by them."

This was written in 1837, before the islands had, by means of steam communication, obtained a market in London for their products of fresh vegetables and fruit, to which it is customary to attribute their present wealth. It represents not less now than then the condition of things, and it embodies the almost universal opinion of the best-informed people in the islands as to the cause of their prosperity.

Of the actual condition of the islands it is not necessary to say much. It has been fully and faithfully described by Mr. Zincke.* I can bear testimony to the accuracy of his account. In the civilised world it is probable that there is no community where there is greater wealth in proportion to the people, or more widely distributed, than in the Channel Islands.

The area of all the islands together does not exceed 50,000 acres, of which nearly one-third is irreclaimable. The population is under 90,000, or relatively about three times more numerous than that of the Isle of Wight. In Jersey the population is 57,000, of whom 30,000 reside in St. Helier, leaving 27,000 as the rural population. Its cultivated land does not exceed 20,000 acres, and there are 2,500 owners of land, with an average of about eight acres each ; these for the most part cultivate their own property, and probably one-half of the heads of families in the rural districts are in this position. In the parish of St. Peter, which is a purely rural district, consisting of 3,030 acres, there is a population of 2,150, or 530 families, and there are 404 persons registered as owners of land, or "rentes." The rateable value of the parish is £13,000 on land, and £1,500 a year for personal property. There is very little pauperism throughout the island.

The soil of the island is good, and the climate is mild ; but these conditions are not more favourable than in many parts of the south of England. The amount of their production is most remarkable. Till a few years ago they were dependent on their dairy produce and their apple orchards, but of late years the opening of steam communication has enormously developed the cultivation of vegetables and fruit for the London markets. In Jersey alone upwards of 4,000 acres are planted with early potatoes, at a cost of cultivation often of £40 an acre, and the produce is said to be worth £300,000 in good years. Land suitable for this cultivation sells for over £200 an acre. In Guernsey every small farm

* See *Fortnightly Review,* January, 1876.

has its range of glass-houses, where the owner grows grapes for the London market. The grapes are generally grown without artificial heat. The valuable breed of cows of the island forms a very important export.

What most strikes a visitor to the islands is the manner in which their population is housed. In Jersey, small but most comfortable farm-houses are spread over the whole country, at short distances from one another. They give evidence of care and of a sense of beauty. There are few cottages, in the ordinary acceptance of the term, or that remind one of those so common in rural England. The people have solved the question of cottage accommodation by housing themselves, and the capital thus invested must be very great. Few persons are there to remind one of the English agricultural labourer. Such rare specimens as there are to be found are imported. The small yeomen farmers form a body of intelligent and independent men. Many of them boast of an ancient lineage. I have the authority of the Lieutenant-Governor for saying that the militia, which is largely composed of these yeomen, is as fine a body of men as could be desired for defence. The islands are greatly favoured by exemption from imperial taxation; they pay the expense of their own administration, and the charge for public works is not low; the tax for the militia, which amounts to a week's service for every able-bodied man, is not to be disregarded.

Everything tends to show that the aggregate wealth of the population is very great. The imports and exports are very large in proportion to the population. In Guernsey, the population of which does not exceed that of an average small county town in England, it has been found possible to raise very large loans for public works. The harbour of St. Peter's Port alone cost more than £300,000, which was wholly raised on loan in the island; the savings' banks show deposits three times more than the relative amount for England.

What, then, is the cause of this general prosperity, of this widely diffused wealth, and of the universal industry and thrift which is so remarkable? Is it due, as the island thinkers believe, to their land laws, which discourage the aggregation of property, and favour its distribution among the members of a family, and to the fact that the island

people have never permitted the introduction of the English
Land Laws, which they believe to have an opposite tendency? What also, we may speculate, would be the present
condition of the islands if the system of English law had
been introduced? if in early days the feudal law, with its
primogeniture and entail, had succeeded in making its foot·
ing in the islands, and had driven out the customary laws of
Normandy, as in England they superseded the old Saxon
laws of equal inheritance? and if they had been followed, as
in England, by all the subsequent complexities of law and
difficulty of transfer of land? Can there be any reasonable
doubt that the island authorities are right in supposing that
in such case the result would have been much the same as
in England—namely, a continually decreasing number of
yeomen farmers, until the class itself should be almost
extinct; and until people try to persuade themselves that
such extinction is due wholly to natural causes, and is in no
way the result of positive law?

It is almost impossible, and therefore almost useless, to
conceive of the English system of large farms in an island
like Jersey, with a cultivated area of only 20,000 acres, in
substitution for the existing small farms; but it is not difficult to conceive the substitution of the Irish system of small
holdings farmed by tenants. There are very many estates
in Ireland belonging to single individuals, of a larger size
than either Jersey or Guernsey, and farmed by a tenantry
almost as numerous as the small owners of these islands.
Some of these must be almost as fertile; but let us suppose
one of average Irish fertility, which is considerably below
that of the islands. Is the production of such average Irish
property what the land is capable of? Are the tenants
prosperous and contented? Are the rights of property safe,
and as unquestioned as they are in the Channel Islands?
On the first of these points, the production of the land, the
latest and best authority we have is that of Professor Baldwin,
head of the Agricultural College of Glasnevin, who has
recently written an interesting paper on the result of the
competition for the prizes offered by Lord Spencer and
others for the best cultivation by the small farmers of Ireland.
It is worth while to refer to it, as the contrast with the state
of things in the Channel Islands is most remarkable. I find
in it the following passages :—

" In most parts of Ireland the agricultural practices of the small farmers are very defective. In some places they are quite primitive. Vast numbers of the occupiers are very poor, while wide areas of land are not yielding a fourth of the produce which could be obtained from them."

* * * * * *

" The dwellings of a vast number of small farmers in Ireland are wretched. In this age of progress it is unsatisfactory to find that there are in Ireland very many small farmers with large families whose dwellings consist of one apartment, in which cattle and pigs are also housed.

" There are four millions of acres of ·medium land now growing poor herbage, which often contains more weeds than grass, and which would pay far better in tillage. At present the gross return of these four million acres does not amount to twice the rent ; if put under a proper system the yield would amount to five times the rent, and the wealth of the country would be increased to the extent of several millions.

" The state of the cultivated land of Ireland is also very defective, as is well known to all persons of experience. It is notorious that on the vast majority of farms the tillage is shallow and imperfect, and that the general management is ex- tremely defective. . . . Tillage is done in a slovenly fashion. . . . The live stock of Ireland is not made as profitable as it ought to be. . . . The want of drainage is a crying defect in Irish agriculture.· In Ireland at least six millions of acres are in need of drainage. This work could be effected at a cost of £5 an acre. The annual letting value of the year would be increased thereby by £3,000,000 a year. Many persons will ask, where is all the capital to execute this work to come from ? I answer that the greater part of it is in the labour of the people. The working farmers of Ireland have a great deal of labour in their families which could be most usefully employed in draining their land.

" Every experienced agriculturalist who carefully considers this category of defects will agree that the smaller farmers of Ireland could, by adopting modes of management which are within their reach, double their income."

Of the district of Monaghan, Mr. Baldwin says :—

" No person appears to take any interest in improving either the agricultural practices of the district, or the condition of the people. I passed tract after tract of land which is not yielding a fourth of the produce which ought to be extracted from it. The rents are low. In some cases neither landlord nor agent has been on the land for years. Yet a land agent on an extensive property, to whom application was made for a contribution to the prize fund, wrote that he thought the money could be better expended."

The result, however, of the competition for the prizes among the farmers brought out many cases which showed that with industry and thrift the small farms of fifteen, or even ten acres were quite capable of producing results most satisfactory, and which in production and profit to their tenants are far beyond the average. In many parts of the country, Professor Baldwin states that he found the greatest objection even to compete for the prizes thus freely offered for good cultivation, arising from a prevalent feeling that the rents would be raised of those successful in the competition, and that the co-operation of the landowners was the result of a settled desire to use the system "as a cloak for raising rents." Everywhere we are met with the same difficulty and hesitation. The owner cannot supply the necessary capital, the tenant will not do so through fear of rents being raised; he will not even cultivate his land to the best of his ability through the same fear. There is, therefore, a vicious circle from which there seems to be no escape.

Comparing, then, this result with that of the Channel Islands, we find in Jersey and Guernsey production evoked to the furthest limit which the land is capable of; we find an universal spirit of industry and thrift; we find content in the highest degree; we find the rights of property never questioned. Is it not, then, a safe inference to draw from the comparison that, in the one case, this happy state of things is due to the stimulating influence of a distributed ownership of land; and that, in the other case, the low rate of production, the chronic discontent, the want of industry and thrift—above all, the fear of improvement lest the rent should be raised—are due to the very limited ownership of land, to the fact that for centuries the law and administration of Ireland have tended to discourage the existence of a numerous proprietary, and to accumulate land in the hands of the few?

The small landowners of the Channel Islands are scarcely of the class which we should call peasant proprietors; they are rather of the class of small yeomen. In proportion to the size of their farms, their land is of considerable value; they rank in status rather with the small farmers of this country than with the agricultural labourer. Their cultivation involves often a great outlay of capital in plant and manure—they are therefore capitalists; they are not above working in the fields themselves—they are therefore labourers; the land is their own—they are therefore land-owners, and have the pride and sense of responsibility and status due to such a position. In fact, they combine together in one person the three functions of landowner, capitalist, and labourer. It is by reason of their combination that there can be no separation or opposition of interest between these functions. English law appears to be framed too much on the principle that these three functions are necessarily distinct, and that the best result must be where they are separated and brought to bear upon the land by three different persons or classes. The hypothesis is then put forward that the interests of these three classes are identical, that they pull together in the same boat, contribute to the same object, and that therefore there is the greatest inducement to all of them to do their best. The hypothesis, however, is founded on an imperfect view of human nature. In the process of working together, the three classes have separate interests, and find themselves in a certain sense in opposition. So long as human nature is what it is, and so long as self-interest prevails over the best ideal of an enlightened regard for the interests of others, so long will men work better for themselves than for others. The agricultural labourer working for wages by the week on another man's land will not work so effectively, or with so much intelligence, or with such a sense of satisfaction, as when working on his own land, and conscious that he must reap the full benefit of his labours. He requires strict supervision, but supervision must be paid for, and its cost must be taken into account; or else he must be paid for by piece-work, but there are many operations in farming which cannot be paid for by piece-work. In illustration of this point, I may mention that in one of the small Guernsey holdings I found the owner thinning his grapes. I asked him how he compared his work with that of hired labourers. His reply was that he could do from twice to three times the amount of work which any hired man could, or rather would, do in the same time; and he believed it to be the same with most of the vine-growers. For similar reasons, deduced from the same imperfect condition of human nature, men will not as a rule expend their capital so freely on the land of another as on their own.

From these considerations it appears not difficult to explain why it is that the combination of landowner, capitalist, and labourer in one person in the Channel Islands has produced so remarkable a result. It promotes the saving of capital, and therefore creates it; it promotes the efficiency of labour, and therefore multiplies its results; and as the most certain mode of creating capital is by the storage of the results of labour, it increases capital in this direction also; it spreads through a large class the pride of ownership, the feelings of citizenship, and the sense of equality. Nor are its results confined to the class immediately interested in the land; they permeate through every class of society, and spread the habits of saving, thrift, and self-restraint.

COMMON LANDS.*

ORIGIN OF COMMONS.

THROUGHOUT England and Wales, and in many parts of
Europe, there exist numerous districts which from the
earliest times have remained open, unenclosed, and uncultivated, where the owners and occupiers of adjoining land
have the right of turning out their cattle, and where the
villagers exercise the privilege of cutting turf and gorse for
fuel. These are not confined in England to mountains and
purely rural districts, but are often in the neighbourhood of
large towns. In the latter case they constitute oases, as it
were, of nature, which now subserve a very different
purpose than that which originated them; rights of
common exist over them, but are of no value except so far
as they help to keep open such places for the health, enjoyment, and recreation of the people living in the neighbourhood. Such Commons are in law, so far as the soil is
concerned, the property of some lord of the manor, but
the rights of adjoining owners create practically a joint
or divided ownership, which has prevented from time
immemorial their appropriation and enclosure.

In Ireland and Scotland there are very rare cases of
common lands in the legal sense. The manorial system was
not extended to these countries; but there are vast districts
of mountain and bog, open and unenclosed, the private
property of large landowners, whose farming and cottier
tenants have the privilege incident to their tenancies, of
turning out their cattle and cutting their peat upon them.

Much light has been thrown in late years on the origin
and legal condition of the English Commons. Till lately
the views of the feudal lawyers were generally accepted; it
was held by them that these open and unenclosed lands

* A part of this was published in the *Contemporary Review*, January, 1879.

were the wastes of manors, which had been originally granted by the Crown; that the freehold of them was originally vested in the lord of the manor, and that the rights of the commoners or adjoining owners had only arisen by custom or grant in derogation of the lord's rights. The investigations of Professor Nasse, Sir H. Maine, and others, have shown that in respect of by far the greater number of commons, the rights of the commoners had a very different origin, and were antecedent to those of the lord of the manor; and that the rights of the latter had arisen by way of usurpation or conquest as against the rights of the surrounding community, and had subsequently received the sanction of the early feudal lawyers.

According to this view, the Commons now existing are to a very large extent a remnant or survival of that collective ownership of land, the prevalence of which in the early stages of all communities has been traced by the above authors, Monsieur de Laveleye, and others. Under this system there was no individual ownership of land; it was owned in common by a village community, originally a family group or a band of settlers who came into a new, or a conquered and devastated country, and there appropriated or received a grant of a district. The land was in such case owned by the community; that portion of it only which was suitable and necessary for the production of corn and other crops, was enclosed and cultivated; this part was generally divided into three great fields, for a three-course system of agriculture, of which one was always in fallow; and each field was divided into a number of equal parts, which were distributed by lot every year among the heads of families constituting the community. The remaining land was open to the cattle of all. Very frequently the cultivated land itself was thrown open to the cattle of all, after the completion of the harvest, or the mowing of the hay, and until it was necessary to shut it off again in the following spring, for the next crop. Small portions of land were attached as gardens to the houses or homesteads of the inhabitants, and acquired the condition of private property; other portions were enclosed from the open or common land only when it was necessary to withdraw it for the purpose of adding to the cultivated part, as the community increased.

Such was the system of common ownership of land

among the early German tribes, when they emerged from the
nomad state, and began to settle permanently upon the land.
It was extended to a great part of Europe as the Teutonic
migration moved onwards; it was introduced into this
country by the Saxons.

It is unnecessary to follow up the changes by which
individuals gradually acquired complete ownership of those
portions of the land which were thus enclosed or separated
from the common property of the community. The process
is still going on to this day in England, for vestiges still
remain of commonable land, or common fields, as distinguished from commons, the true wastes of manors, and
Acts of Parliament are still occasionally passed for dividing
such common fields, and converting them into separate
ownerships.

Even before the Norman Conquest, individual ownership had supplanted the system of common ownership, in
respect of a large proportion of the enclosed or commonable land, but the open land still remained the property of
the community, and was called the *folk-land*, or the people's
land, and the villagers, whether owners of land or not, had
the right of turning out their cattle there, according to some
well-defined proportion, and of cutting there the turf, or
gorse, or wood for fuel.

COMMONS UNDER THE FEUDAL SYSTEM.

The introduction of the feudal system effected a great
change in this condition. It had its origin in military necessities. The chief led his men to battle and acquired a
supremacy which was afterwards localised, and became
attached to the community and the district. The villagers
became the subjects, as it were, of a petty sovereign, who
first reigned over the district, and then assumed the rights
of property over it. The larger freeholders became, in a
sense, the subjects, and were later considered the tenants of
the feudal superior or lord, bound to render him military
service in return for the protection he afforded to them.
They held, however, their lands on certain tenure, and not
at the mere will of the lord. An inferior class of people,
the holders of smaller plots of land by commendation,
conquest, or usurpation, fell into a much lower status.

They were completely subject to the lord; they were considered as having no real right independently of his will; they held their lands and houses at his caprice; they were liable to be turned out at his pleasure. They continued, however, in possession of their holdings, subject to payments or services to their lord. Their ancient rights over the common lands of the community were considered as appurtenant only to their holdings. These people became the villeins of the manor. A yet inferior class of persons, with no land, became the mere slaves or serfs of the lord, without any rights whatever, but continued probably to exercise the old custom of cutting turf, &c. Indeed, the supply of fuel in those days must have been purely local, and without these common lands, where turf or gorse could be cut, the villagers could not have obtained fuel.

The feudal lord thus became lord-paramount of the district or manor. The common land or folk-land was held to be his property, subject only to the acknowledged right of turning out cattle by the larger free tenants of the manor who held direct from him, and subject to the licensed, but no longer legal, rights of the inferior villeins or serfs, of turning out cattle and cutting turf. This was the mode in which, in imitation of what had taken place over a great part of the continent, the feudal system was gradually introduced into this country, and by which the lordship over the common lands became vested in the feudal superior.

The process by which this took place is well described by Monsieur de Laveleye. "The fief having been granted by the Sovereign to the lord, the latter assumed as a consequence that the whole soil belonged to him. He did not on this account suppose himself able to despoil the peasants of the enjoyment of their lands, or of their right of using the common forest or pasturage, but these rights were regarded as privileges exercised over the property of the lord."

Already before the Norman Conquest this substitution had begun to take place; but, as the result of that event, the feudal system was thoroughly established throughout England; a vast proportion of the land was confiscated and granted out anew to the military followers of the Conqueror, to be held on military service, and they in their turn introduced the feudal system into the manors so granted to them.

From this change, caused by the introduction of the feudal system, and the subordination of the rights and customs of local communities to those of feudal lords, most important results followed, which have made themselves felt down to the present time, by creating a difference between popular conceptions and traditions, and legal theories.

The first result of the new position of the feudal lords as regards the Common Lands, now termed the waste of their manors, was their claim to enclose, for their own particular use and benefit, any portions of it. The claim was resisted by the freehold tenants of the manor, who had rights of pasture. Ultimately it was decided by Parliament, under the well-known Statute of Merton (20 Henry III., A.D. 1235) that the lords of the manors should have this right of enclosure or approval, as it was called, provided it should appear on complaint of the tenants of the manors, that there was left as much pasture as was sufficient to satisfy these rights, with free access thereto. The Act threw the onus of proof upon the lords who should make the encroachments, which has had an important influence up to the present time. At the date of this statute also, only the freehold tenants of the manor had any acknowledged rights as against their feudal superior. The villeins, and still less the serfs, had no right or position at law as against their lords ; the Act, therefore, strictly applied only to the freehold tenants, and did not at that time prevent the lord enclosing as against his villeins and serfs.

It is certain that at this early time a very large proportion of England was unenclosed, and consisted either of common pasture, heath, or forest land. The right of approval, therefore, was of great value, and frequently gave rise to disputes between the lords of manors and their tenants. The early law books are full of such cases. Frequently enclosures were made for the purpose of making parks for deer or other game. Even more frequent were enclosures of a *pastura separabilis*, which it was often added, *fuit quondam communis et quæ solebat esse communis totius villæ.*

Later, a much greater restriction was practically imposed upon these encroachments by the legal recognition of the

villeins to an ownership of the land which they occupied.
This conversion of villeinage into tenure by copy of court-
roll, which was the origin of copyholds, came into existence
almost imperceptibly, without the intervention of the legislature, and by the gradual expansion of legal doctrines,
borrowed by the judges from the Roman law.   It cannot
be traced earlier than the time of Henry IV.

These copyholders, who added largely to the class or
yeomen in this country, had rights of common over the
waste of the manor.   When their interests were recognised
as permanent, they were able to maintain suits against their
lords, and, by asserting their rights of common, to prevent
enclosure.

About the same time (or perhaps rather earlier) the
lower class of dependants on the manors—the serfs—became
freemen.   Some of them may have possessed houses and
plots of land inscribed in the court-rolls, but by far the
greater number of them lived in cottages, the property of
their lord, and on their emancipation from servitude did not
acquire any rights of property.   They were the progenitors
of the agricultural labourer of the present day.   It might
have been expected that on the emancipation of this class
the law would recognise as legal and valid the ancient right
or custom of the village community, by which this class
enjoyed the privilege of cutting their turf or wood on the
common land or forest, and of turning out cattle on the
common pasture.   The courts of law, however, refused to
acknowledge this.   The case of such inhabitants of a village
was finally decided by the judges in 1603, when a claim
was made by the villagers of Stixwold, in Lincolnshire, to
turn out cattle in the waste of the manor, and it was held that
it could not be maintained.   It appears that no reference was
made in the proceedings of this case to the ancient customs
of the village community, before the introduction of the
feudal system ; the judges were probably quite ignorant of
them ; the case was decided on the most technical and
narrow points of feudal law ; it finally shut out for ever the
right of inhabitants, as such, to claim, by prescription, a
right of pasture or turbary upon common lands.   It is
certain that this case has justified and enabled the extinction
and destruction, in thousands of cases, of rights or customs
which villagers, from time immemorial, had exercised and

enjoyed. The ingenuity of lawyers subsequently invented modes of saving such customs in some individual cases; the principal grounds on which the decision had been given were the uncertain character of the class of persons who might claim as inhabitants, and that there would be no person who could extinguish such rights ; it was therefore contended that the inhabitants of a town, which had been incorporated, might claim such a right, on the ground that the grant had been originally made by the lord of the manor or the Crown to the corporation, in trust for the benefit of the inhabitants ; this view was conceded. It was then attempted to set up the theory of a lost grant from the Crown to the inhabitants of a manor or district, in the view that a grant from the Crown would be a sufficient incorporation of the inhabitants to enable them to hold and enjoy such rights ; and where the forest, manor, or district had in ancient times been in the ownership of the Crown, this theory was at times successful. But these instances have been few in comparison with the vast number of cases where, by virtue of the above decision, the inhabitants of villages and parishes have been deprived of rights, which they undoubtedly enjoyed from immemorial times, and which were of the greatest value to them. It also enabled lords of manors to enclose under the Statute of Merton, or with the consent of the recognised manorial tenants, without consideration for the interests of the general inhabitants in the manor ; and on the same view was based the practice of the older Enclosure Acts, which gave little or no compensation or consideration, except in rare cases, to the inhabitants generally, for the injury done to them by enclosure.

Notwithstanding this decision, the inhabitants of villages and manors, where Commons still remained unenclosed, continued to exercise the privileges of turbary and pasture, though not as of right. They were generally tenants of houses, belonging either to the lord or to some of his freehold or copyhold tenants, to which these rights attached. It was only, therefore, on enclosure that they suffered ; any compensation in land for the enclosure, where effected by legislative sanction, was given to the owner of the land, and not to the tenants of it. The bulk, therefore, of the inhabitants secured no benefit from the enclosure, but were mulcted of their previous rights of pasture and turbary.

N

Reverting again to early times, after the full recognition of the customary right of the copyholders, the rural system of landownership was generally as follows : there was the lord of the manor, with his castle or castellated mansion, and with his demesne lands ; these he either cultivated himself by hired labour, assisted in part by customary services rendered by the tenants of his manor, or he let them out on farming leases to the class we now call farmers. There were next the freehold tenants of the manor, the better class of yeomen, owning land which they cultivated themselves, with or without the aid of hired men. There were the more numerous copyholders, with small holdings of land, seldom more than twenty acres in extent ; these formed the great bulk of the class of yeomen, for which England was so famous in olden times. Lastly, there were the cottagers, with small gardens, some of whom may have been copyholders, but most of whom were merely tenants-at-will of the lord or his principal freehold tenants. Beyond the land thus occupied in severalty, there was always a large expanse of common land, whether pasture, heath, or wood. Here the tenants turned out their cattle and cut their fuel. The right of turning out cattle on this waste land was of enormous value to the copyholders ; it added greatly to the value of their properties ; in proportion to the extent of their holdings, they were able to rear and maintain a large number of cattle, which lived in summer on the open land, and in the winter were stalled on the small farms.

Where the right of turning out cattle on the waste was cut off, the holding was greatly depreciated in value, because without such right it would not be sufficient to sustain the owner and his family. Equally valuable was the Common to the smaller tenants, who could turn out cows upon it and cut their fuel. If the Common was enclosed they were deprived of the privilege, without compensation, and without the means of supplying the deficiency. It is not difficult from this view to understand the discontent which arose in the middle ages from the enclosure of Commons. The enclosure, by adding to the extent of cultivated land, might be of great value to the lord, and be of importance from a public point of view to the general public, by adding to the power of producing food, but it was generally productive of great loss to the smaller tenants of the manor and to the labouring people.

The extent of Commons, however, in early times was very great, and there can be no doubt that they suffered much shrinkage under the Statute of Merton, without seriously affecting the condition of the small yeoman class or labourers. It was not till the fifteenth century we find that enclosures began to cause general discontent, and to affect the general status of the rural community. A great rise in the value of wool appears to have been the main cause for a general movement towards appropriating the common lands and for turning arable land into pasture.

The previous enclosures had already so reduced the extent of the common land that these fresh enclosures began to press most severely upon the smaller copyholders. They rendered the tillage cultivation of the lands of these people impossible, and led to their being bought up at a small price. A great reduction consequently took place in the number of these yeomen. Houses were pulled down ; sheep took the place of cattle, and pastures of arable land. The movement was mainly an economic one, but it was too often carried through by fraud and violent invasions of right. The smaller copyholders were unable to protect themselves by law proceedings against the wealthy wrong-doers ; and the judges appear to have lent their aid to the wealthy suitors, who were willing to pay for it.

The earliest record we have of this change is to be found in Bacon's " History of Henry VII." He says :—" Inclosures at this time began to be more frequent, whereby arable lands, which could not be manured without people and families, were turned into pasture, which was easily rid by a few herdsmen ; and tenancies for years, lives, and at will, whereupon much of the yeomanry lived, were turned into demesnes. This bred a decay of people, and, by consequence, a decay of towns, churches, tithes, and the like." He justified the wisdom of the King and Parliament in legislating against this evil, and describes the method adopted. " Inclosures they would not forbid, for that had been to forbid the improvement of the patrimony of the kingdom ; nor tillage they would not compel, for that was to strive with nature and utility ; but they took a course to take

away depopulating inclosures and depopulating pastures"
indirectly, by ordaining that all farmhouses with twenty
acres attached should be kept up with "a competent proportion of land."*

The complaints against enclosures continued through the
reigns of Henry VIII., Edward VI., and Elizabeth, and frequent statutes were passed with the object of minimising the
evil, but without much effect. In 1549, Bishop Latimer, in
his well-known "Sermon on the Plough," preached before
Edward VI. and his court, brought the question prominently
before the public. He reproached the nobles who were
among his audience as "inclosers, graziers, and rent-raisers,"
who made dowerless slaves of the English yeomanry.
The sermon was perhaps due to the fact that in that
year an insurrection of an agrarian character broke out in
the Eastern Counties against the new fences and enclosures.
It was put down, but other disturbances followed.

Sir Thomas More complained that "noblemen, gentlemen, and even abbots, in their eagerness to swell their
revenues, leave no ground for tillage. They inclose all into
pasture ; they throw down houses ; they pluck down towns ;
and leave nothing standing." He declared that "tenants
were got rid of by force or fraud, or tired out by repeated
injuries, into parting with their property."

The Protector, Somerset, had already appointed a Royal
Commission "for the redress of enclosure," and to inquire
into the violations of law in ten counties whence the main
complaints came.

Among other things the Commissioners were directed to
enquire "Whether any person hath taken from his tenants
their Commons, whereby they be not able to breed and
keep their cattle and maintain their husbandry as they were
in times past." In an explanatory statement issued by the
Commission, it was said : "But first to declare to you what
is meant by this word 'enclosures.' It is not taken where a
man doth enclose and hedge round his own proper ground,
where no man hath commons ; for such enclosure is very
beneficial to the Commonwealth ; it is a cause of great
increase of food ; but it is meant thereby when any man
hath taken away and enclosed any other men's commons,

* See "English Land and English Landlords," by Hon. G. Brodrick,
p. 26.

and hath pulled down houses of industry and converted the lands from tillage to pasture." *

"The miserable and unsatisfactory result," says Professor Nasse, "of this commission, originally hailed with intense delight by the rural population, is sufficiently well known.. The power of the nobility in the country was so great, and the hand of the executive so weak, that in some cases the witnesses summoned did not dare to appear, and in others, those who had given truthful evidence were subjected to ill-treatment by the landlords. If the Protector's extraordinary Royal Commission could not effectually resist the power of the ruling class, it may naturally be inferred that the protection of the ordinary courts could not much avail the sufferers. Their rights rested on the customs of each estate, to be proved by the rolls in the hands of the lord of the soil, and they were liable to forfeiture by an indefinite number of acts on the part of the copyholders. The small copyholders were doubtless unable to substantiate their rights in courts of law, opposed by expert lawyers. Latimer, in fact, charges the judges with injustice and the receipt of bribes, and says that money was almighty, even in courts of justice. A period of such tremendous revolution in Church and State as the reign of Henry VIII. could certainly not have been favourable to the protection of customary rights. Such a sudden change as the secularisation of Church lands must have shaken the whole traditional order of property. Thus, a pamphlet, published in 1546, complained that the new owners of Church property generally declared the ancient rights of the copyholders forfeited. They were compelled either to relinquish their holdings, or accept leases for a short period." †

Numerous quotations from writers of that period might be made for the purpose of showing how strongly stirred was the public mind on this subject. It may be interesting to point out that the only recorded saying of Shakespeare which has come down to us, apart from his dramatic and poetic works, is in a letter from his relative, Thomas Greene, the clerk to the corporation of Stratford, who had been sent by them to London to oppose in the law courts the enclosure

---

* Strype's Memorials, vol. 2, 359.
† "The Land Community of the Middle Ages," by Professor Nasse, p. 92.

of Welcombe, a common immediately adjoining Stratford, and which Shakespeare must have crossed daily on his way to his farm. He states that his "cozen Shakespeare had said that he was not able to bear the enclosing of the Common."[*] The enclosure, after some years of litigation, was pronounced to be illegal, and was abated. Nevertheless, it has since been enclosed, and is now a part of Welcombe Park. It is also said that the first speech which Cromwell made in the House of Commons was against an Enclosure Bill.

ENCLOSURE BY PRIVATE ACTS.

The general practice of enclosure under the Statute of Merton, or by arbitrary proceedings in defiance of the rights of the smaller commoners, trusting to the venality of the judges for protection against legal redress, appears to have come to an end; and in the reign of Queen Anne we first meet with private and local Acts of Parliament for enclosure by legal sanction, and with some regard to the interests of those concerned in them. It may be presumed, then, that long before this time the powers conferred by the Statute of Merton were practically exhausted; and from that time it has become a well-established maxim with lawyers, that no enclosure is practically possible under the Statute of Merton or otherwise, or without the authority of Parliament ; and although here and there portions of Commons have occasionally been filched, or have been enclosed under customs with the consent of the peerage, yet in the main, for the last 200 years, no enclosures have been effected, except under sanction of the legislature. Two main difficulties were opposed to enclosure under the Statute of Merton ; the one that the onus lay upon the encloser of showing that a sufficiency of Common was left for the commoners ; the other that the statute only applied to rights of pasture, and not to rights of turbary, and consequently the existence of rights of turbary was in all cases sufficient to prevent enclosure. The best proof, however, of the necessity of parliamentary sanction lies in the multitude of Enclosure Acts which have been passed with this object.

As the country became more populous and wealthy, and

---

* Dyce's Shakespeare, vol. 1, p. 109.

as manufactures increased, so the inducement to enclose the open land became stronger ; later, foreign wars and the high price of wheat enormously increased this, and made it a matter of the greatest national importance, and even necessity, that the area of corn-fields should be increased ; thus it was that from the fall of the Stuarts, when the country began to intervene more actively in the affairs of the continent, and was seldom for many years without a foreign war, till the General Enclosure Act of 1845, which immediately preceded the adoption of free trade, there was a continually increasing number of enclosures. At the commencement of this period, Macaulay estimates that only one-half of the area of England and Wales was under cultivation. Between 1700 and 1845 it is an ascertained fact that 7,175,000 acres were enclosed under about 4,000 separate Enclosure Acts, or enclosure awards.

The addition of this vast extent of land to the enclosed and cultivated fields of England and Wales, has doubtless been of great benefit to the country, by adding to its productive power, and by affording additional employment in rural districts ; but it has unquestionably had other effects of an opposite character. It was one, if not the principal of the causes of the extinction of the class of small yeomen, of those who cultivated small properties of their own ; these holdings were for the most part of such a size that the appurtenant right, of turning out cattle on the waste, was an almost necessary condition of their existence, and when this was taken from them, they could no longer stand in the economic race for existence. It is interesting to observe that the only parts of England where this class still exists, in any conspicuous number, namely, in Cumberland and Westmoreland, and on the borders of the New Forest, the open Commons and forest also still exist, and render the continued existence of such small holdings possible. It cannot be doubted then that the enclosure of commons has been a powerful factor in the process of extinction of the small yeoman class, during the last two hundred years ; this force has not been counteracted by any opposing influence resulting from the free dispersion of larger properties, which would have occurred but for the laws of inheritance and entail. Professor Nasse, speaking of the effect of the movement in favour of enclosure in the six-

teenth century, says, " Powerful as it was it did not then reach
its limit. The small landowners did not all disappear in the
sixteenth century: The majority of freeholders doubtless
held their ground, and even the copyholders were not all
driven out or converted into tenants for terms of years.
Lord Coke declared in the seventeenth century that one-third
of England was copyhold. The revolution, however, thus
inaugurated, has lasted down to our own day. Sometimes
the progress has been slower, sometimes faster, until by
degrees the close connection in which the two phenomena,
enclosure and expulsion of the peasantry originally stood, has
ceased."

Another result has been the depressing effect upon the
agricultural labourer. It has already been shown that the
law recognised no right or interest in the villagers or
labourers of a manor over the common land, apart from
the houses which they occupied, no matter how ancient and
how certain their custom of cutting turf or turning out
cattle may have been. On enclosure, therefore, no consideration was due to their interests. They were simply
deprived of the privilege which they had previously enjoyed,
and the compensation for the right went to the owner of
the property. Not unfrequently, however, Parliament made
it a condition of its sanction that small plots of the enclosed
land should be set apart for the benefit of the labouring
poor, as an equivalent for this loss of privileges. These
were called fuel allotments ; sometimes they consisted of a
part of the common, where peat and turf could still be dug ;
at other times they consisted of land which was of agricultural
value, and which could be let on lease, with the object of
distributing the proceeds in the shape of doles of coal.
These, however, were most inadequate, and were often
forgotten. The labouring people had no *locus standi* to
object to enclosure, and the smaller commoners or copyholders were unable to afford the cost of resisting such Acts
by appearing before Committees of the House of Commons
to oppose the enclosures. Great and grave injustice resulted,
and this, added to the cost of enclosure bills, was the main
cause of the General Enclosure Act of 1845, which was
passed before the withdrawal of protection to agricultural
production, and the adoption of Free Trade, and when the
general opinion of the country was still strongly set in

favour of enclosure, and of adding to the means of production of the country.

THE ENCLOSURE ACT OF 1845.

The main object of the Act of 1845 was to substitute local enquiry, through Enclosure Commissioners, as to the expediency of enclosure, thus affording an opportunity to the smaller commoners of making their views known, and greatly reducing the cost by avoiding expensive Parliamentary enquiries, and, at the same time, to lay down as a condition of enclosure, that certain very moderate appropriations of land should be made to the labouring people, for recreation and for garden allotments, in lieu of their fuel rights. In moving the second reading of the Bill, Lord Lincoln, who had charge of it, stated that "in nineteen cases out of twenty, Committees on Enclosure Bills in the House of Commons had neglected the rights of the poor."

The Act of 1845, however, though an improvement over the previous practice of enclosure by private acts, inasmuch as it secured a far greater measure of justice to the smaller commoners, was, in its practical working, quite as detrimental to the interests of the labouring people. No regard also was had to the interests of the public. The Enclosure Commissioners acted upon the principle that their function was to stimulate the enclosure of commons, whether any public interest was involved or not, and even in cases where it was the utmost advantage to the public that the land should remain open and unenclosed for the purpose of health and recreation. Between the years 1845 and 1869, 614,800 acres of common were enclosed, under orders approved by the Enclosure Commissioners, and sanctioned in General Acts by Parliament. Of this great extent, less than 4,000 acres were set apart for public purposes—namely, 1,742 acres for recreation grounds, and 2,220 acres for garden allotments for the poor. In a great number of cases this provision was miserably scanty and inadequate. As a general rule, the plots selected for garden allotments or recreation were the least suitable for the purpose, and remote from the villages. No regard was had for public interests. Commons were enclosed which were in no way suitable for cultivation, and which in their natural state were far more valuable to the

nation, many of them being within easy reach of large popu-
lations.

Until, however, the year 1865 no public attention was
directed to the subject.   The general bent of public opinion
was in favour of enclosure, on the ground that it added to
the value of the property so dealt with, and increased the
productive power of the country.   So late as in 1848 a Committee of the House of Commons recommended the enclosure of Epping Forest.   The neighbouring forest of
Hainault was actually enclosed, and converted into farms.
The New Forest and the Forest of Dean were threatened
in the same utilitarian spirit; and no attention was ever
given in Parliament to the enclosure schemes which came
before it annually in a general Bill.   Between the years
1865 and 1870, however, there arose two very distinct
movements with respect to commons, the one of opposition
altogether to their enclosure when within reach of large
towns, especially of London, on the ground of the enormous
importance to the public that such spaces should be kept
open for health and recreation ; the other, from the point of
view of the agricultural labourer, whose interests had been
so shamefully neglected in past enclosures, and which
claimed that no enclosures should henceforth be permitted,
unless it could be distinctly shown that they are in the
general interest of the public, by adding to the production
of the soil, and in such case only, with great consideration
for the interests of the labouring people of the district.

The first of these movements was initiated mainly by
myself, the latter by Mr. Fawcett, and after a time we
united our efforts with a view to a common object.   Before,
however, describing this movement and its results, it may be
well to point out what has been the course on the Continent
of Europe with respect to common lands.

COMMON LANDS IN EUROPE.

The early history of common lands in most parts of
Europe was very similar to that in England. · In pre-
feudal times, in Teutonic countries, the system of ownership
of land by the community existed as already described.   In
those parts where the civilisation and law of Rome prevailed,
as in France and Italy, the uncultivated lands and open

pastures belonged to the local community in whose district they were situate.

In both cases, when the feudal principle was introduced, either by the growth, in the one case, of a new military system within the Teutonic tribes, and, in the other case, by the Teutonic invasions, a claim was alleged on behalf of the feudal chief or lord to a paramount right over the common lands of his fief. This right, however, appears to have been rarely put in force in early times, save for the purpose of creating great forests for the preservation and ·pursuit of game. When, however, population and cultivation increased, and land became more valuable, the same contest arose in France between the feudal seigneurs and the people living in their fiefs, as has been described in England. There, as here, the feudalist lawyers founded a claim of right for the seigneurs, to at least a third part of the common lands, which they called a right of " triage." They contended that, when after the Teutonic conquest, the property of the fief was granted to the seigneurs, it was only by their liberality that the inhabitants were permitted to continue in the enjoyment of these common lands ; that the seigneurs in doing this had not renounced their own rights ; and that in demanding a third part of the land for their exclusive property, they were only claiming that which was their due.

It was in the 15th century, in the reign of Francis I., that the seigneurs began generally to make appropriations of the communal property. It appears to have been effected by violence and fraud, and by the destruction of title-deeds. The latter course was the more easy, as the archives of the manor were in the keeping of the officers of the seigniory; and when the titles were destroyed, the land to which they applied was claimed as the property of the lord, by virtue of the legal maxim, " Omnia censetur moveri a domino territorii." Even where the titles existed, it was often contended that the lord had the right to enclose the common land, and to add it to his demesne, in the interest of cultivation. In numerous instances the communities were threatened, bribed, or cajoled into parting with their lands for very low prices. In contradiction of what took place in England, the State, represented by the more arbitrary power of the Sovereign, took part with the people

against the seigneurs. With the object of reducing as much
as possible the power of the nobility, a claim was asserted
on behalf of the Sovereign for enormous power over inferior
fiefs, and feudal property of all kinds. Frequent royal
ordonnances of the 16th and 17th centuries forbade
encroachments on the common lands by the seigneurs, and
directed that lands thus enclosed and robbed from the community should be restored.

An ordonnance of 1667 annulled all alienations thus made
in the previous fifty years, and authorised the communes to
re-enter upon their lands, upon restoring the sums which they
had received. It abolished the right of "triage." Its
preamble accused the nobles and the judges of having
profited from the feebleness of the commoners to deprive
them of their lands. "To disguise these usurpations, they
have made pretence of debts, and have abused the formali-
ties of justice." Notwithstanding this, the abuse continued,
and we find that at the outbreak of the Revolution of 1789
the claim of "triage" on the part of the seigneurs was still
a grave subject of complaint.

By successive laws in 1791, 1792, and 1793, the right of
"triage" was abolished; all enclosures made under it since
1669 were annulled; the communes were restored to the
possession of such properties, and to the customs of which
they had been deprived, and were declared to be the owners
of all open land, save in the cases where authentic evidence
was produced that they had sold such lands at a full price.

The Convention of 1793 proceeded further. By a law
of June 10, 1793, it directed the division of the communal
property among the inhabitants. By virtue of this law, a
considerable extent of communal land, mostly of the better
quality, was sold. In very numerous cases, however, no
action was taken upon it, and at the Restoration the process
ceased, and it was found that there still remained ten
millions of acres of communal property, of which four millions
acres consisted of wood, and the remainder of open pasture
or heath.* The general opinion of late years has been
opposed to the sale or division of such lands, but for the

* This account of communal lands in France is taken mainly from
Monsieur de Laveleye's work, "De la Propriété;" from Championnière,
"De la propriété des eaux courantes;" and from Dalloz: "Jurisprudence
Générale v. Commune."

improvement of such as is capable of cultivation, by letting them on long lease for the benefit of the commune.

In Germany the same system of ownership by the community existed till a very much later period than elsewhere ; the feudal system, though it over-rode the general rights of individuals composing the community, and reduced them to a state of dependency, in which they were subject to every kind of base service to their feudal superiors, interfered very much less with the general system of agriculture ; and, till the great changes effected in the beginning of this century, a great part of the country was owned and cultivated on the principle already described as that of commonable lands, save that the tenants of the manors had acquired individual property in their shares of the common fields.

For the most part the unenclosed districts, not brought into cultivation, consisted of forest, where the inhabitants claimed the right of cutting wood for fuel, and of turning out their cattle and pigs ; this right, however, was generally of little value except when there was an abundant crop of acorns. In very early times these forests were owned in common by the communes in which they were situate. In many cases, however, the feudal lords asserted a right to them, subject to the customary privileges of the inhabitants. In others the State claimed this right ; but in not a few cases the communes still retain their right of ownership. Of a total area of 71 million acres in Prussia and Saxony, there are 17,800,000 acres of forest, of which 4,720,000 are owned by the State, 2,364,000 by communes, and the remainder by individuals. Since the reforms commenced in the beginning of the present century, the general tendency has been to free private property, whether forestal or agricultural, from any rights of common with which it is burthened. The communal forests are placed under very strict regulations of the State for their proper management, and power is given to redeem those rights which are injurious to them.

In Switzerland the feudal system was introduced at a much later period, as compared with its neighbours. It never succeeded in taking any strong hold upon the institutions of the country, or in destroying the previously-existing system, and it was completely driven out again before the close of the middle ages. The communes, therefore, have retained possession of all the forests and the mountain pastures. In many parts of the country some of the cultivated land also belongs to the commune under the name of "Allmend." The right to it is generally vested in the descendants of those families only which have been from time immemorial resident in the district, and is divided equally among them. The rights of pasture on the mountain, and of firewood in the forest are conceded more generally to . all the inhabitants, irrespective of their place of birth, but in the case of pasture in proportion to the holdings of land which they possess.

Generally then, it may be said that in Europe the feudal system found on its introduction the same principle of common ownership of the community of the land, which was not set apart and appropriated for individual cultivation, and that although the feudal chiefs did their best to assert an ownership over this common land, they did not succeed in this to the extent which they have done in England. The communes have in most countries succeeded in maintaining their right to this open land in trust for the general exercise of customary rights, either by the occupiers of land within the district or of the inhabitants at large, according to the nature of the right.

Ireland and Scotland, however, are exceptions to the general rule of Europe. They were not subjected to feudal law or to the manorial system. The old tribal laws of property which prevailed in the Celtic parts of Scotland, and throughout a great part of Ireland, were not very different from the system of community of property under the Teutonic system. Property in the land was vested, not in individuals, but in the tribe. The chief had great authority over the individuals, but he could not alienate the land. When they were subjected to English rule, the main features of feudalism had already ceased to exist in England, and the principle of individualism had already taken its place. The feudal lawyers would doubtless have recognised the occupiers of land in Ireland and Scotland, as tenants of manors, and have conceded to them permanency of tenure, as they did to the copyholders ; the more modern lawyers, though still imbued with many feudal notions, treated the newly-conquered countries upon the principle of absolute ownership. The English landlord took the place of the Irish tribal chief; and the Scottish chief found himself invested with full ownership according to the English law. No recognition or consideration was given to the ancient claims of the tribal members; they were reduced as tenants to a position of absolute dependency.

The conditions, however, of the population in the Highlands of Scotland and in the west of Ireland were very similar to those of many countries in Europe, and the essential conditions of agriculture were the same. Only the better parts of the land could be cultivated, the rest necessarily remained open and unenclosed. The power of turning out cattle on the mountains was necessary to the existence of the cultivator, who had his five or ten acres of better land in the sheltered valleys, and who could only find his fuel on the bog or peat moor, open to all.

It has followed then, that whenever these rights or privileges have been interfered with, great hardship has been done to the small tenants of the district, and the conditions of their very existence have been made almost impossible. The great landowners, by introducing the system of sheep farming in the mountainous districts of Ireland and Scotland, have not unfrequently done grave injury to the small tenants, and have been the cause of the extreme depression and poverty to which many of these people have been reduced. In Ireland, the first Whiteboy rising in 1762 was mainly due to this cause. A great rise in the price of meat had given inducements to landowners to let their land for grazing; and the small tillage tenants were consequently deprived of their privilege of turning out their cattle on the waste lands. Arthur Young, speaking of this rising, says: "It began in Tipperary, and was owing to the enclosure of commons, which the people threw down, levelling the ditches, and were first known as levellers."

URBAN COMMONS.

In England, as already shown, the process of enclosure had gone on with increasing activity for upwards of 200 years, until the year 1865. The consent of three-fourths of the freeholders and copyholders of the manor was a condition of the enclosure. The common, when enclosed, was divided among them in proportion to their holdings, the lord of the manor usually being awarded one-sixteenth only of the common, in respect of his manorial interest, and taking another share in proportion to the quasi-right of common exercised in respect of his demesne.

The lord of the manor had an absolute veto upon the enclosure, and without his consent nothing could be done. As he enjoyed the exclusive right of sporting over the waste, it often happened that he was an obstacle to enclosure, preferring to retain the exercise of this right. It was the universal opinion that the powers conferred by the Statute of Merton had long been exhausted, and it was seldom that any, except small and insignificant enclosures or encroachments, were made under it.

About this time, however, the enormously increasing value of land in the neighbourhood of London, and the growing unwillingness of Parliament to assent to the enclosure of commons within the Metropolitan District, offered a great temptation to the lords of manors to revive the obsolete power of the Statute of Merton, and by arbitrary enclosure without the sanction of Parliament to realise the great value of this land, to the exclusion of the neighbouring people, and without consideration of public interests. Several of the most important commons in and near London were threatened with extinction in this manner.

It has been the fortune of London to be peculiarly favoured in respect of its surrounding Commons. Within twelve miles of its centre there are not less than 14,000 acres of commons, including 6,000 acres of Epping Forest. Some of them, such as the London Fields and Hackney Downs, are now entirely surrounded by a dense population; others, such as Hampstead Heath, Clapham Common, and Blackheath, are on the very edge of densely populated districts, and are as important for health and recreation as the London Parks; a little beyond, but still within reach of a walk, are numerous other Commons, such as Wimbledon, Tooting, Barnes, Chislehurst, and the greater expanse of Epping Forest. Irrespective of the latter, there are 60 Commons averaging 130 acres each, and 120 smaller spaces, often former village greens, averaging 10 acres each. It is difficult to exaggerate the importance of these to London. Every year as the great city expands they become more so. They supply natural parks for recreation. They are reservoirs, as it were, of pure air, whence the breezes may blow freshly into the crowded districts.

The growth of London, while it made these Commons even more important, added to their danger; as houses grew up round a Common, and population increased, the user of the Common altered in character; it no longer became possible for commoners to turn out their cattle there, still less was it possible or profitable for the householders to cut turf there as of old ; people took the place of cattle, and used the common for recreation and games. The owners of the villas which were built round the Common no longer valued their rights for their intrinsic importance in the pasture of cattle, but only as a means of keeping it from being enclosed.

It might be supposed that the law would not be so little flexible as not to recognise this practical transfer of user from cattle to people ; and that as the great population grows up round a space which has been open from time immemorial, and as more and more every year the maintenance of such a space becomes an essential condition of the health of the neighbourhood, the law would permit the growth of a right by way of custom or user. Here, however, the very technical rules of the old law with respect to customs opposed a difficulty to the assertion of a right of the public.

The law, it seems, has fully recognised the right of a village to its green, where the inhabitants have been in the habit of playing games from time immemorial, but it has failed as yet to recognise the analogy between the great city and its common, and the village and its green, however close that analogy may be. The difficulty consists in this, that the law of old laid down the principle that a custom must be local and confined to the inhabitants of a particular place, and that if it be general and enjoyed by all the world it cannot be sustained. Sir Matthew Hale laid down in the time of Charles II. that the inhabitants of a village could maintain a right to the village green by evidence of user for the purpose of dancing ; but later it was held that such a custom must be strictly local ; and it has been laid down that a custom which may be general, and extend to all the subjects of England, and which is not warranted by the common law is void.

o

It is the development of this doctrine which has made it difficult to assert a right at law for the people generally to the user for the purposes of recreation of open spaces and commons, which from time immemorial have been open and used by them. Indeed, this very technical rule has opposed a great difficulty in asserting a right even to the green of a village, which has been absorbed by the greater town ; for it is held that the evidence must show that the user of the green is confined to people of the immediate district, and if it shows that all the world came there for games and recreation, it fails to comply with the technical rule of law.

In the face of these absurd and pedantic doctrines it is very difficult to assert a right on behalf of the inhabitants adjoining such a common as Blackheath or Hampstead, no matter how great the user of it for games and recreation, or how necessary it has become for the health of the people. While, therefore, the importance of such commons has greatly increased, the danger to them has also increased, for the disuse of common rights has been alleged by the lords of the manor as a justification for enclosure, under the Statute of Merton.

The growing danger to the London commons from these causes led, in 1865, to the appointment of a Committee of the House of Commons to inquire generally into the condition of the commons and open spaces in the neighbourhood of London, including Epping Forest. Their report was the turning-point of a new policy. It fully recognised that the public interest required the maintenance of these open spaces in their integrity. It showed that, large as is the area of the commons round London, it is so valuable, immediately and prospectively, to the population of London for health and recreation, that it cannot safely be reduced ; and that every means should be taken to prevent the enclosure of any part of it.

Two opposite views were maintained before the committee as to the legal position of these commons, and as to the best mode of preventing their enclosure. According to one view, that of the lords of manors and their legal agents, the Commons, including Epping, were practically their private property, free from any right of, or obligation to the public or the commoners. It was contended that the public, by immemorial user, had acquired no right; that the rights of the commoners had vanished by non-user; and that under the common law, and by the Statute of Merton, the lords were justified in enclosing and appropriating these open spaces. On the other hand, it was maintained that whatever might be the right of the public, the Commons were practically protected from enclosure by the common rights still existing and vested in the owners and occupiers of adjoining property; that these rights, though little used in consequence of the growth of population, were dormant, not extinct, and could be maintained for the purpose of abating enclosures; and that all the experience of the past, as represented in thousands of private Enclosure Acts, and the General Enclosure Act of 1845, showed that all enclosures, whether by common law, or under the pretence of the Statute of Merton, however theoretically possible, were practically impossible and illegal unless sanctioned by Parliament. The committee, taking this last view of the subject, advised against a scheme, propounded by the Metropolitan Board, for the compulsory purchase of the forest and commons, which would have resulted in a vast expenditure of the ratepayers' money, to secure that which had always, *de facto*, been enjoyed. They recommended a scheme for placing these spaces under proper regulation and management, so as to prevent nuisances, and to preserve order, leaving all existing rights untouched. This suggestion was subsequently adopted by the Government of the day, and was embodied in the Metropolitan Commons Act. With respect to Epping Forest, the committee recommended that the Crown should put in force its forestal rights for the abatement of enclosures.

The report of this committee was followed by important consequences, and led to a course of litigation respecting the London Commons without parallel for its duration, the importance of its issues, and its historical interest. Each party to the great controversy before the committee proceeded to act upon its views. The lords of manors of numerous commons round London commenced a wholesale course of enclosure, which put in issue their contention as to their rights in the most practical manner, and which, if uncontested, would have speedily led to the disappearance, not only of Epping forest, but of all the most valued commons near London. Within a short time, nearly three thousand acres of the forest were abstracted from it, and enclosed with fences. The Commons of Berkhampstead, Plumstead, Tooting, and Bostall, were wholly, or in great part, enclosed; Hampstead Heath and many others were threatened, and would, doubtless, soon have been engulfed.

The opponents to this view of the right to enclose were equally determined to resist, in the interest of the public. In the autumn of 1865, I formed a Society for the Preservation and Protection of the Commons in the neighbourhood of London, with the object of resisting, or advising and assisting in resistance to their enclosure. Of this society I acted till the year 1880, with one short interval, as chairman, and chiefly advised and directed its motions and proceedings. In 1866 Mr. Fawcett joined the society, and by his advice its operations were subsequently extended generally to the question of Commons, whether urban or rural. Among the most prominent aiders in the movement which was thus originated have been Lord Mount Temple, Sir Charles Dilke, Mr. E. N. Buxton, Lord Edmund Fitzmaurice, Miss Octavia Hill, Mr. Philip Lawrence, who acted as the legal adviser to the Society during the first four years of its existence, during which many of the principal suits were brought to an issue, and to whom the origin of the movement is greatly due, and Mr. Robert Hunter, who succeeded him in the position, and who was employed by the Corporation of London to assist in the great suit respecting Epping Forest, for which his great knowledge of the law relating to Rights of Common eminently qualified him.

What the committee of 1865 had predicted came to pass. As each Common near London was enclosed or threatened, local opposition was aroused, which only needed the advice and assistance of the parent society to commence active proceedings against the wrong-doers. In most cases the resident owners of villas adjoining the commons formed committees and raised funds to oppose the aggressors in the law courts, or public-spirited men took upon themselves the burthen of resistance. In the case of Berkhampstead, where six hundred acres were enclosed by the late Earl Brownlow, and added to his park, the late Mr. Augustus Smith, well known as the Lord of Scilly, vindicated his right

as a commoner, after the manner well recognised by the law
as a legitimate method of dealing with an illegal encroachment. He sent down two hundred men to Berkhampstead,
who in one night removed the iron fences which engirdled
the stolen common. At Plumstead, Sir Julian Goldsmid
took the leading part against the enclosure. At Hampstead
the late Mr. Gurney Hoare joined with his neighbours in
organising resistance. At Tooting, Wimbledon, Wandsworth, and other suburban places committees were formed
for protecting the Commons.

EPPING FOREST.

In Epping Forest, where the enclosures were on the largest
and most threatening scale, great difficulty was found in
making effective resistance. The local landowners who had
rights of common were, as a rule, more in favour of enclosure
than opposed to it ; they were not unwilling to share in the
spoil, and many of them received allotments of the forest.
As the case is a good illustration of the dangers which beset
such districts, and of the difficulties in preserving them, it
may be of interest to describe it at greater length.

Epping Forest was in bygone times a part of the much
wider range of Waltham Forest, a district extending over
sixty thousand acres, to which Manwood's definition of a
royal forest applied, "a territory of woody grounds and
fruitful pastures, privileged for wild beasts, fowls of forest
chase, and warren, to rest and abide there in the safe protection of the king, for his delight and pleasure." This
district was not all woodland or waste, probably not more
than one-fifth of its area, even in early times, was in this
condition. The remainder was cultivated and enclosed
land, but it was forest in the sense that the forest laws were
applied to the whole of its area. These laws were framed
with a view to maintain the right of the sovereign to sport
over the district. No fences could be maintained high
enough to keep out a doe with her fawn ; no buildings could
be erected without the consent of the authorities. Game,
great and small, and especially deer, was protected by most
severe laws, enforced in courts peculiar to the forest, by
officers responsible to the Sovereign.

What was strictly forest in the district of Waltham was

confined to two wide ranges, the one known as Epping
Forest, which consisted of about six thousand acres; the
other, Hainault Forest, of four thousand acres. There
nature was allowed an undisputed sway; the forest trees
existed much as they had from before the time of Edward
the Confessor; the public had everywhere access, and the
only right conflicting with that of the Crown was that of the
freeholders and occupiers within the range of Waltham Forest,
by way of compensation for their subjection to forest law, to
turn out their cattle (not offensive to the deer) in the waste and
woodland. The Crown, beyond its forestal rights, had little
property within the limits of Waltham Forest. Before the
Reformation the greater number of the manors were in the
possession of the wealthy Abbeys of Waltham, Stratford,
and Barking; on the dissolution of the monasteries, in
the reign of Henry VIII., most of these manors came into
the possession of the Crown, and were subsequently re-
granted to private individuals, favourites of the Sovereign,
from whom they have descended to their present owners.
The extensive waste belonging to the Abbey of Barking,
constituting the greater part of what has been popularly
known as Hainault Forest, was retained by the Crown, and
the forest was preserved till 1851, when it was disafforested,
enclosed, and converted into arable lands and farms.

The motive which induced the destruction of this forest
was the improvement of the revenues of the Crown lands;
and probably the same fate would have overtaken the Forest
of Epping—at a time when the value of such a district from
an æsthetic and sanitary point of view was not as yet recognised—had the Crown been the owner of its soil. Fortunately,
however, the interest of the Crown in Epping consisted only
in its forestal rights. The ownership of the soil was vested
in the lords of fourteen different manors within the area of
the Forest of Waltham. This ownership was little more
than a barren and valueless right, for it was subject in the
first place to the forestal rights of the Crown, which forbade
the cutting down of any trees in the forest, and ousted them
from the privilege of other lords of manors, that of sporting
over the waste; and secondly, to the rights of the commoners
of turning out cattle on the waste.

The law of the forest was maintained and put in force by
special courts, and by an elaborate machinery, intended to

preserve the rights of the Crown and to prevent enclosure or trespass. Four verderers, elected by the freeholders within the forest, assisted in this duty, and the whole was under the authority of an hereditary lord warden, responsible to the Crown. At the commencement of this century these courts appear to have fallen into disuse. The growth of London and the immediate proximity of a large population made it more difficult to maintain the forest laws, and the Sovereign ceased to visit the district for sporting purposes. The old use of the forest, therefore, came to be disregarded, while its new value in relation to the great population of London was as yet scarcely perceived or appreciated. It is only within recent years that this has been recognised, and till then public opinion was decidedly adverse to the continued existence of such forests, mindful rather of the vices and hardships of the forest laws, sympathising rather with the owners of property against the claims of the Crown, and looking with utilitarian views to the greater return which might be obtained from so much waste land, if enclosed and cultivated. So late as 1848 a committee of the House of Commons, presided over by Lord Duncan, took this view of the forest, and recommended that the Crown should sell its forestal rights to the lords of manors within the forest, a course which was unfortunately adopted by the Commissioners of Woods and Forests. The Crown rights over about half the forest were thus parted with to those lords of manors who would buy them, at the rate of £6 per acre. The deer were killed down, and no efforts were made to maintain the Crown rights over the remainder of the forest.

Even before this, the Earl of Mornington, a dissolute spendthrift, who through his wife had become hereditary lord warden of the forest, and owner of four of the manors within its range, had done his best to ruin the forest. He reduced the verderers' court to impotence by appointing his own solicitor to be its steward, and in lieu of maintaining the forest, as he was bound in duty to do, led the way him-' self to its destruction, by enclosing and appropriating a great part of its waste within his own manors. His example was followed by most of the lords of the manors. They contended that the forest consisted of a number of distinct and separate manors, and was not a common waste over which all the landowners of the forestal district of Waltham had rights. In this view they had each to deal only with the comparatively few tenants of their own manors, and could disregard the great body of commoners over the wider district. The contention had no historical or legal justification, but the prize within their grasp was enormous. The forest land was worth from £300 to £1,000 per acre for building purposes. It was scarcely to be wondered at that greedy hands were laid upon this tempting prey, and that difficulty was found in rousing any action among the local landowners against the spoliation.

Impunity in the earlier cases begat recklessness. Enclosures were made wholesale, and in a short time the whole forest would have disappeared. In one of the largest manors of the forest, that of Loughton, the lord, who was also rector of the parish, enclosed in one swoop 1,300 acres, and commenced to fell the trees. Three hundred of these acres he was good enough to divide among those of his neighbours whose common rights he recognised. A pitiful plot of twelve acres was set apart for the school-children and the public. The magnitude of this trans-action, the scandal it created, and the alarm it gave rise to as to the remainder of the forest, assisted in working its own retribution ; and the first attempt, therefore, to deal with the Epping enclosures arose out of this Loughton case.

In this manor the inhabitants had from time immemorial, claimed and exercised the right of lopping the trees for fire-wood during the winter months. The tradition was that the right had been granted by Queen Elizabeth to the in-habitants of the parish, on the condition that on the 16th of November of each year they should at midnight commence their lopping. Certain it is that this custom had been maintained for many generations, and the labouring poor derived great advantage from this privilege, though of late years it had been somewhat abused by the sale of firewood, and by the intrusion of persons from a distance. In defiance of the enclosure, an old labouring man named Willingale, whose name is now associated with the preserva-tion of the forest, persisted with his two sons in exercising this right. They were summoned by the lord of the manor before the local justices, and were sent to prison with hard labour, although they protested their right, which should have ousted the jurisdiction of the justices, of whom one at least, had received a share of the stolen forest.

These high-handed proceedings roused public attention, and Willingale was advised to commence legal proceedings in support of the right of the inhabitants to lop the forest trees, a right which, if maintained at law, would have preserved and kept open the forest. An interim injunction was obtained on behalf of Willingale, to restrain the lord of the manor, pending the determination of rights, from felling the forest trees, and cutting up into building plots the great area he had enclosed. A thorough investigation was then made of the court rolls of the manor, and of the legal position of the forest; and although Willingale died before his suit could be decided, the proceedings in his case, extending over four years, during which the forest was practically protected from further devastation, were greatly instrumental in saving it.

In the meantime the other great suits respecting the London commons were proceeded with. It resulted from the movement, and from the exertion and assistance of the parent society, that a community of interest was established between them; the important suits, eight or nine in number, were conducted by the same solicitor, Mr. Philip Lawrence, the legal adviser of the society; and this gave a great advantage in the general direction of the proceedings. The law involved in the maintenance of common rights was intricate and almost obsolete; much of the older law had seldom come under the attention of lawyers of the present day. It was necessary to be very careful not to force decisions upon the Courts with undue haste. Even the highest tribunals of the country are not impervious to public opinion representing the general tone and sentiment of the community. The insistance of a technical right, for the purpose of keeping open a Common for a totally different object, might at one time be considered as scarcely worthy of the aid of the courts of law; whereas, at another time, and with an universal desire to save the Common, it would be grasped at and welcomed as a most timely and efficient weapon for the purpose.

In this view, then, the Commons' cases were purposely marshalled in such an order as gradually to lead the Courts of Law back to the older view of the value of rights of

Common; and decisions were obtained which strengthened public opinion in favour of the course pursued. In the Berkhampstead case, the first to come to a hearing, the proceedings of Mr. Augustus Smith were fully justified. It was shown that the pulling down of fences was not so violent an act as that of putting them up, where there was no right to do so. It was decided that the lord of the manor who encloses must take the burthen of proving that he has left sufficient waste for the commoners, happily a thing which is generally impossible. The investigation showed that a similar enclosure of this Common had been made by Charles I. when Prince of Wales, and in virtue of the Duchy of Cornwall, lord of the manor of Berkhampstead, and that one of the commoners had then summoned five thousand of his neighbours, who forcibly destroyed the fences. For this act the commoner was imprisoned by the House of Lords for contempt of the Prince's prerogative; but, not the less, the Common was left open till Lord Brownlow, in the present generation, made a fresh assault upon it. The Plumstead case decided that freeholders of a manor had equal rights with copyholders. The wrongful enclosers in this case were the Fellows of Queen's College, Oxford, and in deciding this case, Lord Hatherley made use of this strong expression :—" The litigation has been occasioned by a high-handed assertion of right on the part of the College, who really seem to have said in effect to those who have been exercising their rights for two hundred years : ' You will be in a difficulty to prove how you have exercised them ; we will put you to that proof by enclosing and taking possession of your property.' I think, therefore, the whole expense ought to fall on those who have occasioned it, namely, those who have brought into question rights which have had so long a duration, and to which I am thankful to be able to discover (because it is the duty of the Court to discover, if it can) a legal origin."*

The case of Tooting Common was also decided in favour of the inhabitants. In other cases satisfactory arrangements were arrived at. Wimbledon and Wandsworth Commons were preserved by securing to the lord of these manors an annuity, chargeable upon the local rates, equal

---

* Warwick *v*. Queen's College, Oxford: "Law Reports, 1871."

to his average previous receipts. The Metropolitan Board, which had never quite abandoned its plan of purchase, intervened in the Hampstead case, and bought the rights of the lord of the manor at a price infinitely below that originally claimed by him before the suit. Other Commons, such as Blackheath, Barnes, Shepherd's Bush, and others, were brought under the Metropolitan Commons Act, and were subjected to regulation and management.

There still remained, however, the case of Epping Forest. The investigation of the legal position of the forest, in the Willingale case, showed that a much longer purse was necessary to unravel its intricacies and deal effectually with its spoliation, than could possibly be provided by private persons and societies.

The claim of Willingale on behalf of the inhabitants of Loughton, although substantiated by evidence extending over 300 years in the manorial records, showing that the custom of lopping the forest trees for firewood during the winter months had been exercised from time immemorial, was subject to the difficulty already alluded to, resulting from the decision in Gateward's case, that the inhabitants of a parish or manor are too vague a body to claim a right or custom of a profitable value. It was certain, however, that the custom could never have been allowed to exist in a Royal Forest, where the forestal rights of the Crown were guarded with the most zealous care, if it had not a legal origin. It was hoped that the theory of a lost grant from the Crown would be adopted by the Court, so as to uphold the custom, and to prevent the enclosure of the forest. A judgment of the late Master of the Rolls, Lord Romilly, on demurrer, appeared to warrant this hope. Funds, however, were wanting to carry on this case in a manner which could alone secure success. It was necessary to look for assistance elsewhere, and the information obtained through the inspection of the Manorial Rolls in the Willingale case led to the confident belief that the enclosure would best be met and defeated by a claim on behalf of commoners. The Metropolitan Board declined to aid or to act in the case, on the ground that the Forest was beyond the limits of its district, and that it could not charge itself with any payments in compensation of manorial or proprietary rights. Fortunately it was then discovered that the Corporation of London, as owners of a cemetery within the range of Waltham Forest, had rights of common which would enable them to fight the battle : application was made to them to undertake this great question in the interest of the public. About the same time, motions were also made in the House of Commons calling for the intervention of the Government. Mr. Fawcett in 1870 carried an address to the Crown praying Her Majesty to take steps that the forest might be kept open for the enjoyment of the public. This was followed by an abortive and unsatisfactory proposal of the Government, by which 5,000 of the 6,000 acres would have been abandoned to the lords of the manors and commoners, and lost to the forest, a proposal which died a natural death in the face of a hostile resolution by Mr. Fawcett ; and in the following year Lord Mount Temple carried against the Government another address to the Crown, calling upon it to preserve those parts of Epping Forest, which had not been enclosed by legal authority.

Personally, I had not been favourable to an application to Parliament on the subject. I had no belief in the possibility of putting in force the forestal rights of the Crown, in view of the virtual abandonment of them, the disappearance of the deer, and the decay of the forest courts ; and I feared a compromise from any scheme which might be propounded by a commission or government department. I believed that the better course was to meet the aggressors in the courts of law on behalf of the commoners' rights, and I was confident that the law, if prosecuted with spirit and with ample funds, would be equal to the task of abating those enclosures. Experience has shown, however, that both courses were expedient, and that both contributed to the ultimate success. On the one hand, in answer to the Commons' address, the Government passed an Act creating a special commission to investigate the legal condition of Epping Forest, and to report a scheme to Parliament for the preservation and management of so much of it as had not been lawfully enclosed, or was still subject to the Crown's forestal rights. On the other hand, the main battle was fought and won in the law courts. The Corporation of London was induced to take up the cause of the public, and to put in force its common rights in respect of its cemetery, for the purpose of abating the forest enclosures. It commenced a suit in the year 1871, against all the lords of manors within Epping Forest who had made enclosures. In the following year a further Act was passed, restraining, while the commission lasted, all legal proceedings in respect of Epping Forest, with the exception of the corporation suit; this was allowed to proceed, with a view to obtain a legal determination of the great interests involved; and hence it resulted that two great inquiries as to the legal condition of the forest were proceeded with at the same time, the one by a Royal Commission, and the other before the Master of the Rolls, at the suit of the Corporation of London.

The main subject of investigation in both cases was the legal relation of the lords of the manors to the forest. Was the forest merely an aggregation of separate manors, each with its own body of commoners, and without connection with others? or was it part of the waste of Waltham Forest, over which all the landowners of the much wider district, embracing no less than forty-eight thousand acres, had rights of common? Both inquiries came to the same conclusion. That before the Rolls Court, which lasted more than three years, ended in a decision which could not have been more fatal to the pretensions of the enclosers. "If I am right in the view which I have taken of the law," said the Master of the Rolls, Sir George Jessel, "the defendants have taken other persons' property without their consent, and have appropriated it to their own use,"—a declaration which Sir Fitzjames Stephen has said closely approximated to the legal definition of larceny: there was the taking of other persons' property; there was an appropriation to their own use; the physical nature of the property alone prevented its being carried away. The judge went on to say that the defendants had disentitled themselves even to any consideration in respect of costs, inasmuch as "the bulk of them had been parties to a litigation in which they had endeavoured to support their title by a vast bulk of false evidence."

The Royal Commission came to the same conclusion. It reported that the enclosures were illegal, that the forest should be restored to its original condition, and be subject to a scheme for maintenance and improvement in the interest of the public. It also fully confirmed the existence of the custom of the Loughton people.

In pursuance of the Report, and upon the sanction of
the legal decision in the suit of the Corporation, an Act was
passed in 1878, finally settling the question of Epping
Forest.   It directed that the forest should be preserved
for all time to come, open and unenclosed, for the benefit of
the people of London.   It appointed the Corporation of
London, by whose energy, public spirit, and liberal expenditure the forest had been saved, as its conservators.
It required that all illegal enclosures or encroachments
should be abated, and appointed an arbitrator, Sir Arthur
Hobhouse, to decide and settle various questions still in
dispute.

It directed that all rights over the forest which are
inconsistent with its maintenance and beauty should be re-
deemed by the conservators ; and it left to the arbitrator to
determine whether the inhabitants of Loughton had a legal
claim to the custom of lopping.   It is satisfactory to add
that the arbitrator ultimately decided in favour of the
custom, on the ground that one so clearly proved and so
ancient must have had a legal origin.   He awarded to the
inhabitants £7,000 in compensation for it.   A satisfactory
and final settlement has therefore been made of the forest.
A magnificent reach of forest-land in the immediate vicinity
of London has been secured for ever.   A most important
moral has been pointed for the benefit of those who contemplate arbitrary enclosures in the future.   In the history
of legal proceedings in this country there has probably never
been a case at all approaching in extent or importance that
which has resulted in the compulsory restitution of 3,000
acres of land which had been illegally taken from the Forest
of Epping.

The success which has thus attended the efforts to
restore and preserve Epping Forest, and others of the
London Commons, has fully justified the conclusions of the
Committee of 1865.   It has shown that there is the strongest
presumption that such enclosures are illegal, and that
adverse rights invariably exist, which if put in force, and
supported with adequate funds, will abate these enclosures.
By what a slender chance, however, was the forest saved !
It was by pure accident that the Corporation of London, in
their capacity of Commissioners of Sewers, were owners of
the cemetery to which such rights attached.   Cattle may be

" levant and couchant " in this place of sepulture, sufficient to maintain the legal right of pasture in the forest ; but it cannot be supposed that the right is of any real value. Yet this almost imaginary right was sufficient when backed by the long purse of the City, and by public opinion, to defeat the enclosure of three thousand acres, and to compel no less than five hundred persons to restore to the forest their share of this stolen land. What a strangely circuitous method of pre-serving the forest, and of securing it for the public use and enjoyment ! Yet many persons who would have considered any direct intervention of the Legislature to prevent these glaring illegalities as an interference with the rights of pro-perty, regarded with pleasure the tortuous and protracted legal proceedings by which the Corporation vindicated their shadowy rights, and thus indirectly effected the object of preserving the forest for the public.

The process must remind us how completely such rights, whether of the lords or commoners, have altered in character and value. In olden times these manorial wastes were of value only for the rough pasture afforded to the cattle of the community, or for the peat or turves which served as fuel. They had little or no intrinsic value as land. The forest was of value only for the sport it afforded to the Sovereign, or for its subsidiary rights of common. As population has grown up around them, the rights of turning out cattle have practically ceased to have any value, the risk to cattle being greater than the return ; sporting rights are equally reduced to zero ; the cutting of turf is superseded by cheap coal, and. has become a nuisance. People and children have taken the place of cattle and pigs, and use for recreation and enjoyment the heath or the forest. If trespassers in theory, they are dispunishable in fact. The law, if it usually fails to recognise such use, however long enjoyed, fails equally to provide any remedy against such trespassers. No one can prevent or interfere with them. The open space becomes an essential condition of health and existence to the sur-rounding population. On the other hand, this urban growth alters entirely the intrinsic value of the manorial waste. In-stead of being the mere refuse of the manor, unworthy of cultivation, it attains, without any expenditure of capital on it, an enormous value for building purposes, if only it can be freed from common rights and appropriated. Hence the great temptation to enclose. But is it right or just to the surrounding population that this should be permitted, without consideration of the interests or the actual user of those through whose existence only the land has acquired this great value? Or is it right that the population should be called upon to pay an immense price for land which they have always in fact enjoyed?

It has always appeared to me that the law, or, if not the law, the legislature, should recognise and sanction the practical transfer of use from cattle to people, and should admit the right of the population to use and enjoy that which they have in fact always used and enjoyed. The rights of turning out cattle on the Commons had their origin in custom, and, together with the copyholder's possessory right to his land, which in early times was merely permissive, were converted into legal rights by the courts of law, recognising the effects of time upon custom. Why should the law be less pliant now than in bygone times? Why should it not recognise the changes which time effects, and give sanction to long-continued customs? Surely rights can have no better origin than immemorial use. The case is much strengthened when it has been proved by so long a course of litigation that, practically, enclosure means the invasion of other person's rights, and that the sleeping rights of common can be revived to prevent such enclosure. Why subject people to the great expense and trouble of putting in force these dormant rights, for a purpose altogether foreign to their origin? Why longer permit enclosures in the face of such strong presumption that they are illegal? Why not directly prohibit them, rather than compel resort to such circuitous methods of resisting them?

RURAL COMMONS.

While this great litigation was being carried on for the protection and maintenance of the Commons round London, another movement was in progress with respect to rural Commons. Mr. Fawcett was the first, in recent years, to call the attention of the public to the injustice and wrong which was too often done to labouring people in the neighbourhood of Commons by these enclosures.

Mr. Cobbett, in his well-known "Rural Rides," had already, in the last generation, pointed this out. He had spoken " of the great advantages formerly possessed by the cottagers from the cows, pigs, geese, and poultry which they were able to keep on the waste over which they had right." As a contrast, he referred to the disadvantage the labourers are often under in a corn-growing country, and to "the dismal and miserable state of those districts, where every inch of land is appropriated to large farms." " No commons, no grassy lanes—the labourer has not a stick of wood, and no place for a pig or a cow to graze on."*

The late Sir Robert Peel also appears to have appreciated the objections to enclosure from the point of view of the labourers, for, speaking on the Enclosure Bill of 1845, he said, " The House of Commons should be cautious how it dealt with these rights of common. It might be a matter of feeling—honourable members have their feelings, and the poorer classes of the community have feelings on the subject. The right of common connected them with the soil ; the right of having even a goose on the common made a man feel interested in the tenure of land. It might be more beneficial to such a man that he should accept £2 or £3, but recollect you are not dealing with the rights of the individual, but with those of his successors."

In 1868 these views were fully supported and explained in the Report of the Royal Commission on the Employment of Women and Children in Agriculture. After tracing their condition from feudal times to the present, the commissioners concluded that " the agricultural labourers have lost opportunities and means of bettering their condition, which belonged to their class in former times." They gave two reasons for their deterioration—

1. The enclosure of waste lands.
2. The absorption of small farms in large farms. They added that "the second cause is undoubtedly dependent, to a great extent, on the first."

In 1869 Mr. Fawcett opposed for the first time, on these grounds, the General Enclosure Bill for the year, which proposed to enclose no less than 6,900 acres of common land in different parts of the country. Of this immense extent, three acres only were to be reserved as recreation grounds for the public, and six acres only as allotment

---

* Cobbett's " Rural Rides," Edition 1853, p. 86.

P

gardens for the labouring poor. The objections to this wholesale enclosure, with so little regard to the interests of the public or of the labouring poor, had only to be stated to make themselves felt, and although the Bill had already reached a third reading, it was successfully delayed and finally withdrawn. From that time till the year 1876 no further enclosures were sanctioned by the House of Commons. In every case resistance was made successfully, on the ground of the total insufficiency of the public allotments set out under the provisions of the Act of 1845. In 1870, a Committee of the House of Commons took the same view, and reported in favour of wide amendments of the general Act. Meanwhile great arrears of enclosure orders, by the Enclosure Commissioners, were accumulated, waiting in vain for the sanction of Parliament; and in 1876, the then Government introduced a general amending Bill. The main purport of the new Bill, as explained by Sir R. Cross, was to substitute, as far as possible, the process of regulation and improvement for that of enclosure. It was hoped that " its effect would be to prevent the enclosure of commons in the future, and to give facilities for keeping them open for the benefit of the people, so that not only those who had right of common should enjoy them, but that the public themselves might enjoy the use of such free spaces of land, improved, drained, and levelled." With these objects, those who had promoted the movement against enclosures, whether from the point of view of urban or rural commons, fully and cordially concurred. They pointed out, however, that the Bill was so framed, as very inadequately to carry them into effect. They showed that the proceedings for the regulation of commons were so cumbrous, and involved so many consents, and were so wholly dependent on the veto of lords of manors, that practically few such schemes, if any, were likely to be carried out; and they contrasted such machinery with that provided under the Metropolitan Commons Act, in respect of commons in the neighbourhood of the metropolis, where no such consents are necessary.

They also contended, that just in proportion as greater impediments were opposed to the enclosure of commons by legal process, so there would be greater inducements to lords of manors to endeavour to effect enclosure without such legal sanction, by arbitrary, and as all experience had shown, illegal processes, and that it was essential to provide some remedy against such acts. They also showed that the provision in the Bill for the consideration of the interests of the public and the labouring classes, in those cases where enclosure should be sanctioned by Parliament, were insufficient and unsatisfactory.

In the course of the proceedings in the Committee on the measure, many efforts were made by members to remedy these defects of the Bill. They failed, however, altogether to make the clauses with reference to regulation of commons more elastic and workable ; more especially, they failed to limit the veto of the lord of the manor.

They failed in many attempts to insert clauses with the object of making illegal the enclosure of commons, otherwise than by the sanction of the Enclosure Commissioners of Parliament. The only advance in this direction was a clause agreed to by the Government, requiring public advertisement in local newspapers as a necessary preliminary of the intention to make any such enclosure. Several important amendments, however, were secured, extending the provisions favourable to the public, where enclosure should be sanctioned.

The experience of four years, since the passing of the Act, has fully confirmed the views expressed in the discussion on the Bill. The regulation clauses have proved to be unworkable, except in cases where the Enclosure Commissioners are able to make their approval of the enclosure of part of a common conditional upon the regulation of the remainder ; or where the common is a mountain district, and where enclosure would be useless. In respect of lowland commons, the veto conceded in the Act to the lord of the manor, the necessity of the consent of two-thirds of the commoners, and the expense of the proceedings generally, have prevented, and will continue to prevent, any action in this direction.

On the other hand the principle laid down in the Act that no enclosure should be sanctioned by the Enclosure Commissioners, without distinct evidence that it will be beneficial to the general interests of the neighbourhood, as well as to the private interests of the persons immediately concerned as lord of the manor and commoners ; the requirements of public inquiries ; the *locus standi* given in certain cases to local authorities of large towns to object to enclosures ; and the greater consideration shown to public interests on enclosure, have proved to be of great value.

In the year 1875, the Enclosure Commissioners had given their sanction to the enclosure of no less than 39 commons, with a total area of 18,600 acres, and provisional orders for these enclosures were awaiting the confirmation of Parliament. In the course of the discussion on the Commons Act, Sir R. Cross consented that these suspended schemes should not be further proceeded with, but should be referred back to the commissioners with a view to their reconsideration, and to the commencement of new proceedings under the new Act.

It resulted from this course, that in their report of 1878, the Commissioners reported that after reconsidering these proposals for enclosure by the light of the principles laid down in the new Act, it was considered not desirable to sanction enclosure in 18 cases. In these cases they added, " it was proved to our satisfaction that enclosure would not be of benefit to the neighbourhood, and we have, therefore, declined to proceed. In each of these cases, when the circumstances appeared suitable, we recommended regulation ; but in only one has regulation been yet applied for." A new policy has thus been instilled into the Enclosure Commissioners, and there is little chance of any common being now enclosed by their sanction and with the approval of Parliament, unless there be some real advantage to accrue to the public.

Recent reports of the Commissioners have also thrown more light upon the quantity of common land still remaining unenclosed. How little was known on this point may be judged by the fact that so late as 1872 the Enclosure Commissioners, in a report to Parliament, estimated that 8,000,000 acres of common and commonable land still remained undealt with, of which they considered that upwards of 3,000,000 acres were in the lowland counties, and the remainder in the mountainous districts of England and Wales. Of this great extent, they considered "that one million of acres of the common, and the greater part of the commonable land might be enclosed with profit and advantage to the country, and that when this was completed, there would still remain about one-sixth of the area of England and Wales, open and subject to common rights, an extent so great as must show how erroneous have been the apprehensions of the speedy enclosure of commons in England."

Two years later they presented another report to Parliament, the result of a detailed examination of the Tithe Commutation Awards, and from this it appeared that there are no more than 2,632,000 acres of common or commonable land in England and Wales, or five and a half millions of acres less than their previous estimate. Of this but a small proportion is in the lowland districts, and by far the greater part in the mountains of Wales and Cumberland. Of the total amount but a very small part is suitable for arable cultivation. It is certain, then, that the extent of common land which can be enclosed with any real advantage to the public is not considerable, and the importance of preserving commons which remain in the neighbourhood of towns is even greater than was supposed.

Many other steps have been taken during the last few years in the same direction as those already described. The schemes of railway companies for intersecting the commons near London by their lines of rails and embankments, to the destruction of the main use and beauty of such commons, have been watched in Parliament and prevented. A proposal for planting the New Forest, in such a way as to deprive the public of access to it, and to destroy its natural features, was defeated; and a scheme for re-affirming the rights of commoners in the forest was carried in opposition to the views of the Commissioners of Woods and Forests. A proposal for enclosing the Forest of Dean was also defeated; and thus the three remaining important forests in England have been secured, in opposition to the more utilitarian spirit which prevailed but a few years ago. The interests of agricultural labourers in respect of numerous allotments of land, under old enclosure awards, have been watched and defended; and the sale and misappropriation of such land have been prevented. Scarcely a Session has passed without some further action in Parliament on these questions, at the instance of a small knot of members, testifying to the increased interest in the question, and to the change of opinion as compared with past times.

By a recent private Act, the Corporation of London are made the guardians of all the commons within twenty-five miles of London. They are authorised to buy up rights of common for the purpose of keeping them alive, and also to contribute from their funds to any litigation towards maintaining them, a provision which might be usefully extended to other corporations.

Much still remains to be done before the question can be considered as finally settled. It will be necessary to make the Regulation clauses of the Act of 1876 more elastic and workable, and not merely dependent on the veto of the lord, or the consent of so large a proportion of the commoners. Above all, it will be necessary to put some further obstacle to arbitrary encroachments and enclosures of commons. As already shown, the difficulty of obtaining Parliamentary sanction to enclosures will give greater inducement to enclosures without such sanction, by persons who trust to the unwillingness of commoners or others to encounter the litigation which is necessary to defeat such action. It is necessary then that enclosure, otherwise than by the sanction of Parliament, should be prohibited. It is time also that the law with respect to Customs of Inhabitants should be brought under review, and that certain and long-enjoyed customs should not be defeated by such an absurd technicality that the inhabitants are too vague a body to enjoy a profitable right ; on the other hand, the right of the inhabitants of a town to recreation on an open common should be recognised as fully as that of villagers to their village green. When these changes are secured the question of commons will be practically settled, and the limit will be reached of a movement which, in its historic bearings, will be as interesting in a remote future, as its results will be beneficial to the community.

THE GAME LAWS.*

ORIGIN OF ENGLISH GAME LAWS.

THE group of statutes which constitute the present Game
Law of England dates no further back than the year 1831,
when, with one exception, all previous enactments relating
to game were repealed, and the right to take or sell game
was based on a new principle. Previous to that year no
person was permitted to kill game unless qualified either by
the possession of freehold or leasehold property of the
annual value of £100, or by holding the status of esquire.
Landowners by virtue of this qualification and irrespective
of agreement, practically exercised the exclusive right of
sporting over their lands let to farming tenants. Lords of
Manors still claimed the right to game on the lands of the
copyhold tenants of their manors, and the sale of game was
wholly illegal, and was punished by severe penalties.

These laws may be traced without difficulty to the feudal
principles which were introduced into this country by the
Norman conquerors.

Under the older Saxon law every freeholder had the full
liberty of sporting over his land, provided he abstained
from the King's forests. The Royal forests were, doubtless,
even then of great extent, but the prerogative of the Sovereign
did not extend beyond their limits, and in no way interfered
with the free exercise of rights by other landowners. We
are told, for instance, that Canute set bounds to the Royal
forests, and made this provision in favour of his subject :—

"Volo ut omnis liber homo pro libito habeat venerem sive
viridem in planis suis super terras suas sine chaceâ tamen et
devitent omnes meam ubicunque eam habere voluero."

A Pamphlet published in 1874.

This was also the ancient law of the Scandinavian continent, whence Canute probably derived it :

" Cuique enim in proprio fundo quamlibet feram quo modo venari permissum."

And in the laws of Edward the Confessor it is laid down :—

" Sit quilibet homo dignus venatione meâ in sylvâ et in agris propriis et in dominio suo ; et abstineat omnis homo a venariis regiis ubicumque pacem eis habere voluerit."

After the Norman conquest, however, a new doctrine was asserted, and the right of taking all beasts of chase or venary, wherever they might be found, and without regard to the ownership of the soil, was claimed by the Sovereign for himself, or for such only as he should duly authorise.

These restrictive laws relating to forests and game had been introduced generally in Europe, at the same time and by the same people, who were the authors of the feudal system. The conquering generals of the northern invaders, when they settled the economy of the countries they had subdued, and partitioned them among their chiefs and feudatories upon the condition of military service, found it necessary to keep the natives of these districts in as low a condition as possible, and especially to prohibit them the use of arms. Hunting and sporting were therefore prohibited, and the generals reserved these rights to themselves or to those chiefs immediately below them, to whom they thought it safe to entrust such rights.

The Norman kings introduced this principle to England after the conquest, and being mighty hunters, carried it out not only as a matter of state policy but of personal enjoyment. In later times the Norman lawyers vindicated this claim of the Sovereign, partly on the principle that the King was the ultimate proprietor of all the lands in the kingdom, which were held of him as Lord paramount of the fee, and that therefore he had the right to enter on any estate and take all wild creatures at his pleasure ; and partly on a maxim of the law that such creatures were "bona vacantia," and having no other owner, belonged to the King by virtue of his prerogative. Bracton states the Royal prerogative thus :

" Habet etiam Rex de jure gentium in manu suâ quæ de jure naturali deberent esse communia ; sicut feras bestias et aves non domesticas."*

And Manwood, an early writer on the Forest Laws, says :—

'· In like manner wild beasts of venary and beasts and fowls of chase and warren being things of great excellency, they are meetest for the dignity of a prince for his pastime and delight, and therefore they do most properly belong unto the King only. And for that cause, it is not lawful for any man within their land to make any chase, park, or warren, in his own freehold, or elsewhere, to keep or preserve any wild beasts or birds in it, without the King's grant or warrant so to do." †

It would appear, however, that these were rather the after-thoughts of lawyers anxious to obtain royal favour, than the true explanation of the origin of the claim asserted by the feudal sovereigns ; the more probable cause is that already alluded to, namely, that as conquerors of new territory, they found it expedient as matter of state policy to enforce this claim, a policy which also coincided with their predilections for the chase.

Whatever its origin, the prerogative thus claimed on behalf of the Crown was exerted with the utmost vigour by the earlier Norman kings, not only in the ancient forests, but in new forests which the Conqueror and his sons made, by laying together large tracts of country, depopulated for this purpose, and without the consent of the owners or any compensation for the damage done. In these forests great oppression and tyranny were exercised by virtue of special forest laws, for the sake of preserving the beasts of chase, and the killing of any animal was punishable in the same manner as the killing of a man. In the Anglo-Saxon Chronicle of the year 1087 there is a piteous description of the result of the Forest laws of William the Conqueror:—

" He made large forests for the deer, and enacted laws therewith, so that whoever killed a hart or a hind should be blinded. As he forbade killing the deer, so also the boars ; and he loved the tall stags as if he were their father. He also appointed concerning the hares that they should go free. The

---

* Bracton " De Legibus," Chap. 24.
† Manwood's " Treatise on the Forest Law," Chap. 2.

rich complained, and the poor murmured ; but he was so sturdy that he recked nought of them. They must will all that the King willed, if they would live or would keep their lands, or would hold their possessions or be maintained in their rights."

Ordericus Vitalis, in the time of Henry I., said of that monarch, " Omnem ferarum venationem totius Angliæ sibi peculiarem vindicavit et vix paucis nobilioribus ac familiaribus privilegium in propriis saltibus venandi permisit."

Until the reign of King John this prerogative applied only to four-footed game, but that monarch extended it equally to winged game. In the words of Matthew Paris, Anno 1209, " Rex Anglorum Johannes ad natale Domini fuit apud Bristolleum et ibi capturam avium per totam Angliam interdixit." The hardships, vexations, and cruelties resulting from these laws became at last wholly insupportable to the general body of landowners, and they pressed for a relaxation of the Forest Laws and for a limitation of the King's prerogative of game with equal pertinacity as for Magna Charta itself; and by the Charta de Foresta (9 Henry III.) A.D. 1225, confirmed by Edward I. A.D. 1299, all the lands which had been afforested by Henry II., Richard I., and John, except the proper demesnes of the Crown, were disafforested and freed from the Forest Laws, and the Royal forests were stripped of their most oppressive privileges and regulations.

The principal clauses of this famous charter are worthy of attention, as, better than any description, they show what must have been the evils they were intended to remedy.

Clause 1.—First, all forests which King Henry our grandfather afforested shall be viewed by good and lawful men, and if he had afforested any other wood than his own demesne to the damage of him whose wood that was, it shall be disafforested, and if he had afforested his own wood it shall remain forest, saving the common of herbage and of other things in the same forest, to them who before were accustomed to have it.

Clause 3 extended the same measure to forests which had been afforested by " King Richard our uncle, and King John our father."

Clause 10.—No man from henceforth shall lose either life or member for killing our deer. But if any man be taken and convict for taking our venison he shall make a grievous fine if he have anything thereof; and if he have nothing to lose he shall be imprisoned a year and a day, and after a year and a day expired, if he can find sufficient sureties he shall be delivered, and if not he shall abjure the realm of England.

Clause 12.—Every freeman may henceforth without hindrance make in his own wood or on his own land which he hath in the forest, a mill, a fish pond, a pool, a marl pit, a dike or arable land without the covert in arable land, so that it be not to the annoyance of any neighbour.

Clause 13.—Every freeman may have in his own woods ayries of hawks, sparrow hawks, faulcons, eagles, and herons, and shall also have the honey that may be found in his woods.

Clause 15.—All persons outlawed for our forest only from the time of King Henry our grandfather, until our first coronation, may come to our peace without let, and shall find good sureties that henceforth they incur no forfeiture unto us concerning our forest.

From the time of the Charta de Foresta following closely upon the more important Magna Charta, the prerogative of the Sovereign sensibly declined. The right of the Crown to the game over all lands, irrespective of ownership, was still maintained as a principle of law, but practically the Sovereign no longer exercised this right, except in the ancient forests and on his own demesnes, and it was no longer legal for him to create a chase or forest over the land of a subject without his consent. It was still held, however, that no right of chase or free warren could be created without the sanction of the Crown, and during the reigns of the first three Edwards an infinite number of such grants were made to the principal nobility, from which it may be inferred that, by law, the game still belonged to the Crown. These grants appear to have extended not only to the demesne lands of the feudal lords, but also to all the freehold lands and copyhold or customary holdings within the manors; and gradually it became understood that a grant of a manor from the Crown, or a grant of a tract of land with jurisdiction constituting it a manor, carried with it the right of sporting; and for many generations it was held that this right of sporting vested in the feudal lord, extended over the freehold and copyhold lands within the manor. After the Charta de Foresta however, it does not appear that the Sovereign ever created a forest or chase for himself without the consent of the owner of the soil, nor could he grant right of chase or free warren to a person over the lands of another in a separate manor. It is recorded that Henry VIII., before making a chase at Hampton Court, obtained the consent of the freeholders or copyholders over whose land the chase was to extend. Later, Charles I. endeavoured to extort money by the enforcement of the Forest Laws, extending the limits of the royal forests by high-handed proceedings, under the colour of inquests, for the recovery of the Crown forestal rights which had been allowed to sleep, and imposing enormous fines on those who were declared to have infringed on those rights. Parliament again interposed, and in the 16th year of this reign an Act was passed which remedied this evil and finally settled the extent of all royal forests, according to their boundaries in the 20th year of James I., annulling all the perambulations and inquests by which they had been subsequently enlarged.

The feudal lords, who had so successfully asserted their own rights as against their Sovereign to kill game in their seignories, were not the more inclined to be lenient to those below them. As already explained, they obtained grants from the Crown of chase and free warren in their manors, and as against the freehold and copyhold tenants, they exercised, until a much later date, the same rigour against which they had themselves rebelled. Sir W. Blackstone, after tracing the origin of the Game Laws, and explaining the early claims of the Sovereign, adds—

"From this root has sprung a bastard slip, known by the name of the Game Law, now arrived to a wantoning in its highest vigour, both founded on the same unreasonable notion of permanent property in wild creatures, and both productive of the same tyranny to the Commons, but with this difference, that the forest laws established a mighty hunter throughout the land, the game laws have raised a little Nimrod in every manor."*

As the feudal system gradually passed away, the rights and duties of feudal lords, or lords of manors, almost imperceptibly diminished, the freehold tenants of manors emancipated themselves from the jurisdiction of their lords, and copyhold tenants by degrees acquired a right to their

* " Blackstone's Commentaries," Vol. II., Tit. Game.

holdings, subject only to the payment of customary rents, fines, or services. It was not, however, till the reign of Queen Anne that a doubt was raised as to the right of a lord of a manor to the game on the lands of the freeholders of his manor, and it was then said by some of the judges that a lord of the manor could not enter on the freehold estate of another, though situate within the bounds of his manor, for the purpose of sporting. The question, however, was never fully argued or finally adjudged. Neither was the right of the lord to sport over the copyhold lands within his manor decided, but till a very late time the better opinion was that the lord retained this right. Mr. Cruise, one of the ablest lawyers of his day, said on this subject :—

"As to copyhold estates they still form a portion of the demesnes of the manor of which they are held, and therefore I presume that the lord has a right to hunt over them unless barred by a non-user. For considering the original baseness of the tenure, it cannot be supposed that the lord relinquished that royalty over these lands or that a right of hunting could have been given to a mere villein. It is, however, very extraordinary that this point has never been settled."*

It was not till 1831 that the question was finally decided. The Act amending the Game Laws provided that lords of manors should have the right of sporting over the wastes of their manors, and by implication this has been held to negative any right of sporting over the freehold or copyhold lands within the manor. Unless, therefore, the lord of a manor can show that under the special customs of his manor he is clearly entitled to the game on the copyholds within it, he cannot now under the general law make claim thereto.

Landowners, however, have ever maintained, either by law or by contract, the right to sport over the lands of their ordinary farming tenants. Till 1831 it was considered that this right was irrespective of any reservation of game in the lease or agreement. The Act of 1831, however, reversed this presumption, and in the absence of any reservation, gave the game to the tenant, leaving the parties free to make what agreement on the subject they should think fit. The Act fully recognised the power of the landlord to reserve

* "Cruise's Digest," Vol. III., p. 257.

the game and the exclusive right of sporting, and the law has from an early time recognised the possibility of a separate estate being created in the game and the land. Not only can the landlord reserve the game in letting his land to a farmer, but he can separate the right of sporting altogether from the ownership of the land, and let or sell the one apart altogether from the land itself.

From a very early date the rights thus vested in the principal landowners by the Crown were supported by legislative enactments, which took the form of requiring a property qualification as a condition to the right of killing game. The earliest trace of such qualication being required is to be found in the 13 Richard II., chapter 13th, which provided as follows :—

"Forasmuch as divers artificers, labourers and servants and grooms keep greyhounds and other dogs, and on the Holy days when good Christian people be at church hearing divine service; they go hunting in parks, warrens and connigeries of lords and others—to the very great destruction of the same, and sometimes under such colour they make their assemblies, conferences, and conspiracies for to rise and disobey their allegiance—it is ordained and assented that no manner of artificer, labourer, nor any other layman which hath not lands or tenements to the value of £40 by year, nor any priest nor other clerk if he be not advanced to the value of £10 by year, shall have or keep from henceforth any greyhound, hound, nor other dog to hunt—nor shall they use fyrets, keys, nets, hare-pipes, nor cords, nor other engines for to take or destroy deer, hares, nor conies, nor other gentleman's game, upon pain of one year's imprisonment."

This statute was followed by many others in the same direction. The 21 Edward IV., c. 2, provided that foresters, porters, and their assistants, should not be troubled if trespassers were killed by them within their liberty in cases of resistance. The 19 Henry VII., c. 4, provided that no man should shoot with a cross-bow without the King's leave, except he be a lord or have 200 marks land. In the 7th year of the same reign is the first mention by statute of pheasants and partridges, and a special provision was passed for their preservation, which was subsequently strengthened by statutes of Elizabeth and James I.

Even in the revolutionary days of the Commonwealth no attempt appears to have been made to reduce the harshness of the Game Laws, and the only law passed relating to the subject was one putting a further penalty on the illegal killing of deer. A statute of Charles II. continued the monopoly in favour of the landed gentry, and subsequent Acts assisted in carefully shutting out not only the persons who cultivated the soil as tenants, but likewise inferior tradesmen and other persons not endowed with a sufficient degree or estate to warrant them in pursuing beasts or birds of game.

GAME LAWS IN EUROPE.

It is to be observed that from a comparatively early time the qualification to pursue and kill game was based upon property and not upon birth, as was the case in many parts of the Continent, where the feudal system was more rigidly followed to a later date.

In France, for instance, the privilege of sporting was, until the Revolution of 1789, reserved exclusively to the nobility. Ordonnances of the years 1395 and 1515 inflicted heavy penalties on the "roturiers" who should indulge in the pleasure of killing game, a privilege reserved solely to the seigneurs. If the offence was committed in a royal forest, the delinquent was flogged at the gate of the prison ; if the offence were repeated he was sent to the galleys ; and if, after return, he showed himself incorrigible, he was subjected to capital punishment.

In 1669 an Ordonnance of Louis XIV. declared that the right to game belonged exclusively to the King ; it gave permission, however, to seigneurs to kill game on their own lands, provided these lands were not inconveniently near to the royal forests, and it forbade 'roturiers' to indulge in any method of killing game even on their own property.

De Tocqueville, in describing the Feudal Rights which existed in France before the Revolution of 1789, says :—

"The right of the chase was not allowed to be farmed out like that of fishing. It was a personal right arising from the consideration that it belonged to the King, and that the nobles themselves could not exercise it in the interior of their own jurisdiction without the permission of the King.

"The right of shooting and hunting was more interdicted to the non-noble than any other right. The fee fief of the non-noble did not even bestow it. So closely observed was the principle, and so rigorous was the right considered, that the Seigneur was not allowed to give any permission to hunt. The Seigneur Haut Justicier possessed the faculty of hunting and shooting on any part of his own jurisdiction, but alone. He was allowed to make regulations and establish prohibitions upon matters relating to the chase throughout its extent. Every Seigneur de Fief, although not having the feudal power of judicial courts, was allowed to hunt and shoot in any part of his fief. Nobles who possessed neither fief nor jurisdiction were allowed to do so upon the lands belonging to them in the immediate neighbourhood of their dwelling-houses. It was decided that the non-noble possessing a park upon the territory of a Seigneur Haut Justicier was obliged to leave it open for the diversion of the Lord. Nobles alone were allowed to keep pigeons and even ferrets."*

Arthur Young, in his description of the state of French agriculture before the Revolution, has told us that the most important operations of agriculture were fettered and prevented by these Game Laws. Wild animals, such as boars, and herds of deer, roamed at large through districts called 'capitaineries,' where no enclosures for the protection of the crops were permitted. In many parts of the country hoeing and weeding were prohibited, lest the young partridges should be killed ; mowing hay, lest the eggs should be destroyed ; taking away the stubble, lest the birds should be deprived of shelter ; manuring with night soil, lest the flavour of the game should be impaired. Complaints for the infraction of these laws were tried by the manorial courts, where every species of oppression and fraud were practised.

These privileges and abuses were put an end to in 1789. In the memorable sitting of the assembly on the 4th of August the noblesse were constrained to abandon their exclusive privilege of sporting with all other feudal rights.

Even the rights of the Crown were not excepted, notwithstanding the favour in which Louis XVI. was then held by the Assembly. The Royal monopoly of sport extended for twenty leagues round Paris, and was the cause of most crying iniquities. After a powerful speech from Mirabeau, and on the motion of the Duke of Orleans, all capitaineries, whether royal or not, and all reserves for sport, under whatever denomination they may have been, were from that

---

* De Tocqueville's "Ancien Régime," p, 469.

moment abolished. The seignorial right to pigeons, which had been one of the most hated of feudal privileges, was at the same time abolished, and it was provided that thenceforward every person might keep pigeons, subject to the rule, that the birds should be shut up in their dovecotes during the seasons prescribed by the Communes, in the interest of agriculture, or if allowed to be at large during the seasons, might be treated as game by others.

The decree which abolished the feudal privileges to game appears to have intended that thenceforward game should be the property of the owners of the soil, but it provided no remedy against those who should trespass in pursuit of it. For a time, therefore, no Game Laws existed, and there resulted over the whole of France a scene of confusion and disorder. Crowds of artisans and mechanics issued from the towns, and, joining the labourers in the agricultural districts, spread themselves over the fields in search of game. Enclosures were broken down, and woods were destroyed. The disorder which resulted from unrestrained trespass was so great that in a few months it was found necessary to repress it ; and in 1790 a moderate Game Law was passed, based upon the principle that every owner of property was allowed the exclusive right of sporting on his own land, subject only to rules laid down in the general interest. The principles adopted in 1790 were confirmed in 1844 by the present Game Law of France ; and the bulk of the cultivators of the soil being owners of the land, these laws, which in many respects closely resemble our own, have not proved to be oppressive either to the cultivator of the soil or to the public.

In Germany the same feudal laws prevailed until a much later period. The right of sporting was generally reserved from the proprietorship of the land, and was vested in the feudal magnates. The exercise of this right created the greatest discontent, and in 1848 the Game Laws, and all enactments as to fence seasons, were abolished throughout Germany by the Frankfort Parliament, which, however, left the legislative bodies of the different states to decide as to the mode in which the new principle, that the shooting should go with the land, should be carried out. In a few states some little compensation was given to the holders of the old seignorial rights of shooting, in others, as in Prussia,

Q

none. There followed a brief period of lawlessness, during which any peasant at any time of the year was free to kill game. After a short experience of disorder, the several states separately proceeded to re-enact Game Laws, the general effect of which was that the sporting over large estates was reserved to the proprietors, and the sporting over small estates was vested in the local communes, to be let for the joint benefit of all.

THE GAME LAW OF 1831.

In this country the feudal principle, modified in favour of property as distinguished from birth, survived to a later period than in France. It was not till 1831 that a successful effort was made to reform the Game Laws. The inquiries and debates which took place in the House of Commons for many years previous to 1831 show how intolerable had become the burthen of these laws. The change then made was one of the first results of the great Reform movement. The Game Law of that year, which swept away all the previous laws based upon privilege, was passed by the Parliament which had been elected under the popular agitation for reform, and before the Reform Act itself became law; but it was a Parliament in which tenant farmers were not represented; the Liberal element of the country was mainly to be found in the county representatives elected by the freeholders, and not by tenants; and the law bore evident traces of the absence of the voice of the tenant farmers in its preparation.

Although the Act of 1831 abolished privilege, and opened the door to tenant farmers, who were previously disqualified as a class, it will be seen that it gave great facilities for the reservation of game by landlords, and by permitting the sale of game, it gave the sanction of property to game in a sense which was previously wanting, and gave further inducements to that over-preservation of which we now hear so many complaints. It also led to a great extension of the practice of subletting game by the landlords to game tenants, who have no common interest with the farming tenants.

Whatever may be the defects of the Act of 1831, it made bold and sweeping changes. It entirely abolished all property qualification for the right of sporting; it repealed a great number of statutes by which these property rights were enforced, and by which the sale of game was prohibited. In lieu it substituted a moderate day trespass law, directed only against persons wrongfully in pursuit of game. It definitely settled the law as to the rights of lords of manors, giving them the right to shoot over the wastes of their manors, and by implication refusing them the right to shoot over the lands of their copyhold or freehold tenants. Recognising the fact that hitherto tenant farmers had no right to kill game, and that landowners as a rule exercised this right over their lands, it reserved to landlords the exclusive right of sporting over all lands held under existing contracts except where the right had been expressly granted to the tenant.

On the other hand, however, it provided that in future lettings the right of sporting was to run with the land, except where reserved by deed or agreement. Whenever such reservation was made by the landlord, it enforced the right of the landlord by imposing penalties of £1 for every head of game killed by the tenant in contravention of such contract. It gave permission for the first time for the general sale of game ; but required that persons should take out a license for such sale. It provided a close time for certain kinds of game, excluding hares and rabbits from this category, and finally it required licenses or game certificates from those who should in future shoot game.

The most important provision of this Act, however, is undoubtedly that which substitutes for previous laws a moderate trespass law directed against persons who should trespass in the day-time in pursuit of game, and enforces it by a penalty of 40s. and costs of the conviction ; if five or more persons should commit the trespass the penalty is increased to £5. Power is also given to require trespassers to give their names and places of abode, and in the event of their refusing, to arrest them for the purpose of taking them before a justice of the peace, where upon conviction the penalty is increased to £5. The penalty is further increased by £5, where five or more persons, any of whom being armed with guns, endeavour by violence or intimidation to prevent any authorised person from approaching them for the purpose of requiring them to quit the land or of ascertaining their names and abode.

This Act left unrepealed the Night Poaching Act of 1828 (9 Geo. IV., c. 69). Under this Act, which is still in force, any person unlawfully taking game by night may, upon conviction before two magistrates, be committed to gaol for three months with hard labour, and at the expiration, in default of finding sureties for not offending again for the space of one year, may be imprisoned for a further six months with hard labour. The penalties are doubled for a second offence, and for a third offence penal servitude for five years may be awarded. Owners and occupiers of land or their servants are empowered to arrest offenders, and if resistance is made, the punishment may be increased to penal servitude for five years ; and if three or more persons, any one of whom be armed, unlawfully enter land for the purpose of taking game or rabbits, they are liable to not less than five years or more than ten years penal servitude.

Lastly, in the year 1862 the Act known as the Poaching Prevention Act was passed by the united support of the county members, and against the strongest protest and opposition of the then Secretary of State, Sir George Grey. This Act enables policemen to arrest and search men going along the high road whom they have reason to suspect of having been illegally taking game, and gives power to Magistrates to convict, if they think that the accused have wrongfully obtained the game which is found upon them. The object aimed at by this Act was to break up the gangs of poachers, who were well known by the police to make a trade of poaching, and who were frequently met by the police on their return from a raid on some neighbouring preserve, with all the loot upon them, but who from want of evidence could not be arrested and punished.

LEGAL STATUS OF GAME.

Before proceeding further to comment on the policy and general results of these statutes, it may be well to say a few words upon the legal status of game, and to point out in what respects game differs, on the one hand, from beasts or birds, which, having been appropriated and domesticated, are invested with the attributes of property, and on the other hand, from those which are so useless, or noxious, that they have not even the protection afforded to game.

It need hardly be pointed out that domesticated animals, such as oxen, sheep, and poultry, have all the true attributes of property. They have been appropriated, bred, and reared, and can always be fully identified. If they stray from the land of their owner they do not cease to be his property, nor can the occupier of adjoining land to which they stray appropriate or kill them, even if they be doing damage to his property; he must drive them back or pound them, and he can recover from the owner any damage done by them. The really wild beasts or birds, on the other hand, such as the fox, badger, rat, or carrion crow and rook, have none of these attributes. They have never been appropriated, they cannot be identified, they are not recognised as of any value, but rather as destructive and noxious. The law therefore declines to regard them as pro perty, or to afford them any protection. It is true that the fox has a fictitious value, and receives a qualified protec tion from country gentlemen, in order that it may afford sport to those who follow the hounds, but is not such a value as is in any way recognised by law. Midway between these and the domesticated creatures lie those specie: which are generally included in the term "game." They differ from the domesticated species in that they have not been appropriated and cannot be identified. They differ from the species at the opposite end of the scale in that they have a value when captured.

More closely, however, to the domesticated creature lies the pigeon or dove. The wild pigeon does not come under the head even of game. Domesticated pigeons and doves closely approximate to the condition of poultry. The law, however, which applies to the latter is not altogether free from difficulty and doubt. In feudal times pigeons were, like game, the special right of the feudal lord; the erection of the dovecote was a "liberty seignorial;" and it was not till a comparatively late period that even a freeholder or a copy-holder could erect one without the consent of the lord of the manor; it followed that pigeons, often kept in such numbers as to be a positive nuisance to the neighbourhood, were fed at the expense of the neighbouring farmers. Under the present state of the law, pigeons are the property of the person who breeds them, they are for the most part capable of identification, they frequent the same dovecote, they fly in flocks together, they can be the subject of larceny if taken in the dovecote; even where they have the full opportunity of getting out and enjoying themselves in the air, if they wander off the land of their owner, they do not cease to be his property, nor is it the right of any person on whose land they light to kill and appropriate them. If they do injury by taking his seed or corn, he may drive them away, and only in the event of their doing repeated and serious - damage to an extent which becomes a positive nuisance would it be right in him to kill them, and even in such case the dead birds remain, it is believed, the property of their owner. The live birds do not appear to have acquired fully the status of property so as to be treated as personal property on the death of the owner. They descend to the heir-at-law with the land. It is not lawful for a man to keep pigeons at the expense of his neighbours, to feed on their crops and their recently-sown corn; but if he keeps no more than is reasonable, having regard to his own steading, and if he provides them with food at home in reasonable sufficiency, he has a right to expect that when they light on his neighbour's land they will he treated as still his property, and not be sacrificed either to a love of sport or to the unreasonable alarm of petty damage. It is doubtful, however, whether, except when in the dovecote, they can be the subject of larceny, and a special statute was passed (7 & 8 Geo. IV., c. 39) imposing a penalty upon persons who should unlawfully and wilfully kill or take house doves or pigeons under such circumstances as shall not amount to larceny at common law. It appears also, that the excessive breeding of pigeons may be a common nuisance, and be indictable as such.

The swan is another bird nearly allied to the domesticated creature. If swans be reduced into possession of a private person, they become his property; but if they be at liberty on a river, they are then the prerogative of the Crown, and in some cases have been granted by ancient charter from the Crown, as in the case of the swans on the Thames which are the privilege of the Corporation of London, although they have been bred on the land of private owners. If a swan the property of a private person be astray, but shows an intention of returning to its own water, it is deemed to be private property. It may be doubted, however, whether it can be the subject of a larceny, except where it is taken from the land of its owner under circumstances which make it certain that it had been appropriated.

The case of deer, again, presents some difficulties and anomalies. In their wild and unappropriated state they are not property, neither are they game within the meaning of the Game Laws ; but they are the subject of special laws, directed against persons who unlawfully kill them. If, however, they have been reduced into possession, and tamed and reclaimed from their wild state, they acquire the status of property, and pass to the executors of the deceased owner, or on his bankruptcy can be seized by his assignees and sold away from the land, and in such case they are the subjects of larceny. In large parks, however, where the deer are not tamed or reclaimed, they cannot be said to be property ; in such cases they pass like rabbits in a warren, or like pigeons in a dove-house, with the land itself to the heir-at-law, and cannot be treated as personal property distinct from the land.

Ducks, when domesticated, are property in the same manner as ˙ poultry, but when wild are not admitted into the category of game. It appears, however, that a decoy for wild ducks is recognised by the law as a kind of trade, giving to the owner a certain right, on the ground that although it tends "to spoil gentlemen's game, yet it brings money into the land ; " it is, therefore, unlawful to fire off guns or otherwise to disturb and injure a decoy, and whoever does so is liable to an action at law for civil damage.

On the other hand, rooks are not recognised at law as birds entitled to any protection, even under the Game Laws. It is said of the rook, "that it is not supposed to cost anything for its maintenance ; its attributes are 'fera natura' and destructiveness, and neither by common law nor by statute is it deemed as a profitable food." Rooks are elsewhere spoken of as "noyful fowl," and though, in modern times, a rookery has come to be considered as a pleasing accessory to a gentleman's park, affording a certain amount of sport at the time when the young rooks are just coming off the nest, yet it does not appear that it has acquired any status in the eye of the law, and no action will lie for the disturbance or destruction of a rookery, however wilful or wanton.

Passing now to the further extreme, the law gives no protection to such creatures as squirrels and hedgehogs; they are not property, and have no protection under the game laws. Badgers and ferrets are considered such noxious animals that not only is no protection afforded to them, but it is held that no action of trespass is maintainable for following them on to the land of a stranger, digging them out and killing them. So, also, it has been held of the fox; but no more should be done than is necessary to kill the fox, if it be followed into the land of another; and this law can only hold good now in those parts of the country where the fox is still considered to be a nuisance, and not the subject of the so-called noble sport of hunting. It was endeavoured, on the same ground, to sustain the right to follow the hounds over the lands of those who objected to hunting; but Lord Ellenborough directed the jury, in an action for civil trespass against a gentleman who was hunting the fox for his own pleasure, that if they were satisfied that the good of the public had not been the sole object, they should find for the plaintiff; thus negativing the right to follow the hounds over another man's land. And in another case of the same kind, where an action for trespass was brought against the huntsman of the Berkeley hunt, it was held that the damages for which he was liable did not extend merely to the individual act of the huntsman himself, but to such mischief as had been occasioned by those who followed him in the hunt.

Of the smaller birds not included under the term game, with the exception of "woodcock, snipe, and quail," the law till recently took no notice. Mr. Auberon Herbert, however, in 1872 persuaded Parliament to give protection during the breeding season to a certain number of the feathered tribe, such as robins, finches, and to most of the rarer varieties of small birds; but Parliament excluded blackbirds, thrushes, sparrows, and even larks from this protection. In respect, however, of both classes, no other protection is given. They are in no sense property, they have no protection under the game laws, and no criminal proceedings can issue for their destruction by trespassers during the open season.

We now came to those birds and animals included in the term game. Properly speaking, the list is a small one, and the definition of game in the Act of 1831 includes only hares, pheasants, partridges, grouse, blackgame, and bustards; and does not include rabbits, woodcock, snipe, and quail. These latter, however, are included in the principal provision which imposes a penalty for trespassing in pursuit of game. Rabbits are also included in the terms of the Night Poaching Act and the Poaching Prevention Act of 1862; they are not included, however, in the clause which imposes a penalty on farmers who in breach of their agreement with their landlords kill game on their farms.

It may be inferred that any civil contract, also, which only specifies game does not include rabbits. In this, therefore, and in the exclusion of rabbits from the provision directed against farmers, constitutes the only difference between rabbits and other game. To all intents, therefore, rabbits may be treated on the same footing as game, for practically they are accorded the same protection.

THE TRESPASS LAWS.

Now, although game, and also rabbits, snipe, quail, &c., are recognised by the law as of a certain value, and are protected under the Game Law, they are equally with the baser species already alluded to, and for the same reasons, not considered as property by the law of England. They differ, it is true, in this respect, that they have value when killed, but they are wanting in the essential elements of property—namely, appropriation and identification. Game, in its wild nature, has *ex hypothesi* not been appropriated; it wanders from field to field, regardless of ownership; it cannot be identified. No gamekeeper can swear to the identity of hares, rabbits, partridge, or even, except in very rare cases, of pheasants. The law, therefore, has rather of necessity, arising from the stubborn facts of nature, declined to recognise them as property, and a poacher who has wrongfully taken game cannot be indicted for larceny. Game, in a qualified sense, is the property of the owner of the land on which it is taken, and not of the person who kills it; and under the Act of 1831, as already stated, the remedy for wrongfully taking game is not larceny, but trespass for going upon land in pursuit of it.

But for the fact that it appears to be so little known, even to many who are in the habit of discussing the Game Laws, and that it is often suggested that the trespass laws would suffice in lieu of Game Laws, it would scarcely be necessary to point out that by the law of England simple trespass is not an offence for which a person can be subjected to any criminal process, however small. To constitute a criminal offence, trespass must be accompanied by some malicious damage to property, such as breaking down fences or trampling crops, and the offence then consists rather in the damage to the property than in the trespass. The only means landowners or occupiers have of dealing with trespassers is to warn them off their property, and if the trespassers neglect or decline to go, it is then permitted to the landowners or occupiers to eject them forcibly, using such force only as is necessary for the purpose. There is also a civil remedy against a trespasser, but only the value of the damage done can be recovered. So careful, indeed, has the law been not to allow harm to be done to innocent trespassers, so long as they do no damage to property, that it has been held to be illegal to set spring guns or dangerous traps in woods, or elsewhere, in the hope of injuring trespassers, and therefore of deterring others from entering. The Act of 1831 is in the main, then, a discriminating trespass law. Trespass, otherwise not criminal, becomes so if the person be in pursuit of game, and is punishable, if in the day-time, by a penalty of 40s., and if in the night-time, by imprisonment with hard labour.

It is important to observe that the offences against the Game Laws are not in the nature of public offences, but rather of private wrongs. It does not at all follow because a man is in pursuit of game on another man's land that he is therefore committing an offence against the law; the offence is in his doing so against the will of the occupier or landowner. The occupier or landowner, if he does not preserve game, may be careless on the point whether his grounds are entered or game taken or not, and if he cares not to enforce the penalty, it is certainly not the duty of any other person to prosecute for the trespass. It is an affair between the landowner or occupier and the trespasser, and it is not one in which the public are interested; and this is so far recognised that the information for trespass must issue at the instance of the person aggrieved, or by his authority, and the costs of prosecutions under the Game Laws form an exception to nearly all other cases, and are never paid by the public. The Game Laws, in fact, afford the means of enforcing private rights, and the wrong committed by a trespasser in pursuit of game is not in the nature of a public wrong which the community is much interested in detecting, preventing, or paying for.

The Poaching Prevention Act of 1862 appears to have made an exception to this rule. It gave for the first time power to the police to act in game cases, and has made them, to some extent, game preservers. Under this Act the police are entitled to arrest and search persons on suspicion that they have been illegally upon land in search of game. It also enables the justices to convict, without any direct evidence that the accused have actually been trespassing on the land of some person who objects, and practically throws the onus of proving his innocence upon the accused. If, for instance, two or more men are observed by the police going along the road in the early morning under any circumstances which raise the suspicion that they have been engaged in poaching, the police may arrest and search them, and if game be found on their persons, the justices are entitled to convict them if the accused should not be able to show that they lawfully obtained possession of the game. The power thus given to the police and to the justices is very great—greater than in the case of any other property. With the exception of a few cases in the interest of the Revenue, where the accused may be called upon to prove his innocence by showing where he obtained the articles, the law requires in all cases proof of guilt to be tendered by the prosecutor, and does not put the accused to proof of his innocence. In this respect, therefore, the Poaching Prevention Act has extended a greater sanction to game than is given to most other property. In Scotland, however, the judges have interpreted the law differently, and have held that neither the arrest nor the conviction is justified unless there be evidence to show that the accused has been trespassing illegally on the land of some person who objects to it. Under this ruling of the judges, the Act has proved to be quite inoperative in Scotland.

It might, perhaps, be presumed that as game is not

property, and as the only process under which it can be preserved against destruction by unauthorised persons is that of trespass, it would follow the land on which it is to be found and on whose crops it feeds, and that no right could be asserted in it independent of the occupier of the land, who owns also the growing crops. It is not so, however. The law fully recognises the possibility of severing the game from the occupation of the land, and the right of sporting from the right of cultivating the soil. It has already been pointed out that by the Act of 1831, in the absence of any reservation by the landlord in his lease, the game and the right of sporting is the privilege of the occupying tenant; but the Act recognised the reservation of game by the landowner, to the exclusion not only of the public, but of the occupier, lesee, or tenant himself. The landowner may also assign this right to any other person, thereby creating two tenants in respect of the same holding, the one a farming tenant, the other a game tenant, without any privity between them or community of interests. The Act has also enforced this right of reservation by making it a penal offence for a tenant or occupier, where the landlord has reserved the game, to take or destroy game upon his holding, punishable by a fine of £1 for every head of game then taken, or by imprisonment in default of payment.

As regards the labourers at work on the farm, who cannot be said to be there as trespassers, it is held that if they neglect their duty and snare or destroy game, they become *ipso facto* trespassers, and can be proceeded against under the Act of 1831, by the occupier of the land or by the landlord if the right of sporting be reserved.

Not only, therefore, can the landlord prosecute an outsider for trespassing in pursuit of game on land which is in the occupation of his tenant, but he can prosecute the labourers at work on the farm if they take game upon it, and he can prosecute the occupying tenant himself for killing game bred upon the land and fed upon the result of his own farming.

What the law thus permits and has thus fortified by unusual precautions (for in very few cases can a breach of contract be punished criminally) has become the custom. It may be said that the all but universal practice throughout the country is, that farming land is let with a reservation of game in favour of the landlord, and with more or less stringent covenants on the part of the tenants, binding them to preserve the game or to enforce the law against outsiders who trespass in pursuit of game.

Judging from the tenor of the debates on the Act of 1831, it would seem that it was intended, by the passing of that Act, to benefit the tenant farmers by securing to them the game on their farms where there was no reservation, and it was evidently expected that in the majority of cases there would be no reservation of game by the landlords. But custom has prevailed against the intention of the legislature, and the all but universal rule is for landlords to reserve the game on letting their lands.

In many parts of the country it is almost impossible for a farmer to hire a farm where he has control over the game ; he would be shut out from his profession if he insisted on this. The severance of the enjoyment of game from the occupation of the land is a well recognised fact and almost a condition of the existing relations of landlord and tenant. It may be traced directly to the influence of the feudal laws, under which the right of sporting was a seignorial privilege. The feudal lords for long strove successfully to maintain their hold over the hunt, the hawk, and the sport, and even when the feudal system was on its decline, the right of sporting was for many centuries confined to the gentry and their servants ; and although it can no longer be claimed as a right by landlords independent of contract, yet the custom which had its origin in right in former days has been stereotyped in our social habits, and in the relations of landlords and tenants. The prevalence of large landed properties, and the all but universal custom for land to be cultivated not by its owners, but by tenant farmers, has also tended to sustain the custom of game preserving and of game reservation by the landlords, and has prevented the more natural combination of occupation of the land and control of the game over it.

DAMAGE BY GAME.

To complete this review of the legal position of game, it should be added, that the law of England gives no remedy to the tenant farmer against his landlord, for damage done to his crops by game, reserved under the lease, however great the damage, and however much the game may have increased beyond what it was at the commencement of the tenancy, unless there be a special agreement on this point. In the absence of such agreement the landlord or his game tenant may allow the game to increase to any extent, and to do any damage to the crops of the farming tenant without fear of having to make redress. In Scotland the law is different, and the tenant can claim compensation where the game has increased beyond what it was at the outset of the tenancy. The cases, however, where such claims have been made good are most rare, and there is admittedly the greatest difficulty in estimating the damage done to growing crops by game. The damage by game is not confined only to the actual value of food consumed by it; hares and rabbits spoil much more than they consume, and the farmer is deterred from doing his best to obtain produce from the soil by the fear that he is only adding to the food for game and wasting his capital and time. In no case does the law recognise a claim against an adjoining proprietor for damage done by his game, unless it amounts to a common nuisance; short of this, the only remedy is to shut out the hares and rabbits by wire netting or to kill them.

The silence of our law on this most important point is in striking contrast to the jurisprudence of the Continent. In France, and in other countries where the Code Napoleon has been adopted, the provisions of the code have been construed so as to give most ample protection to landowners and occupiers against damage done by game coming from the lands of their neighbours. It is recognised as the obligation of the proprietor of a wood or forest to keep down the game, and especially rabbits, by all reasonable means, so that his property may not become the harbour, from which the game may make incursions upon the crops of neighbouring proprietors. If the proprietor, by preserving the game, by abstaining from shooting it, by putting down rabbits and other game to breed, or by allowing old warrens and rabbit holes to exist where rabbits may be harboured, allows the game to be in excess, he must pay the penalty by recompensing his neighbours for any damage done by it; and the game tenant of a wood or forest stands in this respect in the same position as his landlord.

It is recognised, however, that a certain quantity of game is a necessary incident to a wood, and that even extraordinary exertions will not entirely remove the evil. To relieve himself of all possible responsibility, it is advisable that the proprietor of a wood should give leave to his neighbours to follow the rabbits into the wood and there destroy them, or should invite them to join in battues for their destruction.

As between landlord and tenant the law is equally explicit and just. If the farmer, by his lease, has agreed to reserve the game to the proprietor, he has no ground of complaint against the latter, when the game of which he complains comes from the land let to him, or the hedges or little covers comprised in his holding ; but on the other hand, the reservation of the right of sporting to the proprietor does not prevent the farmer from destroying the game, which comes from beyond his holding to ravage the produce of his land, and the farmer may employ engines of destruction against such game during the harvest time, without committing an offence against the game laws, or infringing the contract with his landlord.

If, on the other hand, the game of which he complains comes from woods in the hands of his landlord, not included in his lease, he has the same rights against his landlord as against any other neighbouring landowner with whom he has no relations. It would appear also that even where the game is reserved, if the landlord does not take reasonable steps to keep it down, the tenant has a claim against him for damage done to his crops ; and even where, under his lease, the farmer has renounced any action against his landlord, either in respect of game bred on his farm, or in respect of game coming from adjoining covers, yet if the landlord, or his game lessee, does nothing to prevent the ravages of the game, and the damage assumes a great proportion, the law holds that the farmer could never have consented to so terrible a condition, which would make his position insupportable, and enables him to sustain a claim against his landlord, notwithstanding the clause in his lease excluding such claim.

Numerous cases have also established the principles on which the measure of damages, in the case of destruction of crops by game, is to be assessed, so as to cover not only the actual loss, but the amount which would have been realised by the farmer if his land had not been overrun by game.*

Such being, briefly stated, the present law on the subject of game and its historical derivation, we may proceed to examine into its results. This task is the more easy as twice within recent years Committees of the House of Commons have taken evidence on the subject at great length, and we have the fullest and most comprehensive view of all the evils which are complained of, whether by the tenant farmers looking at the question from their own point of view, or from others in the interest of the general public. The latest Committee sat throughout the sessions of the years 1872 and 1873, and comparing the evidence taken before it with that taken by the Committee of 1845, it is impossible not to come to the conclusion that the preservation of game has increased in the interval, and that all the evils complained of in the earlier year have since been aggravated. The complaints are twofold—those in the interest of the tenant farmers, and those in the interest of the more general public. The complaint of the tenant farmers is to the effect that preservation of game presents great and increasing obstacles to good farming and to agricultural improvements, and that it is highly unjust that game should be fed at their expense, especially in the case of hares or rabbits, which spoil far more produce than they consume. The complaint from the more general view of the public is, that preservation of game leads inevitably to poaching, that the labouring class do not and will not be persuaded to regard poaching as a crime, and that consequently large numbers of young men are tempted to break the law, and are subsequently led on to more serious offences; and further, that by the obstruction to good farming, caused by over-preservation of game, the gross produce of the soil of the country is much less than it ought to be. Making every allowance for the highly coloured statements of many of the witnesses, it must be admitted that there is much ground for these complaints.

It is a matter of common knowledge that the preservation of game is on the increase, that the reservation of game

---

* In Belgium a special law provides that the indemnity to be recovered by the farmer, in the event of damage to his crops or fruit by rabbits, shall be estimated at double the actual loss.

by landlords is almost universal, and that leases contain often elaborately-devised covenants, binding the tenants not only to refrain from killing game themselves, but to assist in preventing poachers coming upon the land for that purpose ; it is also certain that the fashion for battues has greatly extended, and that where some years ago it was thought a good day's work for a party of sportsmen to kill 100, or at the utmost 200 head of game, at the present time such bags are considered below the average, and not unfrequently upwards of 1000 head of game are killed within the day. The increase has undoubtedly been mainly in the direction of winged game. It is true that many of the best landowners have waged war upon their hares and rabbits, and that some game preservers have devoted their energies mainly to winged game ; but it is clear that there is still great ground for complaint on the part of the tenant farmers, and the growing necessity for improved and more scientific farming has rendered the nuisance of ground game and of excessive preservation yearly more felt. It is also certain that the practice of letting the shooting by the owner of the land has increased of late years, and is the cause of greater complaints on the part of the tenants.

As between themselves and their landlords, the tenant farmers do not always raise or feel the same objections. They retain the hope that the interest of their landlords, where not obscured by an excessive love of sport, may protect their tenants from an overplus of game. But where the shooting is let by the landlord, an outsider comes in who has no relation with the tenant, who looks only to his sport, and to whom it is matter of indifference what happens to the crops provided he gets his game ; and it need hardly be said that the farmer views with aggravated bitterness the destruction of his corn and turnips by the rabbits and hares bred for the amusement, not even of his landlord, but of an outsider with whom he has no relation or sympathy. Colonel Robertson, the Chief Constable of Hertfordshire, alluding to this subject, said :—

" Too many covers are let to extraneous people, who come from all parts of the country, mostly from London, who do not care one single pin about the farmer or his crops. If you could do away with that there would be no complaint about the game."

R

It is not as it used to be in olden time, when country gentlemen were more at home and had less facilities for travel. Then the squire was content if he could go out with a friend and shoot a moderate head of game over his tenant's land, and take the opportunity of talking with his tenants and looking at their crops. In these days shooting has become a more serious affair. The fashion of battues has given a taste for blood, and in many parts of the country sportsmen are not satisfied unless game by the hecatomb fall to their guns ; and it has resulted that not only pheasants, partridges, and grouse are strictly preserved with a view to secure these great bags, but in order to fill up the day's sport hares and rabbits must be equally prolific. Save for hares and rabbits, the balance of evidence is to the effect that but little complaint would be made by farmers. Partridges, it is admitted, do little or no harm ; they probably do more than an equivalent good in destroying insects. Pheasants can only do harm during the very short interval when the harvest is ripe ; at other times if they are to be preserved in any number they must be well and frequently fed in the covers. Grouse only come down to the cultivated grounds for purposes of mischief during a late harvest. The true enemies to the farmer are the hares and rabbits. The rapid multiplication of rabbits is well known, and has been from the earliest times the subject of complaint by farmers. Pliny tells us that the inhabitants of Minorca petitioned the Emperor to send them troops to aid in ridding their island of the rabbits, who destroyed their trees and undermined their houses ; and even in these days on some soils the pest of rabbits can only be kept down by constant exertions and by using every implement of destruction against them. Not only is the amount of food they eat very considerable, but they destroy a great deal more. Where a farm is over-stocked with hares and rabbits, no excellence of farming will avail.

That farmers themselves are not averse altogether to game is abundantly clear, not only from the evidence but to everyone who has any knowledge of the class. In the rare cases where, holding under corporations or under non-preserving landlords, they have the right to shoot over their own farms, they generally become game preservers ; but with this difference, as is alleged, that while maintaining sufficient for sport, they do not allow their farms to be over-run with game. There is also every difference between the feeling that your own game is eating your own crops and the feeling that the crops which you raise fall the prey to the game of others, suggestive of the old line ;

" Sic vos non vobis vellera fertis oves."

As a further illustration of this, it is stated that where the farmer has a right to the game no man looks better after the poachers ; in fact no poacher dare venture upon such farm. Poaching is mostly done by the people in the imme-diate neighbourhood of the farm. The farmer very soon · finds out who the poachers are, and can guard against them, and he can make it the interest of his own labourers to pro-tect the farm against trespassers.

It is also admitted that where the game is reserved under the farmer's lease, whatever covenant there may be as to preserving the game and warning off poachers, the farmers, as a rule, trouble themselves very little about it. No one ever hears of a farmer prosecuting a poacher for killing the game of the landlord ; he leaves all this to the gamekeeper. In many parts of the country the farmers look upon the poachers as their friends, as the natural cor-rective to an overtendency to accumulate game. The fact is, that in the artificial condition of things, where the occupation of land is severed from the right of sporting, the interest of the person best able to watch and preserve the game is lost ; the duty falls to the gamekeeper, while the increase of game, the result of his exertions, ends in in-creasing the number of poachers. The more keepers, the more game ; the more game, the more poachers, and the less interest taken by occupiers in resisting their attacks. Such is the vicious circle which results from high preserva-tion of game, under the condition of its complete severance from the land on which it is bred, and on whose produce it is fed.

EFFECT OF GAME LAWS ON LABOURERS.

Looking at the effect of the Game Laws from the more public point of view, it can scarcely be denied that there is some truth in the complaint that they lead many people into a course of crime who would not otherwise be tempted.

The same feeling which is the essence of sport with gentlemen, which sanctions the killing of game when it does not sanction the killing of domesticated creatures, except with some eccentric tastes in the case of pigeons, is also at the root of that which makes the labouring classes, as a rule, look upon game as a fair subject of capture. The taking of game is not, in the public opinion of those classes, a serious offence. The better class of workmen will generally refuse to work with a man who has been convicted of theft. They do not consider conviction for poaching in the same light. Poaching, therefore, presents many attractions to the active young men in the country districts. It is restrained, not by any public opinion, but only by the fear of detection and punishment. It leads many men, therefore, into a course of action which ends in worse company, and in the gaol ; and once in gaol, they speedily become contaminated by contact with men of criminal habits. The number of commitments to gaol, however, is not so large as is often represented. The statistics laid before the Committee show that in England and Wales on the average of three or four years—

7,000 persons are annually fined for simple day trespass in pursuit of game.

1,500 are imprisoned for short periods of under three months' duration.

70 are imprisoned for upwards of six months.

10 are sentenced to penal servitude.

In Ireland the convictions under the Game Laws average under 500 a year.

The convictions in England and Wales appear to be very steady in number, and the Poaching Prevention Act of 1862, whatever its other effect, has not reduced the number of these convictions.

Another serious result of the Game Laws, or rather, it should be said, of excessive preservation of game, is the very large number of persons who, during many months of the year, successfully practice poaching as a means of livelihood. In the county of Herts alone, there are stated by the Chief Constable to be not fewer than 300 men who for several months of the year maintain themselves in a great measure by the illegal taking of game. If this be a fair specimen of other parts of the country, the number of professional poachers must be considerable.

If hares and rabbits were kept down, by far the greater proportion of the present cases of poaching would not take place. If other game were only preserved in moderation, it would certainly not be worth while for men to make a living out of poaching; while if the sympathies of farmers were enlisted on behalf of the game on their farms, we should hear little of the poaching which is due to the neighbouring labourers, and which could not be carried on if the farmers were really in earnest to prevent it.

Many of the ulterior effects of game-preserving in its exaggerated form are also very mischievous; it leads to cases of local tyranny, such as forcing men out of the country who are known or suspected to be poachers. There is also some ground for complaint of the administration of the law by the unpaid magistrates, who are so often themselves preservers, and who at times impart into judgments on the subject of game a degree of acrimony and prejudice which results in injustice.

A further ulterior effect of exaggerated game-preserving is the impetus it gives to the aggregation of properties and to the squeezing out of small freeholders. There is nothing so hateful to the game preserver as the small freehold, where the game may be taken *in transitu*. It is therefore a great object with such men to buy up such small freeholds even at extravagant rates wherever it be possible, and this action accounts to some extent for the diminution of the number of small freeholds.

Another indirect evil of the present state of game-preserving is that so many men of the upper classes are brought up in the belief that sporting is the great end and object of civilised life. Hundreds of young men of the present generation have been ruined by this folly. This country is not large enough for them; they ransack the world for fresh fields for their gentle prowess; they roam over the world to the centre of Africa or the hills of India in search only of game; and all this enterprise and activity is thrown away upon the most useless sport without leaving a trace of any benefit to the actor or the world. The same fashion has also created a false ideal of life. It is considered by many engaged in industrial pursuits that one of the highest objects of ambition which can be aimed at in life is to become a game-preserving landowner on a great scale.

The conclusion which is justified on review of all that has been written and said about the Game Laws, and especially from the evidence taken before the Select Committee, is that the grievance of the Game Laws is first and mainly a farmer's grievance.

In Ireland, where the practice of strict preservation h⁴s never been followed, probably on account of the very small extent of the farms and the number of persons always on the land, there is no game question. Game is by no means extinct, but no complaints are made either by farmers or by the public.

In England, however, it is very different, and there is strong ground for Legislative interference. Excessive preservation has become a great impediment to good farming, and therefore to the production of food, while it has greatly increased the inducements to poaching, and the putting in force of laws, some of which are still very severe, and too often administered with harshness or carelessness.

PROPOSED REMEDIES.

To point out an evil, and to devise a remedy, are two very distinct tasks, and to many the difficulties of interfering with the existing Game Laws have appeared so great, that it has seemed to them preferable to leave the question to the force of public opinion, acting slowly upon the customs and habits of landowners and game preservers, rather than attempt legislation which might, in its result, disappoint those who are most interested.

The question, however, has passed beyond this stage, and as the Select Committee has proposed many and important, though it is believed inexpedient changes, and as other schemes of legislation have been proposed, and will doubtless be again proposed in substitution for that of the Committee, it is necessary to submit them to a careful scrutiny.

The proposals to deal with the Game Laws may be ranged under three heads :—

1. The repeal in whole or in part of the Game Laws.

2. The giving to game the status and sanction of other property.

3. The amendment of the Game Laws so far as they affect the relations of landlord and tenant.

I. It is uncertain how far those who advocate the total repeal of the Game Laws wish to see the entire extinction of game, and whether they include in their objects the repeal of those provisions only which protect game during the breeding season. It may be presumed that they contemplate at least the repeal of those provisions which make it penal for any person to trespass on the land of others in pursuit of game, whether by day or night, and whether with or without guns, nets, or other implements of destruction.

It is not difficult to foretell what would be the effect of such a measure. The experience of France and Germany has already been adverted to. It can scarcely be doubted that the same results would follow in this country. Multitudes of people from both urban and rural districts would avail themselves of the licence, and would wander freely over the cultivated districts, woods and moors, in all directions, with guns and other implements of destruction. If, within a reasonable time, all species of game could be totally extinguished, this free spirit of trespass might come to an end, and the ordinary trespass laws might suffice in the future ; but, in fact, game is not likely to be wholly extinguished, however great the number of persons in pursuit of it. There are parts of the country where it is impossible to exterminate rabbits ; there are some species of game birds, such as snipe, woodcock, and wild duck, which are only birds of passage, and which, bred in remote countries, only visit our shores for a brief season. It is also not probable that partridges would soon become extinct, however great the exertions made to destroy them. It would, therefore, result that some of the inducements to sport would remain, and we must look forward to an indefinite prolongation of the disorders which would result from unrestrained trespass in pursuit of game. Some would pursue game only for sport, others for gain ; and we might expect to see gangs of unauthorised persons beating covers or netting fields, in such numbers as to amount to a nuisance, not only to farmers, but also to the rest of society.

There would also still remain the ordinary law of trespass. The law, though it does not visit upon an ordinary trespasser who does no damage to property any penal consequences, gives full power to the owner or occupier of the land to drive trespassers off the land by the exercise of such force

as may be necessary for the purpose. He might still, therefore, by manual force eject the poacher from his ground, and
it might be possible in many of the more thinly-peopled
districts, by increasing the number of watchers, and by
arming them with guns and life-preservers, to keep strangers
off the land, or to make it dangerous for them to attempt a
raid. It is, however, certain that such action would lead to
constant and dangerous conflicts, and the remedy might
soon. prove worse than the disease. It would still
be possible for landlords to require covenants in their leases
forbidding their tenants to kill game or rabbits, and requiring them to drive off trespassers. The tenants might,
therefore, find themselves in the condition that, while de-
barred themselves from killing game on their farms, they
could not prevent any number of disorderly persons from
coming on their land in pursuit of it.

To legalise the universal destruction of game it would be
necessary to do more than simply repeal the existing Game
Laws ; it would be neccessary to provide expressly that all
the world might trespass anywhere and everywhere in pursuit
of game, so long as they should not do damage to other
property, and it would be further necessary to make illegal,
by express enactment, any contract between landlord and
tenant respecting game.

The Game Laws, as now consituted, not only protect
game, but act as a very moderate trespass law. It is a
general presumption, that persons trespassing in woods or
at night, with nets and guns are in search of game ; and
magistrates, not without reason, refuse to believe that they
are in search only of sparrows, crows, or any other non-
valuable species, but under the new regime persons would
have free license to trespass in pursuit of any kind of bird
or animal not included in the term property.

It is, doubtless, in view of these probable results of an
unconditional repeal of the Game Laws, that almost all
those who advocate it, are also prepared, when questioned
on the point, to admit the necessity of adopting a more
stringent general trespass law, as a sequel to the repeal of
the special Game Laws. It has not, however, occurred to
them that a more stringent trespass law would in fact be a
game law under another name. With a stringent trespass law,
game, as well as any other product of the soil, would be

protected; but there would be this addition, that whereas at present trespassers doing no damage cannot be punished, under a stringent trespass law, innocent persons, merely walking over open fields and meadows, or wandering off a footpath, without doing damage to any property, would be equally liable to prosecution. It is not conceivable that such a law would be maintained; if passed, it might be the engine of greater oppression than the Game Laws themselves, and would be a dangerous power to put into the hands of an unpaid magistracy.

The law of England most wisely holds that a person trespassing over land without doing any damage to property, is not liable to any penal action. To alter this law and to subject simple and innocent trespassers to fine and imprison-ment might be very agreeable to some landowners, and even farmers, and would give great facilities to game preservers, but it would lead to much local tyranny, it would be oppres-sive to the general public, and it is not too much to say that it would not long be endured.

It should never be forgotten that the essential feature of the present Game Law is that it is a trespass law directed against those trespassing on land in pursuit of game; as the greater contains the less, a general trespass law would include the main portions of the present Game Law, and would also include a hundred other cases which are not now subject to criminal process.

On the one hand, therefore, the repeal of the Game Laws if coupled with a more stringent trespass law would lead to intolerable strictness. On the other hand, if without a trespass law, it would lead equally to intolerable license.

II. It is thought by some that to make game property would give it a greater sanction in the public estimation, and lessen the inducement to take it unlawfully.

The question, however, at once arises, whose property is it to be? Is it to be considered the property of the person on whose land it is bred, or on whose land it is found? Is it to be the property of the owner of the land, or of the occupier?

Game is now, in some sense, the property of the person on whose ground it is found, but it is not vested with all the sanction of other property. To call it property while it changes ownership in going from one person's land to another, and to give it the same sanction as other property, would involve changing the game trespass law into a game larceny law; in other words it would greatly strengthen the penalties for taking game.

If, on the other hand, game is to be the property of the person on whose land it is bred, we are met at once by all the difficulties of identification. Pheasants that are reared by hand, and afterwards turned out into a wood for sport, might possibly be so treated. They would then continue the property of the person who bred them, although wandering on to the land of a neighbour; but if the neighbour were himself a breeder and preserver of pheasants, there would at once arise the difficulty of identification. It would generally be impossible to distinguish the pheasants of the one from those of the other, and disputes of a serious difficulty would occur. If difficult, however, as regards pheasants, how much more so with other descriptions of game—such as partridges, hares, and rabbits. The idea of treating these creatures as pigeons are now treated may be at once discarded as impossible.

The arguments in favour of this proposal appear to justify a very different conclusion—namely, that hares and rabbits should be the property of the person who feeds them; that is, of the farmer whose crops they eat, and not of the landowner. They would also justify the giving permission to the farmer to follow the hares and rabbits which are gorged with his turnips into the neighbouring wood from which they issued forth to feed, and there to kill and appropriate them. If, however, it is really intended that game is to be the property of the landowner on whose land it happens to be, the only effect of such a proposal would be to increase the penalties of the Game Laws, and to make game the subject of larceny, notwithstanding that it cannot be identified.

III. It has already been shown that the main objection to the Game Laws from the public point of view is not so much due to their existence as to their abuse—to the multiplication of game to such an extent that good farming is hindered, and the inducements to poaching greatly increased.

It has also been shown that the practice of excessive preservation has greatly increased, and is mainly due to the complete separation which exists in this country between the right of sporting and the occupation of land; that this separation is the cause of wrong to the farming tenant, in that the produce of his labour is consumed by the game for the benefit of another.

It can scarcely be doubted that if the farmers, as a rule, had control over the game, there would be no complaint of over-preserving, they would preserve only so far as was consistent with their farming interests, and they would also protect the game against unauthorised trespassers in a far more effectual manner than any keeper could do ; and the preservation of game being less, there would be less inducement to poach. The question, therefore, arises, whether, by any legal process, the game may be annexed more closely to the land, and whether it is just or expedient to take this course.

The law, undoubtedly, now recognises a separate estate and interest in the game apart from the ownership and occupation of land. It has been shown that this is itself an inheritance of the feudal laws. It is enforced by the penalties which the Act of 1831 imposes on the tenant who, in breach of his agreement under which the game is reserved by the landlord, takes game when feeding on his crops. It is recognised in the validity of all contracts reserving the right of sporting, and it is further confirmed by the power which the law gives to the owner of the land, or his assignee, who has parted with the possession of the land, to prosecute a poacher for trespassing on the land in pursuit of game. Although, therefore, the owner has parted with the possession of the land, the law enables him to retain dominion over it so far as the game is concerned ; and it fully, therefore, recognises a separate property in the game and the land, in the farming produce and the game produce.

It would be possible in many ways to legislate so as to prevent this separation, or at all events to give no legal sanction to it. It would not be inconsistent with legal principles to forbid the separation of the game from the ownership or occupation of land, on the ground of public policy, or on the principle that the separation of these two interests results in bad cultivation, in over-preservation of game, and in the consequent increase of offences.

To effect this object in the most complete manner, it would be necessary to enact that the sale of land and the letting of a farm should always carry with it the game, that no interest in the game separate from the land should be acknowledged by the law, or be the subject of any contract. It might be further necessary to enact that any prosecution under the Game Laws should issue at the instance only of the occupier of the land * ; and it would further follow that the penalty by which the Act of 1831 enforces the reservation of sporting should be repealed.

A change of this nature, although, it must be admitted, of a radical character, would be in harmony with the historic changes which have been made in times past, as illustrated first by the decay and destruction of the King's prerogative of sport over the lands of his subjects; secondly, by the emancipation of the freehold and copyhold tenants from the same pretensions of lords of manors; and lastly, by the abolition of privilege and qualification. These changes have been all in the direction of preventing the separation of game from the ownership of land. It is but a step further in the same direction to prevent the separation of game from the occupation of land.

It would appear, then, that the ultimate end which should be aimed at in any modification of the Game Laws is the annexation of game to the land, the preventing of any severance at law between the occupation of land and the right of sporting. There are, however, degrees of legislation short of this, though in the same direction, which are worthy of consideration ; and as in this country compromises are often come to between rival principles, it is not improbable that some half-measure may be found more acceptable to all parties than the more complete and logical one submitted above. The tenant farmers of England and Scotland have not generally put forward a claim to all the game on the farms they occupy, but to the hares and rabbits only ; and they appear to be content that their landlords should have the power to sever the right of sporting in respect of winged game from the occupation of land. They ask that they may be invested with an inalienable right, concurrently with their landlords, to take and destroy hares and rabbits on their

---

* Till 1864 every prosecution in Ireland for trespassing in pursuit of game was required to be in the name of the occupier of the land ; and where a landlord had reserved the right of sporting, and prosecuted a poacher in the name of the tenant, it not unfrequently happened that the tenant came into court and disavowed the proceedings. In 1864 an Act was passed enabling a landlord in Ireland who had reserved the right of sporting to prosecute under the Game Laws in his own name.

farms. It is from these animals that damage accrues to their crops; and their special grievance is confined to them. On farms of moderate size the partridge shooting would not be of much value from their narrow limits; and the sport could scarcely be enjoyed, except over an extent of land which embraces many farms of moderate size. Pheasants are not commonly reared, except in woods and plantations, which are usually in the hands of the landlords.

The tenant farmers, therefore, do not lay much stress upon the winged game; they rest their case mainly upon the grievance of hares and rabbits. It would, then, be quite consistent with the principles already indicated, and would be a long step towards the full realisation of them, if legislation, as between landlords and tenants, were confined in the first instance to hares and rabbits.

Such a remedy, if adopted, would have this further advantage, that it would bring the law into harmony with the existing practice on the best managed estates. There are many landlords who do now concede to their tenants the right of killing hares and rabbits, reserving only the exclusive right of winged game; this practice is decidedly on the increase among those landlords who have the interest of their estates and of their tenants really at heart. There is no safer guide for legislation than the growing practice which a higher morality or better experience inculcates among those for whom it is intended to legislate.

The concurrent right of landlord and tenant would have this further advantage—that the landlord could prevent the undue multiplication of rabbits and hares upon the holding of any of his tenants, which might result either from the negligence or love of sport of such tenant, or which might, in its turn, become a nuisance to neighbouring tenants or an obstruction to good farming.

If this partial remedy should be adopted, the main provisions of the existing Game Law would still remain. The law would still prohibit trespass on land in pursuit of game against the will of the owner or occupier. The day trespass law would remain unaltered. The Night Trespass Act would need a careful revision; the penalties attached to it are too severe. It is reasonable enough that men who go about in armed bands at night should be punished with more severity than simple unarmed trespassers in the day time; but the punishments of the Act are too severe, and should not be administered by justices.

The Poaching Prevention Act of 1860 should also be repealed. The Act is founded on a wrong principle. It enables the police to act on suspicion, and authorises the magistrates to condemn on suspicion only. It introduces a principle novel to the law in throwing the onus of proof of innocence on the accused. If the principle be worthy of trial, game offences are not those which should be selected for the experiment. Further, there is the great objection that it turns the county police into gamekeepers. It is most important that the principle should be maintained that it is no part of the duty of the state to preserve game for landowners. It does not at all follow that all land-owners object to their game being taken, or would desire to prosecute trespassers. The offence should in no way be treated as one of public interest.

CONCLUSION.

In what has been hitherto said, care has been taken to avoid any expression of opinion as to the merit of the institution known as sport. It is sufficient for the purpose to acknowledge that game now exists in large quantities, that numerous persons are interested in its preservation and derive great pleasure in searching for it themselves or by their beaters, and in destroying it. It is also a not unimportant article of food; though hares and rabbits, if excessive in number, displace a greater value of animal food of better quality, and pheasants as a rule cost more to rear than they sell for when dead. It is not possible to accept the theory that the Game Laws must be maintained on the ground that game is the only inducement to country gentlemen to live in the country. Considerable numbers of gentlemen do now contrive to pass their time and to enjoy themselves in the country without sport. It may be admitted of sport, also, such as it used to be, or such as it is now for the most part on the moors, consisting in the search for game with the aid of dogs, and involving considerable exertion and the exercise of some skill and knowledge of the country, that it has exerted no bad influence, but has given a taste for active life, which may have reacted to advantage upon the habits and life of many families.

But when for sport of this kind is substituted the modern battue, with its army of beaters, its massacre of hares, or its bouquet of pheasants, and where the sportsmen line the wood and have all the labour done for them, it is difficult to avoid the conclusion that true sport has vanished. There is no longer the uncertainty of the chase, or the exercise of skill in finding the game. It has degenerated into a system where the sportsman can prescribe the number of head of game he wishes to be driven into the shambles, and where the only skill is in killing in rapid succession at what is called a hot corner.

It is not probable that the craze for sport of this kind will long continue. It is contrary to the better instincts of English gentlemen and true sportsmen.

It has often been said that Shakespeare has, in the course of his great dramas, left nothing unnoticed of the varying phases of life, and of the customs of his days. Not the least happy among his descriptions is that where he expresses his manly contempt for the battue shooting of his period, which was directed against deer.

In " Love's Labour Lost " the Princess of France says to her forester—

. . . " Where is the bush
That we must stand and play the murderer in ?
The Forester.—Here by, upon the edge of yonder coppice ;
A stand where you may make the fairest shoot.
The Princess.—But come, the bow : now mercy goes to kill,
And shooting well is here accounted ill ;
Thus will I show my credit in the shoot,
Not wounding, pity would not let me do't;
If wounding, then it was to show my skill,
That more for praise than purpose meant to kill ;
And, out of question, so it is sometimes ;
Glory grows guilty of detested crimes ;
When for fame's sake, for praise, an outward part,
We bend to that the working of the heart,
So I, for praise alone, now seek to spill
The poor deer's blood, that my heart means no ill."*

The irony of these lines was not improbably directed against Queen Elizabeth, who was much addicted to shooting deer driven past a stage. Her slaughters on these occasions

* Act 4, S. I.

must often have shocked public opinion, as they did still more the sensitive mind of Shakespeare, himself a sportsman of the truer type, who has shown in his touching and beautiful description of the hunted hare in "Venus and Adonis," how keenly he could feel for brute nature.

The rebuke he thus administered to the ignoble sport of the day would apply equally in the present day to those who indulge either in tournaments of doves or in battues of pheasants or hares.

Whatever theoretical views, however, may be entertained by the few as to sport, it is certain that the great majority of Englishmen have no wish to see the extermination of all game. They will not, however, treat with much consideration that right of sporting which is carried to excess at the expense of suffering tenants, to the discouragement of good farming, and which results in diminished produce of the soil. The public, it is equally certain, will not readily give up any freedom which they now practically enjoy, of wandering freely over land where they do no damage, or agree to substitute a severe general trespass law for a game law, which is directed against trespassers who are in pursuit only of game. It is therefore in the relation of landlord and tenant that we must look for a remedy of admitted evils. The ground for such change will not be any objection to Game Laws in the abstract, but the more solid one that as now constituted they do grave injustice to a great body of tenant farmers, not only in causing destruction to their crops, but in making it impossible for them to put forth those exertions to increase the produce of the soil from which we may hope for increased results to labour in this country.

In 1880 "the Ground Game Act" carried into effect one of the principal of the above recommendations. It provided that "Every occupier of land shall have, as incident to and inseparable from his occupation of the land, the right to kill and take ground game thereon, concurrently with any other person who may be entitled to kill and take ground game on the same land."

CASSELL, PETTER, GALPIN & CO., BELLE SAUVAGE WORKS, LONDON, E.C.

www.ingramcontent.com/pod-product-compliance
Lightning Source LLC
Chambersburg PA
CBHW030345270326
41926CB00009B/963